THE BRITISH
IN THE
CARIBBEAN

THE BRITISH
IN THE
CARIBBEAN

Cyril Hamshere

HARVARD UNIVERSITY PRESS

Cambridge, Massachusetts

1972

ISBN 674 08235 4

Library of Congress Catalog Card Number 77–178079

Printed in Great Britain

CONTENTS

*This book is dedicated to the boys of
Papplewick School, Ascot*

ILLUSTRATIONS

Sir Thomas Picton *(Mary Evans Picture Library)*.
The Old Naval Hospital, Port Royal *(Jamaica Tourist Board)*.
The British capture of Trinidad, 1797 *(British Museum)*.
The fort on Brimstone Hill, St Kitts *(D. Leigh)*.
On deck off Port Royal *(Jamaica High Commission)*.
A West Indiaman *(National Maritime Museum)*.

III   THE SUGAR INDUSTRY *(between pp. 96 and 97)*.

Holeing a cane piece in Antigua. From R. Bridgens, *West Indies Sketches*, 1851.
Planting the canes. From Bridgens, *West Indies Sketches*.
Cutting the canes. From Bridgens, *West Indies Sketches*.
A sugar mill *(Mary Evans Picture Library)*.
Diagram of the two main processes of sugar manufacture. *(Mary Evans Picture Library)*.
A rum distillery in Antigua *(National Maritime Museum)*.
Shipping sugar *(National Maritime Museum)*.
Testimonial to the popularity of rum *(Public Record Office)*.

IV   SLAVERY AND ABOLITION *(between pp. 128 and 129)*.

A group of newly arrived slaves *(Mansell Collection)*.
Diagram of a French slaver *(National Maritime Museum)*.
The breadfruit tree *(Mary Evans Picture Library)*.
The ackee *(Jamaica Tourist Board)*.
Anti-slavery propaganda *(Mary Evans Picture Library)*.
Branding slaves *(British Museum)*.
Branding irons *(Fot Library)*.
Manacles for slaves. From Bridgens, *West Indies Sketches*.
Negro heads. From Bridgens, *West Indies Sketches*.
Mission in Antigua *(British Museum)*.
Slaves receiving news of their emancipation *(Mansell Collection)*.
'The New West India Dance' *(Mansell Collection)*.

V   THE PLANTERS' SOCIETY *(between pp. 160 and 161)*.

Planter, attended by his negro driver *(Mansell Collection)*.
John Gregg *(Royal Commonwealth Society)*.
A slave-owner and his slaves. From P.J.Benoit, *Voyage à Surinam,* 1839.
A funeral in Dutch Surinam. From Benoit, *Voyage à Surinam*.
A man of quality with his wife and slaves. From Benoit, *Voyage à Surinam*.
Rose Hall, Jamaica. From James Hakewill, *Picturesque Tour of Jamaica,* 1825.
Holland Estate, Jamaica. From Hakeville, *Picturesque Tour of Jamaica*.
Cardiff Hall, Jamaica. From Hakewill, *Picturesque Tour of Jamaica*.
Gracehill, Antigua *(National Maritime Museum)*.
Spring Garden Estate, Jamaica, by James Hakewill *(National Maritime Museum)*.

The Jamaican earthquake of 1692. From a seventeenth-century broadside *(British Museum)*.

Lewis Galdy's tombstone, Port Royal *(Author's Collection)*.

Guns sunk in the Great Earthquake *(Jamaica Tourist Board)*.

Pewter implements sunk in the Great Earthquake *(Jamaica Tourist Board)*.

VI ISLANDS AND TOWNS *(between pp. 192 and 193)*.

View over Kingston, 1870 *(National Maritime Museum)*.

King Street, Kingston, in 1850. From J.Duperly, *Daguerrian Excursions in Jamaica,* 1850.

The Court House, St John's, Antigua *(British Museum)*.

Port George, Scarborough, Tobago, 1793 *(National Maritime Museum)*.

Scarborough Bay, Tobago *(National Maritime Museum)*.

Kingstown, St Vincent, by Lieut. Caddy, R.A. *(British Museum)*.

The Pitch Lakes, Trinidad. From Bridgens, *West Indies Sketches.*

Looking down on Falmouth Harbour, Antigua. A greetings card of 1830 *(Royal Commonwealth Society Library)*.

Brimstone Hill, St Kitts, by Lieut. Caddy, R.A. *(British Museum)*.

The Blue Mountains, Jamaica *(Jamaica Tourist Board)*.

MAPS AND PLANS

The maps were drawn by Claus Henning

PREFACE

Between Cuba to the north and Colombia and Venezuela to the far south, an immense galaxy of islands, islets and minute uninhabited atolls sweeps across the Caribbean Sea. The British have been active here since 1622, when Captain Thomas Warner, who had already attempted to found a settlement on the verge of the Amazonian wilderness, decided with some friends to seek a new home, 'free from the disorders that did grow in the Amazons for want of Government among their Countrey-men', and finally reached St Kitts, in the Lesser Antilles, which became the first British Caribbean colony. Thence merchant adventurers moved down the chain of the Antilles; and in February 1627, a ship named the *William and John* carrying eighty colonists, arrived at Barbados, where they planted yams, cassava, maize and plantains, and sowed cotton and tobacco seeds. Jamaica, both the most varied and the most beautiful of Caribbean territories, did not fall into English hands until the year 1655.

The Caribbean has had a bloody history. About a century before the appearance of Columbus, the fierce Caribs, a race of cannibal warriors, had partly dispossessed the peaceful Arawaks, but were themselves nearly exterminated by the almost equally ferocious Spaniards; and they, in their turn, were harried and plundered by the bands of roving Buccaneers – squatters and beachcombers, English, French and Dutch, who waged an unholy crusade against the Spanish settlements, robbing, torturing and raping. An especially intrepid Buccaneer chief was the Welsh adventurer, Sir Henry Morgan; but, as 'nothing succeeds like success' – beside ravaging the coastline of the Spanish Main, he had captured and sacked the city of Panama – Morgan was appointed Deputy-Governor of Jamaica, an office he continued to hold from 1674 to 1682. He had many admirers, despite his horrible early record both in English aristocractic society and in the island that he governed. He was 'an honest brave fellow', said his good-natured London acquaintances, and cut a picturesque figure while he swaggered around Port Royal – damning and cursing 'most extravagantly' upon the smallest provocation, 'lean, sallow coloured, his eyes a little yellowish, and belly jutting out . . . not being able to abstain from company, much given to drinking and sitting up late'.

By the eighteenth century, however, the 'West India trade of plundering and burning towns . . . long practised in these parts' had been more or less discredited; and, as the planters grew increasingly rich, privateering lost its patriotic aura. At the same time, the 'indentured servants', the poor white bondsmen, who had previously worked the plantations, were replaced by imported black slaves. 'In 1700,' writes Cyril Hamshere, 'there were about 32,000 white inhabitants and 112,000 slaves in the English West Indies'; in 1800, the whites were nearly twice as numerous, and they dominated half-a-million blacks. Mr Hamshere's book devotes a series of particularly interesting chapters to the exotic social system that resulted. At home, no one could quite decide how far civilized man was justified in building a civilization upon servitude. Dr Johnson referred to the West-India planters as 'barbarians'; and the traveller and memorist, William Hickey, was shocked and disgusted by the barbarities he witnessed. But other observers thought that the bad treatment of slaves had been wantonly exaggerated; and that English abolitionists drew an unnecessarily alarming picture. Meanwhile, the planters built their splendid houses, of which one or two magnificent examples have survived until the present day, with spacious exterior galleries and huge, mahogany-panelled halls; and a number of English plantation-owners, who had never visited the Caribbean, collected princely annual revenues.

Among these absentee landlords was William Beckford, author of *Vathek* and builder of Fonthill Abbey. In 1797, the income Beckford drew from his West-Indian estates amounted to £155,000 per annum, which enabled him to spend over a quarter of a million pounds on his beloved Gothic fantasy. His fellow-novelist, 'Monk' Lewis, though he, too, had inherited vast Jamaican holdings, was a good deal more scrupulous, and paid a couple of visits to the island, where he made determined efforts to improve his wretched slaves' existence. Such is the social background of Mr Hamshere's study. It is written without prejudice, but with a keen sense of his subject's historical and moral values. No one who intends to visit the West Indies – surely some of the most delectable places on earth, an exquisite blend of tropical and temperate landscapes – should fail to include this book among his luggage.

PETER QUENNELL

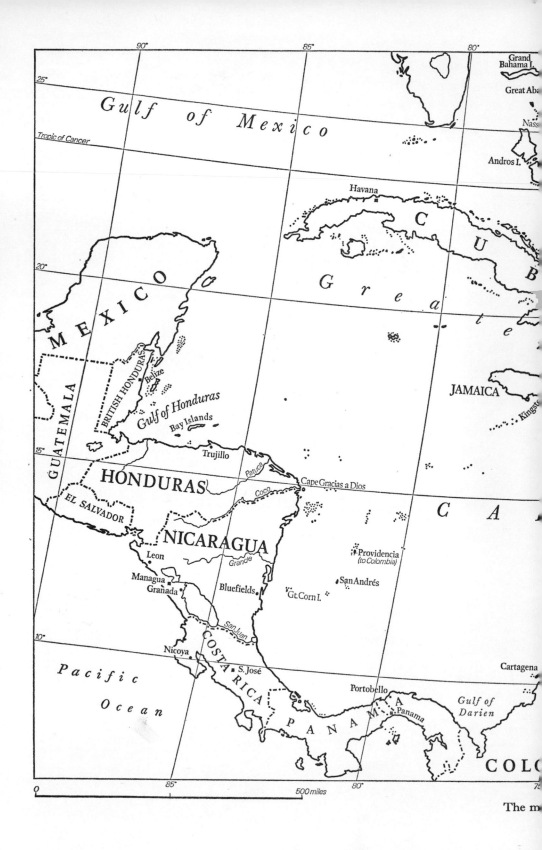

The m

ra I.
BAHAMA
Cat I.
ISLANDS *UK*

San Salvador

Atlantic

Long I.

Ocean

Acklins
I.

Caicos
Is.

Great Inagua

HAITI   DOMINICAN
REP.

PUERTO RICO

Virgin Is.   Anguilla*UK*

Barbuda
UK

St.Croix
US

Nevis
UK   St.Kitts*UK*   Antigua*UK*

Montserrat
UK

n   t   i   l   l   e   s

Leeward
Islands

Guadeloupe
Fr

Marie
Galante
Fr

Dominica
UK

L   e   s   s   e   r

Martinique
Fr

B   B   E   A   N

St.Lucia
UK

BARBADOS

St.Vincent
UK

Bridgetown

E   A

A   n   t   i   l   l   e   s

Windward
Islands

Grenada
UK

Curacao
Du   Bonaire
Du

Tobago

Los Roques
Ven.

Margarita

TRINIDAD

P.of Spain

Orinoco

A   V   E   N   E   Z   U   E   L   A   GUYANA

Orinoco
Barama
Essequibo
Georgetown
Mazaruni
Demerara   Berbice
Courantyne

GUYANA

0   200 miles

ean

1

THE TUDOR SEAMEN

There is no certainty who the first Englishman was to arrive in the Caribbean. It is possible that there were English or Irishmen among the motley crews of Columbus, but if there were their names are unknown. A Bristol man sailed with Magellan and died in the Pacific. During his voyage to the Rio de la Plata in 1526, Sebastian Cabot, then Pilot-Major of Spain, had two Englishmen among his crew named Roger Barlow and Henry Latimer. They had been sent by Robert Thorne of Bristol to spy out the land. Thorne was one of a number of English merchants trading with the Canaries and Spain, where several of them had settled, principally at Seville and San Lucar. By the time of Cabot's voyage Thorne had an English agent by the name of Thomas Tyson living in Hispaniola. It was through these merchants engaged in the Spanish trade that information about the West Indies first reached England. Those were the days of Anglo-Spanish friendship, cemented by the marriage of Henry VIII and Catherine of Aragon. There was no objection to English merchants going to America in Spanish ships, but when an English captain sailed into Santo Domingo harbour in January 1528 there was great consternation.

Again there is uncertainty. In 1527 two ships of Henry VIII's navy sailed across to Newfoundland under the command of one John Rut who is otherwise unknown, unless he was the same Jean Rotz of Dieppe who was employed by the King as a pilot and wrote a book about navigation. The voyage started as an attempt to find the North-West Passage, but masses of ice forced the ships to turn back to Newfoundland. There John Rut gave a letter to the master of a fishing vessel saying that he was heading south to the islands 'as we were commanded at our departing'. This is the last English record of the voyage, but Spanish reports from Hispaniola mention the arrival of an English ship there about three months later. As this was the first interloping ship to appear in the West Indies, the Spanish officials did not know what to do. There was some misunderstanding and the

Englishman moved away, plundered a plantation and was seen no more.

In 1530 the picture grows clearer with the appearance of William Hawkins of Plymouth. In that year he made a voyage to West Africa and from there crossed the Atlantic to Brazil. Repeating the voyage in 1531, Hawkins returned with an Indian chief whom he showed off at the court of Henry VIII, where he created a sensation. As a hostage Hawkins had left one Martin Cockeram, who had volunteered to live with the Indians while their chief accompanied Hawkins. A year later Cockeram was allowed to leave in peace, although the chief had died at sea. Meanwhile he had collected a cargo of Brazil-wood, which was to become a principal trade commodity for the useful dye it provided. Martin lived on in Plymouth until, as an old man, he watched the Armada sail by. Charles Kingsley made him the old man talking to the captains on the Hoe, and others have identified him as the old sailor yarning to the boys in Millais's picture *The Boyhood of Raleigh*. Fiction perhaps, but so much of the early adventurers' story is left to conjecture.

By 1540 Hawkins had established a profitable trade. In February of that year his 250-ton *Paul* sailed for Africa and Brazil with what a later age was to describe as a cargo of 'Brummagem goods': 940 hatchets, 940 combs, 375 knives, 5 hundredweight of copper and 5 of lead made into bangles, 10 hundredweight of copper and 10 of lead in the lump, 3 pieces of woollen cloth and – the English trader has always been enterprising – 19 dozen nightcaps. The whole cargo was valued at £23 15s and paid £1 7s 3d export tax. Six months later the *Paul* was back with one dozen 'olyfantes tethe' and ninety-two tons of Brazil-wood valued at £615, on which £30 15s. duty was paid. Small wonder that William Hawkins became the richest merchant in Plymouth!

Other merchants of Plymouth, Southampton and Bristol also made voyages at this time of which few records have survived. When Hawkins died in 1554 his two sons, William and John, inherited the family business. While William stayed at home as manager, young John – he was twenty-two when his father died – went on his famous voyages.

While his father William had operated between West Africa and Brazil, John Hawkins transferred his interest to the Caribbean. On his voyages to the Canary Islands he struck up a friendship with a Spaniard named Pedro de Ponte who lived in Tenerife, and it was Pedro who aroused his interest in the West Indies. Meanwhile at home John had moved to London where in 1559 he married Katherine, daughter of Benjamin Gonson, Treasurer of the Navy. With ideas given him by his Spanish friend and support from the influential friends of his father-in-law, John Hawkins set sail in October 1562 with three ships on the first English trading voyage to the West Indies. He chose to trade in slaves. It is ironic that the reign of Elizabeth I, in which the last vestiges of slavery in England were abolished by the emancipation of the serfs, saw the start of the nefarious African slave trade, yet neither in the lifetime of John Hawkins nor, with a few exceptions, in the following century did Englishmen suffer any qualms about it, although they were very religious people. It is a measure of the difference in outlook between then and now. In fact John Hawkins seems to have been proud of his idea, for when he came to be knighted in a later year he had incorporated in the crest of his coat of arms 'a demi-Moor proper bound in a cord'. It is unfortunate that the bad name awarded him during the nineteenth-century obsession with the horrors of the slave trade has obscured the recognition of Hawkins's great contribution to the efficiency of the Elizabethan navy. During his years of office as Treasurer of the Navy he drew on his experience of the West Indian voyages to improve the design of the navy's fighting ships and to make modifications to the capstan and the chain pump. He also introduced elm-sheathing for the ships to counter the depredations of the tropical worm.

On his first voyage Hawkins called at Tenerife where Pedro de Ponte supplied him with a Spanish pilot who knew the Indies. After collecting between three and four hundred Negroes in the region of Sierra Leone, Hawkins's ships safely crossed the Atlantic and reached the north coast of Hispaniola in April 1563. There the agent of Pedro de Ponte had arranged for his reception and a brisk trade ensued, so much so that Hawkins chartered a Spanish ship to assist in carrying his cargo of pearls, ginger, sugar and hides. This and a Portuguese vessel he had chartered at Sierra Leone he sent direct to Spain with the licences to trade he had obtained from the Spanish officials and their receipts for the customs duties he had been punctilious in paying. But the Spanish and Portuguese authorities refused to play; the ships and their cargoes were confiscated. It is a proof of his aim to establish a legitimate trade that Hawkins openly protested and was backed by his Queen – all to no avail.

In spite of the two lost ships, John Hawkins had made such a handsome profit that for his second voyage he received the backing of Queen Elizabeth and the leading figures of her court; Sir William Cecil, the Earl of Pembroke and Lord Clinton the Lord Admiral all invested in the venture. The Queen's stake took the form of a ship of her navy, the *Jesus of Lubeck*, set down in the accounts as the equivalent of a £2,000 investment. The *Jesus* by sixteenth-century standards was a very large ship at seven hundred tons, whose inclusion in the expedition left no doubt about Hawkins's official backing, even though she was old and rotten. Leaving Plymouth on 14 October 1564, with three ships in addition to the *Jesus*, Hawkins called at Ferrol where he spent five days without rousing any Spanish protests.

3

After a troublesome collection of Negroes Hawkins reached Dominica with between four and five hundred of them in early March 1565. After watering there he steered south-west for his first visit to the Main. This was the occasion for the first English comment on the potato: 'the most delicate roots that may be eaten, and do far exceed our parsnips or carrots'. The trading went well, in spite of some official protests, and Hawkins took orders for more slaves on future voyages. The ships returned to England safely in September, but the *Jesus* required repairs costing £500, which the syndicate had to pay. All the same the voyage was profitable: the Spanish ambassador calculated that it had returned sixty per cent on investment. Hawkins was pleased with his own record, as he reported to the Queen: 'I have always been a help to all Spaniards and Portugals that have come in my way without any harm or prejudice by me offered to any of them, although many times in this tract they have been in my power. . . .'

It is obvious that both John Hawkins and Queen Elizabeth were hoping that Philip II would come to an agreement allowing the continuation of the trade that Hawkins had started illegitimately. In 1565 Spain and England were at peace and Hawkins took pains to point out to Spanish officials that not so long before Philip had been his master (when Philip was married to Mary I) and that he still wished to serve him, especially against the terrible French corsairs who had been plundering the Caribbean for thirty years. For her part Elizabeth treasured Spanish amity as a counterbalance to the alliance between France and Mary Queen of Scots that was directed against her. But it was not to be. Although the Spanish ambassador invited Hawkins to dinner and was notably impressed by his guest, he wrote to his King: 'It may be best to dissemble so as to capture and castigate him on his next voyage.' Next year Hawkins came to dinner again, after which Don Guzman de Silva wrote to Philip: 'It will be advisable to get this man out of the country, so that he may not teach others, for they have good ships and are greedy folk with more liberty than is good for them.' Ignorant of this secret advice, Hawkins continued to press for Philip's recognition. He undertook not to sail to the West Indies again unless he was granted Philip's permission. Instead he offered his services against the Turks in the Mediterranean. Philip was unmoved. He took steps to destroy the French settlement in Florida and decided against any encouragement to the Protestant English.

Meanwhile, although he had engaged not to sail to the West Indies himself without Philip's permission, Hawkins sent out four ships in 1566 under the command of John Lovell. Lovell was less particular about his dealings with the Spanish colonists and so was Hawkins's young kinsman, Francis Drake, who made his first acquaintance with the Caribbean on this voyage. He came home smarting from the loss of his stake through Spanish trickery and quickly enlisted in the new venture that he discovered Hawkins was preparing on his return.

The third voyage of John Hawkins to the Caribbean was the most ambitious, the most eventful and the most disastrous of his three trading ventures. It is therefore worth following in some detail for the light that it throws on his motives and methods and the conditions under which he sailed. Once again Hawkins enjoyed the Queen's official backing. This time she contributed two ships of her navy, the *Minion* of 300 tons and the old *Jesus of Lubeck*. Why Hawkins accepted the *Jesus* after his experience with her on his previous voyage has always been a mystery. It was through her dangerous unseaworthiness that disaster befell him. They had a narrow escape in the Bay of Biscay, where she leaked so much that she nearly sank, and only by stuffing cloth from the cargo into the numerous leaks could

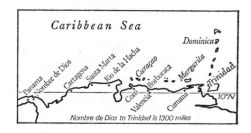

The Spanish Main in Hawkins's day

they keep her afloat. If she had foundered it would have been the end of Francis Drake, for he was on board her at the opening of the voyage. Hawkins had sailed on 2 October 1567. As well as the royal two ships, he had with him the *William and John* (150 tons), the *Swallow* (100 tons), *Judith* (50 tons), the *Angel* (33 tons), and a total of 408 men. The Spanish ambassador knew about the preparations but the official destination was said to be a newly discovered gold mine in Guinea to which two Portuguese were going to lead the way. When they disappeared shortly before the expedition sailed, it was too late for anything to be done.

While collecting five hundred Negroes in West Africa Hawkins added an allegedly abandoned Portuguese caravel to his fleet and was joined by two French ships. Seven weeks later when his nine ships appeared at Margarita the Spanish colonists panicked, thinking they were French. Hawkins wrote a reassuring letter to the governor, which is illuminating:

Worshipful,

I have touched in your island only to the intent to refresh my men with fresh victuals, which for my money or wares you shall sell me, meaning to stay only five or six days here at the furthest. In the which time you may assure yourself and so all others that by me or any of mine there shall no damage be done to any man, the which also the Queen's Majesty of England, my mistress, at my departing out of England commanded me to have great care of, and to serve with my Navy the King's Majesty of Spain, my old master, if in places where I came any of his stood in need.

A number of authorities have found this proclamation too glib: if the object of the enterprise was to serve the King of Spain, why was his acceptance of the offer not obtained first? He had already turned a cold shoulder to Hawkins's earlier overtures. Did the Queen and Hawkins seriously hope to convince him of the value of their service and the innocence of their trade?

However unenthusiastic King Philip might be, his subjects at Margarita gave the English a welcome reception and trade was done. At Borburata there was a new governor, Pedro Ponce de Leon. Writing to him on arrival Hawkins said:

I know the King of Spain, your master, hath forbidden that you should give licence for any stranger to traffic. I will not therefore request any such thing at your hand, but that you will licence me to sell 60 negroes only and a parcel of my wares, which in all is but little, for the payment of the soldiers I have in my ships. In this you will not break the commandment of your prince, but do him good service and avoid divers inconveniences which happen oftentimes through being too precise in observing precepts without consideration.

This sounds like a veiled threat, and it worked. Although official permission was refused, Hawkins stayed two months trading with the Spanish colonists under the most cordial conditions. Of course they were only too pleased to be able to buy slaves. It was the officials who were faced with the dilemma of acquiescing in the trade which the colonists needed but which was forbidden by their king. As many of the officials were planters they found Philip's regulations extremely tiresome, especially as they rarely saw a Spanish trading vessel.

From Borburata Hawkins sent Drake ahead to Rio de la Hacha. Since they had left Africa he had been in command of the *Judith*. Younger and far less patient than Hawkins, Francis Drake had a score to settle with Miguel de Castellanos, Treasurer of Rio de la Hacha, for it was he who had cheated him on Lovell's voyage. Shots were exchanged and Francis seized a caravel that arrived from Santo Domingo. When Hawkins arrived he supported his lieutenant and attacked the little town because permission to trade was refused. Two Englishmen were killed before it fell, and then Hawkins threatened to burn it if de Castellanos still refused to trade. Eventually the colonists pressed him to concede, whereupon the Treasurer said he had tried to hold out because Hawkins 'is such a man as that any man talking with him hath no power to deny him anything he doth request . . . and not through any villainy that I know in him, but great nobility'. It was an unsolicited testimonial for John Hawkins. Later de Castellanos's show of resistance saved his skin when he was asked to explain why he had allowed trade with the English.

After a month at Rio de la Hacha, Hawkins moved west to Santa Marta, where he went through a show of capturing the town to save the governor's face. At all these ports Spanish colonists and English sailors entertained one another at frequent banquets, until at Cartagena Hawkins met with a blank refusal and the town was too strong for him to take. As it was then August when hurricanes could be expected Hawkins decided it was time to go to home. He found he had dallied too long. Near the western end of Cuba his fleet was struck by a '*furicano*'. The *William and John* parted company with the fleet and made its own way home. Somehow the rest kept together, with the terrible *Jesus* opening and closing its timbers to such an extent that fish swam in and out of the bilge. It was nothing but concern to save the Queen's ship that made Hawkins follow a Spanish ship he had encountered across the Gulf of Mexico to the only possible haven for refitting at San Juan d'Ulloa.

San Juan was a wretched port, no more than a sheltered anchorage protected by a low island 240 yards long, a quarter of a mile off the mainland. Hawkins's first action was to seize the island and then ask permission to make use of the port for the repair of his ships. He asked to be allowed to buy victuals and as an earnest of his peaceful intentions a messenger was sent to Mexico City to announce his arrival. The Spaniards explained that they had mistaken his ships for the annual *flota*, which was expected daily. On 17 September 1568, two days after Hawkins had arrived, the *flota* appeared and the fat was in the fire.

John Hawkins's dilemma was this : if he let the Spanish fleet in, they would probably attempt to arrest him ; if he kept them out of their own port in time of peace he would be in serious trouble when he reached home. As in previous difficult situations on the voyage he took a firm but conciliatory line. The Spanish captain of the island battery was used as an envoy to inform the *flota* commander that it was the Englishman's intention to leave as soon as his ships were repaired, but he demanded a guarantee of safety from attack, otherwise he would defend the island. All along the Main John Hawkins had been dealing with minor Spanish officials; it was his double misfortune that in his latest predicament he was faced with senior officers of the highest rank, for on board the Spanish flagship was none other than Don Martin Enriquez, the new viceroy of Mexico. To him the situation was intolerable and he dealt with the impudent intruder in the same way that he would have behaved if held up by a highway robber : he would keep his hands up until the first opportunity offered to over-power his opponent. After three days of negotiation an agreement was reached which left the island and its eleven guns in English hands with the proviso that no armed Spaniard should set foot on it. In the meantime Don Martin had had all available soldiers at Vera Cruz, fifteen miles up the coast, ferried under cover of night on to his largest merchantman.

When the thirteen vessels of the *flota* finally came in the little port was packed tight with twenty-eight ships, lying side by side with bow anchors secured to the island. Hawkins's seven ships were together at one end with the *Minion* and *Jesus*, in that order, closest to the Spanish vessels, the nearest of which was a dismasted hulk into which concealed soldiers moved. For two days all was peaceful and there was fraternization, but on 23 September Hawkins had his suspicions aroused by overmuch activity aboard the large hulk, which was being warped a little nearer to the *Minion*; gun-ports were being opened and there were far too many Spaniards about. Hawkins sent Robert Barret, master of the *Jesus*, who spoke Spanish, to remonstrate with Enriquez. Don Martin smoothly replied 'that he in the faith of a Viceroy would be our defence from all villainies'. But the Spanish activity continued, so Barret was dispatched a second time. It was the last Hawkins saw of him.

As Hawkins went to his cabin for a hasty meal, Job Hortop recounted to Richard Hakluyt how a Spanish guest there was found with a dagger in his sleeve with which he had intended to kill Hawkins. When Barret reached the viceroy he was arrested. Back on deck Hawkins recognized the Spanish Vice-Admiral Ubilla on the merchantman and shouted to him that trickery was not the work of a gentleman. Ubilla replied that he was doing his duty as a fighting man. Hawkins shot an arrow at him. Then a

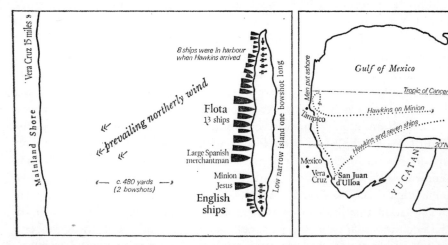

San Juan d'Ulloa: possible situation at 10 am, 23 September 1568, and Hawkins's advance

trumpet sounded on board the Spanish flagship and men came pouring out on to the island and the fight was on. It was 10 am.

Hawkins's vigilance saved the *Minion*. Ordering her headfast cut he had her warped from the shore by her sternfast while the three hundred Spanish soldiers who had sprung aboard were beaten off. The *Jesus* too was cut loose and floated out, but on the island the Spanish surprise was successful. The guns were captured and all the Englishmen except three were slain. The survivors, among whom was Job Hortop, swam out to the *Jesus*. A fierce gun-battle lasted through the rest of the morning and afternoon until four o'clock. The key to it was the island guns which Hawkins, with his three hundred men, had no hope of recapturing, outnumbered as he was by three or four to one. Nevertheless they sank the Spanish admiral and a merchant ship, but by then the *Jesus* had been reduced to a dismasted hulk and 'her hull was wonderfully pearced with shotte'. Still she floated and her great hulk was at last made useful, for the *Minion* was brought under her lee and much of the valuable cargo was transferred. While this was being done the Spaniards sent two fireships, which caused a panic on the *Minion*, so that her crew cut her adrift and nearly left their general behind. Once aboard the *Minion* Hawkins rallied his men, but before he transferred Hortop remembered a lovely incident on the *Jesus*.

Our Generall couragiously cheered up his souldiers and gunners, and called to Samuel his page for a cup of Beere, who brought it him in a silver cup, and hee drinking to all men willed the gunners to stand to their Ordinance lustily like men. He had no sooner set the cup out of his hand, but a demy Culverin shot stroke away the cup and a Coopers plane that stoode by the maine mast, and ranne out on the other side of the ship: which nothing dismaid our Generall, for he ceased not to incourage us, saying, feare nothing, for God, who hath preserved me from this shot, will also deliver us from these traitours and villaines.

Meanwhile the other English ships were captured or sunk, with the exception of the *Judith* which Francis Drake managed to cut loose. This small fifty-ton vessel had only twelve guns and could do little against the heavier armament on the island. She stood off out of range until nightfall and in the morning she had gone. This has always been held against Drake. In his official account Hawkins said tersely that the *Judith* 'the same night forsook us in our great miserie'. Job Hortop's account described how Hawkins lay up behind the *Jesus* all night and 'he willed Mr. Francis Drake to come in with the Judith, and to lay the Minion aboord, to take in men and other things needfull, *and to goe out*, and so he did'. The last thing Drake would have done was to desert a comrade. When the difference between the 300-ton fighting *Minion* and the tiny 50-ton barque *Judith* is remembered, there seems little he could have done to help Hawkins. He certainly could not have carried the hundred men Hawkins later put ashore. There are no details of Drake's voyage home, but afterwards he and Hawkins were good friends.

About ninety Englishmen died at San Juan d'Ulloa. With two hundred survivors on board the *Minion* Hawkins crept up the Mexican coast as far as the Tropic. There was no food to be found and without provisions it was madness to sail. After a fortnight half the men asked to be put ashore and Hawkins reluctantly agreed. He provided them with cloth and some money for trading with the Indians and, promising to send help as soon as he was able, he sailed away. After a terrible voyage he reached home on 25 January 1569, with not more than fifteen of the hundred men who had sailed from Mexico. Ashore, some of the party set out northwards with indomitable courage to walk across to Newfoundland and find a fishing vessel, and three of these actually reached home after being picked up by a French ship in Nova Scotia. The remainder, including tough Job Hortop, fell into Spanish hands. No less than twenty-four were eventually rescued by the efforts of John Hawkins. Robert Barret and two or three more were burnt at the stake in Seville and Job Hortop, after twelve years in the Mediterranean galleys, reached home in 1590, twenty-three years after the disaster at San Juan d'Ulloa.

John Hawkins's efforts to save his captured men read like a chapter from the adventures of James Bond. With the connivance of the Queen and Cecil, Hawkins won the confidence of the Spanish ambassador with whom he plotted to supply a fleet to carry the Duke of Alva across from the Netherlands with an army to put Mary Queen of Scots on the English throne. In repayment Philip released twenty-four of the San Juan prisoners and issued a patent of Spanish nobility to Juan Aquines, as the Spaniards called him. Then the plot was blown and the Spanish ambassador was sent home.

History has its fashions no less than women's clothes. San Juan d'Ulloa used to be regarded as the turning-point in Anglo-Spanish relations in the reign of Elizabeth I. Recent writers have disagreed, pointing to other factors. While these are accepted it would be mistaken to decry the effects of the Spanish treachery on that September day. The ordinary seamen never forgot, and one extraordinary leader chose to remember San Juan for many a long day. Ten years later while plundering the Pacific coast on his circumnavigation, Drake told his prisoner San Juan de Anton that he was collecting debts owed to him by Don Martin Enriquez. Hawkins collected nearer home, not only by bamboozling Philip and his ambassador, but by joining in the privateering attacks of French corsairs and Dutch sea-beggars on Spanish shipping in the Channel. He did not return to the Caribbean until 1595.

There is no room in this book for the story of the exciting raids of Drake and his imitators. His example set one half of the pattern of the first phase of English activity in the Caribbean that continued on into the exploits of the Buccaneers a century later. As for his personal exploits, never was so much disturbance and damage done to a whole empire by any other single man. It was a coincidence, perhaps, that the Spanish form of his name (Draque) spelt Dragon. So he became El Draque, a creature with super-natural powers and a magic mirror that enabled him to see exactly the plans that any Spaniard might prepare for his defeat.

Indeed the exploits of Drake and his contemporary sea-dogs were almost magical in the nature of their achievement. Let the conditions be known under which the first Elizabethans sailed and it becomes a wonder that they ever reached and returned from their destination. In recent years the world has admired a number of lone voyages of circumnavigation that would have been impossible in the days of Drake, because his age lacked the technical equipment that has made the modern exploits possible: self-steering gear, tinned food, glass-fibre hulls and radio. If there is a common feature between the sixteenth- and twentieth-century voyages it is the size of the ships, for the lone sailors of today have reminded the world of giant liners and even bigger tankers that long voyages in ships of under a hundred tons have always been practicable.

The largest English ship to enter the Caribbean during the sixteenth century was the *Jesus of Lubeck* of seven hundred tons, whose misfortunes have already been described. The average displacement of English ships crossing the Atlantic in those days was about a hundred tons, which means they were a little over fifty feet in length, eighteen to twenty feet in beam, with a depth in hold of nine or ten feet. William Hawkins's *Paul* at 250 tons was large; Drake was happy in a 50-tonner. His *Golden Hind* in which he sailed round the world displaced only 120 tons. Ships of this tonnage upwards were classified as galleons, but both Drake and Hawkins valued the smaller pinnaces of 15 to 80 tons, sometimes only half-decked, but very useful because of their shallow draught in uncharted waters. When Hawkins sailed along the Main for the first time, he sailed inshore in a pinnace while the *Jesus* and his other ships kept company in the deeper water to starboard. For his attack on Nombre de Dios in 1572 Drake took out three pinnaces in pieces and had them assembled at Port Pheasant. On the circumnavigation he took four. While the *Golden Hind* was being careened north of Valparaiso he went scouting in a pinnace for the long-lost *Elizabeth*.

On long voyages careening was essential, and the smaller the ship the easier it was. Brought right in to a convenient beach, the ship was hauled over on one side. Between high tides the carpenter and his men went over the hull, cleaning off the barnacles and seaweed, taking out rotten planks and replacing them with new timber, recaulking the seams and greasing the hull to keep off the destructive worm.* When one side had been treated the ship had to be floated off, turned round and brought in for work on the other side. Ballast and guns were removed before work started. Sails, masts and rigging were gone over at the same time. It was a lengthy process over which Drake usually spent about a month.

On board the ships there was no comfort at all. Royal Navy sailors slept on the bare boards of the gun-decks, covered with blankets and coats; they were grouped in messes divided by canvas screens. There was no ventilation except through open gun-ports in fair weather. Pervading the ship below decks foul stenches rose from the bilge, above which, on a brick platform, the galley was situated. Here in one of hell's antechambers the cook sweated over a wood fire, struggling to produce a meal from the stinking salted beef, pork and fish, the weevil-ridden biscuit and beans, the rancid butter and crawling cheese. Later, under the influence of gentlemen-adventurers like Sir Walter Raleigh, the galley was moved into the forecastle. Navy rations sounded generous: a pound of meat or fish a day, and a whole gallon of beer. These were the regulations for home waters. Atlantic voyages proved them totally unsuitable, yet there was little improvement that could be made. The best course was to carry a stock of live animals and replenish them, if possible, at intermediate ports of call like the Canary Islands. Stops for 'wood and water' were routine and European countries allowed foreign ships to make these calls provided permission was requested. In Patagonia Drake had his men catch penguins and seals. Elsewhere they ate crabs, lobsters and sea-birds. Coleridge's Ancient Mariner was not the first to shoot an albatross. There were always fish to be caught on a line over the bulwarks, while some, like the flying-fish, served themselves over the low freeboard. The Elizabethans were tough. When rations ran low they tightened their belts, chewed leather and dropped their pet parrots and monkeys, the ship's cats and rats, into the pot.

In the great cabin off the quarter-deck (the galleon's equivalent of the modern bridge) the officers and gentlemen-adventurers dined in style. Hawkins ate off silver plate and Drake on the *Golden Hind* dined off silver and gold to the strains of viols. Even in the great cabin there was no comfortable furniture: hard wooden chairs were the order of the day, as they were in Elizabethan houses, where the only soft item of furniture was the feather-bed. Not until the adoption of the West Indian hammock in the seventeenth century could sailors sleep in any comfort. Whenever they were careening, most of the crew slept on shore. No details exist about sanitation.

* After his experience of the Caribbean Hawkins introduced elm sheathing as an outer skin. In Charles II's reign lead was tried, and one hundred years later, copper.

A sailing ship required a large crew to provide enough men in the usual two four-hour watches to trim the sails at all hours of the day and night. John Hawkins and Francis Drake, who was greatly influenced by his older kinsman's seamanship, believed in keeping the numbers aboard to a minimum to avoid the ill-health that, they saw, resulted from overcrowding. On the ill-fated *Jesus* the normal complement was 300 men; Hawkins cut it to 180. Later, when Treasurer of the Navy, he worked on a basis of one man to two tons of ship. When bound for Nombre de Dios in 1572 Drake took 73 men on two small vessels. For the circumnavigation he sailed out of Plymouth with 164 men on five ships.

In the navy, as a result of the reduction in the size of crews, Hawkins was able to raise the sailor's pay from 6s 8d to 10s a month, exclusive of rations. To Welfare State ears such figures sound sub-minimal, but Sir Julian Corbett calculated in 1917 that this was better than the naval pay of his day, which stood at 1s 7d *a day*. In war, of course, there was the attractive bonus of plunder.

It is necessary to scratch for details of the sailors who crossed the Atlantic with Hawkins and Drake. In his first great exploit at Nombre de Dios Drake and all his seventy-three men were under thirty. He kept them well exercised as young man like to be. They had their moments of doubt, their grey strokes of fear, but they rallied to their leader's encouragement. They possessed the sailor's droll sense of humour. How they must have roared when retelling the Spaniards' surprise at Valparaiso as Thomas Moon, the first Englishman to disclose himself by shouting, 'Down, dog!', struck a flabbergasted Iberian with the flat of his sword! And further on they appreciated the Spanish sailors' nickname for their treasure galleon with the sonorous name of *Nuestra Señora de la Concepción*. To the Spaniards who had to handle her she was the *Cacafuego* ('Shit-fire'), and when her priceless cargo had been removed they roared again when their cheerful victims said she was now the *Cacaplata* ('Shit-plate').

And so the Elizabethan sea-dogs sailed the seven seas in their little ships, sweating across the frightful equatorial doldrums, shivering past desolate Patagonia, half-starving, half-naked and often half-hearted. There could be no more lurid illustration of the experiences of sixteenth-century sailors than the closing page of John Lane's narrative concerning the remnant that returned from the last voyage of Thomas Cavendish in 1591–2. After struggling through the Straits of Magellan, Captain Cotton decided to turn back owing to the depletion of his numbers and the dangerous condition of his ship and rigging. Stopping halfway back through the Straits to stock up with dried penguin meat – Lane said they slaughtered fourteen thousand of the birds – Cotton crept back along the coast of South America, losing men in Portuguese and Indian attacks until they struck north on the last leg homeward, short of food:

Being thus at sea, when we came to Cape Frio, the wind was contrary; so that three weeks we were grievously vexed with cross winds and our water consuming, our hope of life was very small. Some desired to go to Bahia, and to submit themselves to the Portugals, rather than to die for thirst; but the captain with fair persuasions altered their purpose. . . .

In this distress it pleased God to send us rain in such plenty, as that we were well-watered, and in good comfort to return. But after we came near unto the sun, our dried penguins began to corrupt and there bred in them a most loathsome and ugly worm of an inch long. This worm did so mightily increase, and devour our victuals, that there was in reason no hope how we should avoid famine, but be devoured of these wicked creatures: there was nothing that they did not devour, only iron excepted: our clothes, boots, shoes, hats, shirts, stockings: and for the ship, they did so eat the timbers, as that we greatly feared that they would undo us by gnawing through the ship's side. Great was the care and diligence of our captain, master and company to consume these vermin, but the more we laboured to kill them, the more they increased; so that at the last we could not sleep for them, but they would eat our flesh, and bite like mosquitoes.

In this woeful case, after we had passed the Equinoctial toward the north, our men began to fall sick of such a monstrous disease, as I think the like was never heard of: for in their ankles it began to swell, from thence in two days it would be in their breasts so that they could not draw breath . . . there was no man in perfect health, but the captain and one boy. . . . To be short all our men died except sixteen, of which there were but five able to move . . . upon us five only the labour of the ship did stand. . . . In fine our misery and weakness was so great, that we could not take in, nor heave out a sail: so our topsail and spritsails were torn all in pieces by the weather. . . .

They made their landfall in Ireland. Many ships never returned to their haven under the hill.

Some of the English came to mysterious ends. Drake's young nephew, John Drake, was a case in point. He had sailed from Plymouth at the age of fourteen as page to Francis on the circumnavigation, during which he impressed Spanish observers with his skill as an artist. It was he who won the gold chain offered by Francis for the first man to sight the 'Cacafuego'. In 1582, when he was only eighteen or nineteen, John Drake sailed with Edward Fenton as captain of the *Francis*, a forty-ton barque obviously the property of his uncle, in a voyage that was supposed to take up the contacts Francis had made in the East Indies. When they reached the Plate, John deserted Fenton, of whom he had formed a poor opinion, because he felt that the voyage was soon to be abandoned – as it was. In the shallow estuary the *Francis* was wrecked and the Englishmen fell into the hands of Indians who kept them prisoners for over a year. Then John and a few others escaped, eventually reaching the nascent Buenos Aires. Here they were kindly treated until John was recognized by a renegade Englishman who denounced him to the authorities as the cousin of El Draque. By slow degrees he was passed from one Spanish official to the next until he reached Lima and the tender mercies of the Inquisition. About the time that Francis was 'singeing the King of Spain's beard' at Cadiz, John was received as a penitent into Holy Church. Ultimately he was freed. Richard, son of John Hawkins, himself taken prisoner by the Spaniards in another disastrous voyage, brought back news of John when he reached England in 1602. It was perhaps as well that Sir Francis was resting six fathoms down in Nombre de Dios Bay, for although he might have forgiven his nephew the loss of his ship he would have been horrified at the change of his religion. John Drake must have married, for none but he could have been the founder of the Spanish noble family of Drake del Castillo, who claim connection with El Draque of infamous (to the Spanish) memory. This story illustrates that the Spanish authorities were not inimical to English-men who became Catholics. John Drake's companions also settled in South America.

In face of all the likely perils of a sixteenth-century voyage – storm, shipwreck and disease, pirates, Spaniards and unpredictable Indians – it may well be wondered how any crews were available. The main reason was the indomitable spirit of adventure that fired the imagination of Tudor Englishmen and their sincere belief in the providence of God. They were content to put their hands in His and let His will be done. Religion per-meated their life as it has ceased to do in the present age of technical perfection. Hawkins's instructions to his officers on his second West Indian voyage were: 'Serve God daily, love one another, preserve your victuals, beware of fire, and keep good company.' Serve God they did at morning and evening prayers, attended by all under pain of twenty-four hours in irons.

There were fortunes to be made in the New World and great excitement to be had in the making of them, but there were times when spirits flagged and a good leader was needed to raise them. Francis Drake knew how to play on the motives and emotions of his men. In a sticky moment at Nombre de Dios Drake cried, 'I have brought you to the mouth of the Treasure of the World, and if you want it [i.e. do not take it] you must henceforth blame nobody but yourselves.' Later at the crisis of the circum-navigation, down at Port St Julian, he told his men, 'If such a voyage as this, which has never before been out of England, goes forward to its end, there is not a cabin-boy who will not become a gentleman.' He explained that the world was watching them. 'We have now set by the ears three mighty princes, as first Her Majesty, and then the Kings of Spain and

Portugal, and if this voyage should not have good success, we should not only be a scorning or a reproachful laughing-stock unto our enemies but also a great blot to our whole country for ever. . . .' Fired by idealism in a crisis, the Elizabethans were sufficiently realistic to know that it might be God's will for them to die as easily from plague or smallpox in Plymouth as from scurvy or drowning at sea.

Once the English coast had dropped below the horizon, the practical problems of navigation pressed themselves on the mind of the ship's master. In the trackless ocean it was essential for him to know exactly where he was before he could set a course that would bring him to his destination. In other words he needed to know his latitude and longitude. With their cross-staff and astrolabe sixteenth-century pilots could determine their latitude to within half a degree (about thirty-five miles) but they had no means of fixing longitude. Familiar with the compass for more than a century, they had to learn about magnetic variation. There were primitive forms of nautical almanack, but the most valued possession was a rutter – a book of sailing instructions that was more highly prized than a chart. On their way round the world Francis and John Drake spent many hours painting and making notes about the principal capes and coastal features that they passed. Spanish captains like Anton and Zarate, who watched them at work, expressed concern about this because they realized that once Drake's log was published in England there would be a train of imitators sailing in his wake who would turn the Peaceful Sea into a pirates' paradise. It was on experienced pilots that the adventurous mariner relied rather than charts and instruments. Thus the first thing that Drake did on capturing a ship was to find its pilot and pump him dry of information or take him for a ride.

Partly because of inadequate navigational instruments and partly because the winds were advantageous, the way to the West Indies lay down the coasts of Europe and Africa as far as the latitude of Cape Blanco or Cape Verde with a call at the Canary Islands for wood and water. Then the master set a course due west across the Atlantic to the Lesser Antilles, where he would check his position, often finding himself at the wrong island, and then go island-hopping, north to Hispaniola or south to the Main. The Middle Passage, later to become so notorious in the peak years of the slave trade, took between thirty-five and forty-five days. As the details of Hawkins's third voyage have shown, trading was done without hurry. On the second voyage when Hawkins left the Main he set course for Hispaniola, but the lack of a local pilot and his ignorance of the westward trend of the Caribbean Current carried him to Jamaica instead, whence it was impossible to beat to windward for the larger island. So he set course for the Yucatan Channel, aiming to call at Havana, but without a chart or a

Exploration and Early Colonization

Sir John Hawkins, who pioneered English trade in the Caribbean between 1562 and 1568 and died off Puerto Rico in 1595. Portrait by an unknown artist.

Sir Francis Drake, by an unknown artist. Following Hawkins and sharing with him the Spanish treachery at San Juan d'Ulloa, he took to privateering in the 1570s, led the Great West Indian Raid in 1585, and died within a few weeks of Hawkins in January, 1596. He was buried off Nombre de Dios.

Sir Walter Raleigh, who made voyages to Guyana and Trinidad in 1595 and 1617.

A family of Carib Indians in St Vincent. An idyllic print from Bryan Edwards's
History of the West Indies, 1794. The Caribs and the Arawaks formed the principal
aboriginal inhabitants of the West Indies. The extermination of the Arawaks by the
Spaniards in Hispaniola, and the intractability of the Caribs as labourers, led to the
introduction of slaves from Africa.

An Arawak village in Guyana, 1833. Descendants of both Arawaks and Caribs are still found in that country today.

The Guyana forests in 1833, as portrayed in *Transatlantic Sketches* by Capt. J. E. Alexander.

Above, left James Hay, Earl of Carlisle, Lord Proprietor of the Caribbee Islands.

Above, right Philip Herbert, Earl of Pembroke and Montgomery (1584–1650), who disputed the proprietorship of Barbados with Carlisle.

Left Robert Rich, Earl of Warwick, promoter of the Providence Island Company and later parliamentary Governor-in-chief of all English colonies in America.

Left John Pym, Treasurer of
the Providence Island
Company, until parliamentary
leadership claimed his full
attention after 1640.

Below Sandy Point, north-east
St Kitts, looking across to
Dutch St Eustatius. From here
post horses could be hired for
travel to Basseterre, fifteen
miles to the south.

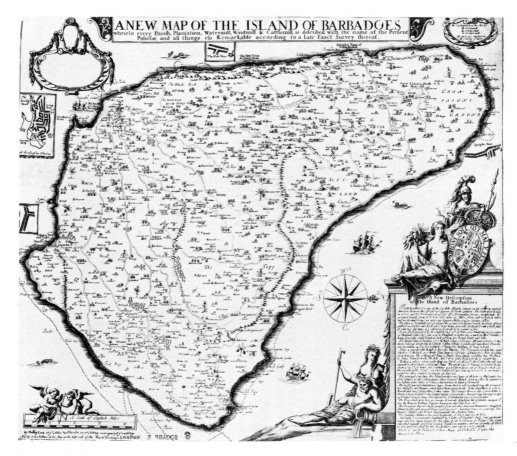

Barbados, 1695.

Curing tobacco, the first export from the English colonies.

pilot he missed it. The Gulf Stream then carried him into the Florida Strait where a Frenchman he had recruited for the purpose guided him to the French settlement of Fort Caroline. Somewhere along the North American coast ships would stop for wood and water before starting on their homeward crossing of the Atlantic. On the voyage just quoted Hawkins sailed as far as Newfoundland, where he bought fish from the fishermen and caught some of his own before making the Atlantic crossing on the westerlies in three or four weeks. Such was the circular pattern of West Indian voyages in the days of sail.

Under such primitive conditions were the first English voyages to the Caribbean made. John Oxenham, a close companion of Francis Drake at Nombre de Dios, returned to Darien on his own in 1576, crossed the isthmus with the guidance of the Cimaroons and raised havoc on the Pacific. He had a plan that anticipated that of William Patterson 120 years later, to hold the strategic isthmus and control its trade, but the fifty-seven men he took with him were far too few to carry it into effect. Over-confident, he allowed himself to be surprised by the Spaniards, who carried him away to captivity in Lima. Drake knew all about Oxenham's raid; he may have hoped to join forces with him after passing through the Straits of Magellan. He asked Spanish prisoners for news of his friend and threatened to kill two thousand Spaniards if any harm was done to him. It was all to no avail. As Drake sailed north to California John Oxenham was executed in Lima.

Thomas Cavendish, the second English circumnavigator, is often ignored. Although he was of lesser calibre than Drake, his voyage was still a remarkable feat. A courtier hoping to rebuild his fortune and aged only twenty-six, Cavendish in July 1586 led 123 men in three ships out of Plymouth along Drake's route to the Straits of Magellen. After a passage of forty-nine days (Drake was to hold the record with only sixteen) Cavendish's men suffered extreme privation, subsisting on limpets, mussels and birds, before they made their way to Quintero north of Valparaiso, where later Admiral Cochrane was to be given a farm. Making their way up the inhospitable coast, they found the Spaniards watchful and no longer sleeping by loads of silver as Drake had done, until, appropriately off the Costa Rica, they met the unarmed galleon *Santa Anna* which they relieved of twenty-two thousand gold pesos and eighty tons of merchandise. Cavendish came back to Plymouth in September 1588, just missing the last remnants of the Armada as they made their broken way back to Spain. In 1591 he sailed again, in company with John Davis of the North-West Passage, but the voyage achieved nothing except the temporary capture of Santos in Brazil. Thomas Cavendish was lost at sea and the experience of some of the survivors in another ship have already been described.

On that voyage John Davis came upon the Falkland Islands. Eighteen months later Richard Hawkins, son of Sir John, also saw them and took them to be part of Terra Australis Incognita. Richard sailed in his comparatively large galleon *Dainty* of 350 tons. He took forty-six days through the Straits, having the luck to suffer no damage after striking a rock. He found the Spaniards more wakeful than Cavendish had done. Out of Callao he was pursued by six ships and two thousand men. He temporarily eluded them. If he had proceeded with the second object of the voyage, the exploration of the Asian side of the Pacific, all might have been well, but his men forced him to stay in the Panama area plundering shipping. Here the Spanish squadron caught him. After a three-day battle in which he lost fifty-five of his seventy-five men he surrendered his sinking ship. This was in June 1594. After eight years in captivity he was ransomed, returning to England in 1602.

Meanwhile Richard's eminent father and Sir Francis Drake had made their last joint voyage to the Caribbean. It was a tragic story in which there was no vestige of glory. Although they sailed with twenty-seven ships they achieved nothing at all. Drake and Hawkins quarrelled. They were repulsed at the Canaries. They were repulsed at San Juan de Puerto Rico. There Hawkins fell ill and died. Drake sailed on to the Main. He captured Rio de la Hacha and Santa Marta but had insufficient men to repeat his capture of Cartagena of 1585. He landed at Nombre de Dios where he had made his name twenty-three years before. In a feeble attempt to cross the isthmus the English soldiers suffered a third repulse. Perhaps it was shame as much as fever that killed the mighty Drake. John Hawkins was so distressed over their failure at San Juan that he left £2,000 in his will to the Queen as a token of compensation.

The year after Drake and Hawkins died San Juan de Puerto Rico was captured by George Clifford, Earl of Cumberland, with a thousand men. It was a short-lived success, for disease so reduced his force that he was compelled to evacuate the town. This was the last considerable expedition of the long, fruitless war. At the end of it England was no better off than she had been at the beginning. Spain still refused free trade. The main English interest had been to plunder the Spanish colonies. This was an unworthy aim and led to nothing. Within a few years of the Peace of London, a more laudable interest developed in the shape of colonization. It was there that the English were to find their true métier.

2
PIONEERS OF ENGLISH COLONIZATION

When Englishmen first thought of the idea of founding colonies, the Spaniards had possessed theirs for the better part of three generations. Indeed the speed at which Spanish colonies had been founded after the discovery of the New World had been remarkable. By the beginning of Elizabeth's reign the Spaniards were in occupation of Mexico and Peru (their principal treasure-mines), Panama on the Pacific coast of Darien, scattered settlements along the Main such as Cartagena and Santa Marta, pearl fisheries at Margarita, Cumana and Coro. In the Greater Antilles, Havana in Cuba, Santo Domingo in Hispaniola and San Juan in Puerto Rico were centres of some importance and Jamaica had a few small settlements. There was also the single outpost of St Augustine in Florida, flanking the homeward route of the treasure galleons. Spaniards had explored the Orinoco where the legend of El Dorado had attracted their treasure-struck attention. In the Lesser Antilles and along the South American coast from the Orinoco delta past the mouth of the Amazon as far as the first Portuguese colonies in Brazil, there were no Spanish settlements at all. Yet Spain claimed all this huge area as part of her exclusive preserve.

From the appearance of John Rut at Santo Domingo in 1528 to the deaths of Hawkins and Drake in 1595 and 1596 there had been a succession of English and French adventurers, at first seeking peaceful trade and, when this was denied them, turning to privateering, as we have seen. The first English attempt to found a colony was made in Newfoundland by Sir Humphrey Gilbert in 1583. It failed when Gilbert was drowned. His half-brother, Sir Walter Raleigh, took over his patent. In 1585 and 1587 two attempts were made to found a colony on Roanoke Island off the Virginian coast. The survivors of the first venture were rescued by Drake on his return from the great West Indian raid. The second colony, neglected through preoccupation with the invasion threat from the Armada, disappeared. The long war that followed rendered any further attempts impracticable.

When James I succeeded Elizabeth in 1603 one of his earliest acts was to bring the long war to an end. In 1604, the year of the Peace of London, the first English settlement was made on the coast of Guiana, or Guyana, the name by which the low swampy river-threaded shore between Amazon and Orinoco was known.

The Spanish colonies were government foundations and their main industry was the mining of precious metals and gems. The first English colonies were founded by private enterprise with limited resources, and involved ridiculously small numbers of men. For these reasons many of the early ventures ended in failure. The first appearance of the English in the Orinoco region occurred in 1592 when Captain Benjamin Wood and John Chudley sailed into the Gulf of Paria. Next year Captain Jacob Whidden, with an advance-party sent ahead by Raleigh, landed in Trinidad and established friendly relations with Antonio de Berrio, the Spanish governor of the small colony of San Josef. In spite of this friendship, however, Whidden's men were ambushed by other Spaniards. Without enough men to retaliate he returned to England where he complained to Raleigh of the Spaniards' treachery. It was a minor repetition of San Juan d'Ulloa. In 1595 Raleigh himself arrived with three well-equipped ships and three hundred men. Inquisitive dilettante that he was, Raleigh sampled the tree-oysters, visited the pitch lake and used the pitch to caulk his ships. When de Berrio refused to welcome him personally, Raleigh attacked San Josef, sacked it and captured the governor. The Englishman was having a general look round, but his greatest interest lay in the discovery of the land of El Dorado, 'the Gilded One', who he hoped would produce for Elizabeth as much treasure as Montezuma and Atahuallpa had supplied to Charles I of Spain. If he had made such a find then England might have founded an empire on the Spanish model, but it was not to be. After navigating the Orinoco for four hundred miles he was driven back by great floods on the river and sailed home to England. In 1667 John Scott, writing from Barbados, suggested that the Spaniards had deliberately fed the story of El Dorado to Raleigh to distract his attention from their richer settlements along the Main.

Before he sailed away, Raleigh left two men on the Orinoco to establish friendly relations with the Indians. The first, Francis Sparrey, was captured by Spaniards, but the second, Hugh Goodwin, spent twenty years with the Indians, only returning home with Raleigh's ill-fated expedition of 1617. Although he made no immediate return to Trinidad and the Orinoco himself, during the next two years Sir Walter dispatched two expeditions to the area. Lawrence Keymis explored the river mouths towards the Amazon. He was followed in 1597 by Captain Leonard Berry, who made a more detailed survey of the rivers Courentyne, Marawine and Wiapoco, where he was well received by the Indians from whom he came home with a cargo of cotton and tobacco. From this reconnaissance came the first attempt at a plantation settlement. A few years before it happened the French and Dutch appeared on the Guiana coast and the stage was set for European activity there for the next two hundred years, featuring a relationship, at first friendly and co-operative, but gradually becoming so competitive that it led first to the surrender of English Surinam to the Dutch and later to the capture of the Dutch colonies of Essequibo, Demerara and Berbice by Great Britain.

The Wiapoco river, or Oyapok as it is named on modern maps, where it forms the eastern boundary of French Guiana or Cayenne, is navigable for fifty miles to the foot of the first falls that break all the rivers of the Guiana region. Here, in 1602, came Captain Charles Leigh on a voyage of exploration. Liking what he saw, he returned to London, where with his brother, Sir Oliph Leigh, he raised sufficient money to back a tobacco-planting colony. On 21 March 1604, Charles Leigh sailed from Woolwich on the fifty-ton *Olive Plant* with forty-six men and boys. At first the colonists tried to live independently of the local Indians, but they were soon driven to seek their help through shortage of provisions. These the Arawak Indians supplied in return for the Englishmen's support against their inveterate enemies, the Caribs. By this time a number of Leigh's men were growing disheartened. They thought it would be more profitable to go off privateering and Leigh was faced with mutiny. But he quelled it by persuasion and the men agreed to give the planting a trial for a full year. In July 1604 he sent the *Olive Plant* home with an optimistic report and a request for another hundred men. He hoped that flax would thrive, yielding between four and eight tons to the acre, and sell for £50 a ton. He also talked of growing cotton and sugar-cane. Soon after the ship left the thirty-five remaining colonists repulsed a Carib attack from the River Cayenne. Then sickness struck. When the *Olive Plant* returned nine colonists had died and the rest were suffering from 'agues and fluxes', but they had learnt a lesson from their Indian allies, sleeping in hammocks off the ground with a fire burning underneath to reduce the damp and the attacks of mosquitoes. It was here in Guiana that Englishmen first met the hammock, taking the Indian word *hamaca* into the language at the same time as *tabaca* or *tabac* came in. In the case of the latter some unnamed Spanish pioneer must have been responsible for a misunderstanding, for to the Indians *tabaca* was the pipe and not the leaf smoked in it. The English word was adopted from the Spanish *tabaco*. Later the Indian hammock was to be adopted by the English navy, but in the pioneer settlements of

Guiana it was a very useful item of furniture, folding away in the daytime to allow a single room to serve for both sleeping and eating.

On its return the *Olive Plant* had brought thirty new colonists under a Captain Huntley. An expedition was dispatched to search for gold further inland, but its members returned not with gold but with fever. Then the blow fell. Charles Leigh had gone on board the ship and there he died. To prevent a panic his death was kept secret and the colonists were led to believe he had sailed home on business. In the meantime Sir Oliph Leigh had sent out a second ship, the *Olive Branch*, of 170 tons with seventy new men, but the captain overshot the mouth of the Wiapoco, and because of the steady easterly current and the Trade Winds could not beat back. The case is a telling example of the importance of the prevailing north-east trade winds in the whole Caribbean area and the inaccuracy of navigation without the means of determining longitude. There was no alternative for the master of the *Olive Branch* but to sail on westwards and turn north into the Lesser Antilles. There the colonists were set down on the island of St Lucia, where most of them were killed by the warlike Caribs. Meanwhile on the Wiapoco, without their leader the colonists gave up hope. A few survivors found their way home on Dutch ships, and the first English plantation in the area came to a sad end. Apart from the small numbers and meagre financial resources failure had come because of the choice of an unhealthy place and the unsuitability of the climate for white labour under a scorching tropical sun; but all this had to be found out by trial and error. In 1607 a French colony was also attempted on the Wiapoco with four hundred men but that too had been 'cut off' two years later. The Dutch, on the other hand, had discovered a more practical form of life so close to the equator: they simply set up 'factories' and traded with the Indians, whom they persuaded to do the cultivation.

The next Englishman to go to Guiana was Robert Harcourt, eldest son of Sir Walter Harcourt of Stanton Harcourt, Oxfordshire. The patronage of Prince Henry brought him a royal commission. On 23 March 1609, he sailed from Dartmouth in the *Rose* of eighty tons, a pinnace of thirty-six tons and a shallop of nine tons, which must have been the smallest ship to set out across the Atlantic of all the many little vessels employed by a generation of intrepid adventurers. It was quite a family party, for with Robert sailed his brother Michael and his cousin, Thomas Harcourt. Travelling by way of the Canary Islands, they made a good passage and arrived at the Wiapoco on 17 May. Accompanying the sixty colonists Harcourt brought an Indian chief who had been in England four years. This man must have been a useful acquisition. As well as interpreting, his authority helped to smooth relations with the Indians. Robert Harcourt had probably been influenced by the Dutch, because he asked the Indians to provide his colonists with food in return for protection against their enemies and a supply of axes, hatchets, knives, beads, mirrors and 'Jewes' trumps'. Settling at the site of Leigh's village, he sent out exploring parties to look for gold. One hundred miles to the west he called on an Indian chief, who was a Christian; he too had been in England, with Raleigh. He told Harcourt that the Wiapoco was known to the Indians as an unhealthy area, but the colony's initial prospects looked bright, for friendly relations were established with all neighbouring Indians, including the Caribs of Cayenne. Harcourt sent home an enthusiastic description of the chief articles of trade, including cotton and sugar-cane. This mention of sugar-cane is intriguing because it is not indigenous to South America. Although the Spaniards had introduced cane-growing in Hispaniola very early, and the Portuguese had brought it into Brazil, neither Spanish nor Portuguese had traded along the Guiana coast, and it was from Brazil that sugar-cane was to be introduced into Barbados in the 1640s. Also mentioned by Harcourt were cotton and 'a natural Hempe or Flax, almost as fine as silk', various dyestuffs, gums and drugs, speckled woods for furniture, 'worth thirtie or fortie pounds a Tun', and tobacco.

On 14 August 1609 Harcourt held a ceremony at which he took formal possession of Guiana 'by Turfe and Twigge in the behalf of our Sovereigne Lord King James'. Four days later he sailed home, exploring other river mouths on the way, leaving his brother Michael in command of the colony. Back in England he decided that the best plan would be to persuade the Indians to grow sugar-cane and cotton under English supervision, but he now had difficulty in raising money. Wealthy London merchants were investing in Virginia and the East India Company, leaving Guiana as the preserve of courtiers and country gentlemen, and courtiers were always short of cash. Harcourt was reduced to sending out a few colonists on Dutch vessels. Although a new patent was issued to Robert Harcourt in 1613, no records survive after that date and it is presumed that the settlement was abandoned. Before the colony's end, however, there is evidence of a remarkable journey conducted by a Captain Matthew Morton, who had been in Virginia with John Smith. Using Indian canoes, he travelled from the Amazon across to the headwaters of the Wiapoco. He followed the river down to the settlement, negotiating thirty-two falls and taking thirteen months over the journey. From there, 'not finding all the West Indies to be full of Gold, as some suppose, he returned by Trenydado'.

Morton had travelled out to the Amazon with Sir Thomas Roe, a man who was later to make his mark in India as an early ambassador. Backed by Raleigh and the Earl of Southampton and others, Roe left Dartmouth with two ships in February 1610. He was the first Englishman to sail up the mighty river, penetrating two hundred miles in his ships and a further hundred by boat. He was probably looking for the kingdom of Manoa and its gilded king. After his return to England in 1611, two more expeditions were dispatched but little is known of them save a report of 1617 in which Sir Thomas Roe's men, it was said, 'are richly retourned in a Holland shippe . . . and mean to retourne.' They had £2,300 worth of tobacco and ingots of gold.

It was the lure of gold that brought Sir Walter Raleigh back on to the scene to play to his final curtain, after his release from the Tower, where he had been confined for twelve years on flimsy evidence that he was implicated in Cobham's plot to supplant James I with his cousin, Arabella Stuart. Eventually the extravagant James also fell under the spell of El Dorado, as a means of escape from his debts, so he let Raleigh go to find the gold mine which Lawrence Keymis had heard of back in 1595. As evidence of the peaceful nature of the expedition, James gave Count Gondomar, the Spanish ambassador, full details of Raleigh's plans and, as Raleigh delayed while a new ship was built for him, Gondomar had plenty of time to warn the governor of San Tomé on the Orinoco that the English were coming. Yet the very size of Raleigh's expedition does not sound as if his intentions were peaceful, for he sailed from Plymouth on 12 June 1617 with fourteen ships and more than nine hundred men. It was ill-fated from the start. Bad weather kept him in home waters until 19 August when he finally saw the last of the Irish coast, and it was not until November that he reached the Wiapoco after losing four ships through desertion. They moved west to Trinidad. Here Raleigh waited with half the force to guard the mouth of the Orinoco, while Keymis went up the river to find the gold mine, taking with him Raleigh's young son Walter and his nephew George. In the long interval the Spaniards had moved the settlement of San Tomé thirty miles downstream. From its new position Keymis was unexpectedly fired upon. Naturally he retaliated. In the fighting that ensued young Walter was killed before San Tomé was captured. It was a barren conquest. Four weeks later poor Lawrence Keymis sailed back to Trinidad, without any gold, without 250 of his men who had died of fever, and without his leader's son. After making his dutiful report, Keymis committed suicide. Raleigh, knowing that his own fate was sealed because his men had fought with Spaniards, did not hesitate to sail home and die on Tower Hill, the last of the Elizabethans.

After the death of Sir Walter Raleigh the interest in the Guiana region survived with a change of emphasis. Gold mines were out and so was the Orinoco, but in 1619, one of Raleigh's captains, Roger North, was instrumental in obtaining a royal patent for the formation of a new enterprise called the Amazon Company, including among its backers the name of Robert Rich, Earl of Warwick, who was to play a leading part in early colonization. Departure of the expedition was delayed by the protests of Gondomar as well as those of Robert Harcourt, who still held his patent and objected that North had been granted some of his allotted areas; authorities in England have been notably ignorant of geography for the better part of four centuries. Eventually North sailed at the end of April 1620 with four ships and had a quick passage of seven weeks to the mouth of the Amazon. In the account that follows a small window is opened on other enterprises of which no accounts have survived, for there on the great river, somewhere near the confluence with the Xingu, North came upon English and Irishmen who had been living there for eight years. One of his pinnaces penetrated possibly as far as the Tapajos confluence four hundred miles from the sea. North's men thought the country delightful. They seem to have been impervious to the heat and he sent back a glowing report of the possibilities of the region:

Sugar-canes, Cotten Wolles, Dyes in grain, Woods of price, Tobacco, Drugges, Oyles, Gummes, wax, some spices, spleen stones, feathers and divers Mineralls . . . islands of wild Nuttmegg trees. . . . The Christians who live in the Countrye take no paines nor labour for anythinge: the Indians both house them, work for them, bring them victualls, and their Commodities for a small reward and price, either of some Iron worke or glasse beads, and such like contemptible things, whereof great vent should be made, and many Artificers mainteyned.

So much for enthusiasm from the man on the spot; when North sailed home shortly afterwards with twenty-five of the settlers he had met he was arrested and thrown into the Tower, for the miserable James had capitulated to Gondomar and forced Warwick to surrender his patent. Fortunately North was soon freed.

Meanwhile disaster had befallen the colonists on the river. In 1615, after hearing of intruders entering the Amazon, the Portuguese had founded the settlement of Para from which to bar the mouth. Now urged on by Spanish pressure, the Portuguese attacked the various English, Irish and Dutch settlements. By 1625, as a result of Portuguese attacks and lack of support from his king, North's colony came to an unhappy end.

But 1625 saw also the end of the reign of James I and his succession by Charles I, who came to the throne incensed against Spain for the snub he and Buckingham had received over their ridiculous attempt to woo the Spanish Infanta. The hopes of English adventurers revived and the new reign opened with a sensible combination of the interests of Harcourt and North.

On 2 June 1627 a royal patent was issued, incorporating 'The Governor and Company of Noblemen and Gentlemen of England for the plantation of Guiana'. It was a highly select company, including among its fifty-five shareholders or 'adventurers' fifteen peers, two bishops, nineteen baronets and knights, seventeen squires and gentlemen, one peeress and one doctor of divinity. To crown the pedestal the governor was no less a personage than the king's favourite, George Villiers, Duke of Buckingham. Roger North was deputy-governor. Among the peers were the Earls of Pembroke, Carlisle and Holland, names that were to become associated with other enterprises a little later. Noble names might add kudos, but there was little money. The company's prospects would have been brighter if its subscription list had included some of the leading London merchants. As it was, the initial capital did not amount to more than £5,000, a sum which today scarcely suffices to build a house, let alone found a colony. Nevertheless, this inconsiderable sum sent out 112 colonists under the leadership of James Purcell, an Irishman whom North had discovered on the Amazon. Landing on the island of Tocujos in April 1628, they built a strong fort, planted tobacco and traded with the Indians. This propitious start did not please the Portuguese. In 1629 they attacked the colony with 1,700 men. Purcell's men repulsed them, but the Portuguese settled down to a regular siege. After four weeks Purcell had no alternative but to surrender: which he did on promise of life and repatriation. Three days later reinforcements of two hundred men arrived from England. As the Portuguese had left a garrison in the fort these new arrivals settled lower down the river. Once again the Portuguese attacked. On 1 March 1631 the last English colony on the Amazon surrendered. In vain the Company petitioned the king to take over and turn the colony into a Crown enterprise, but Charles was as pushed for money as his courtiers and he had by 1631 embarked on his rule without Parliament. Together, a national enterprise could have succeeded, but for such a venture England had to wait until Oliver Cromwell became Protector. Meanwhile another voyage had been undertaken by Robert Harcourt. Instead of going to the Amazon, however, he had against his instructions sailed to his beloved Wiapoco. There on 20 May 1631 he died at the age of fifty-seven, and the colony disappeared shortly afterwards. No more voyages were undertaken after 1631. Although the company continued to exist it did nothing until it was dissolved in 1638.

So a forgotten chapter of English colonization came to an end. In the early seventeenth century Guiana had been regarded as of equal potential with Virginia. Although the Wiapoco colonies had proved unhealthy, those on the Amazon had not suffered seriously from ill-health. It was Portuguese antagonism that led to their collapse, and so Englishmen turned towards Virginia as a place free from both Portuguese and Spanish attack. Yet it was action from men who had been on the Amazon with Roger North that led to the successful foundation of the first permanent English colony in the Caribbean.

3
THE CARIBBEE ISLANDS

Among Roger North's company on the Amazon there had been numbered Captain Thomas Warner, a Suffolk man of good family but no fortune. In 1622, accompanied by John Rhodes and Robert Binns, he left the Amazon to look for a place of his own, 'free from the disorders that did grow in the Amazons for want of Government among their Countrey-men, and to be quiet among themselves'. Their homeward voyage took them through the Lesser Antilles, that archipelago of small, beautiful, mountainous islands trending north and north-west from Trinidad to Puerto Rico, until to-wards its northern end they dropped anchor off the island which Columbus had named St Christopher and was later conveniently abbreviated by the English to St Kitts. Here on this tadpole-shaped island, twenty miles long, six miles across at its broadest, and rising in such a short distance to more than 3,700 feet, the first permanent English colony in the Caribbean was founded.

In 1622, however, Thomas Warner was only on reconnaissance. He made friends with the Carib inhabitants and stayed with them for six months, planting an experimental crop of tobacco. When this had been harvested and cured, he sailed home to find financial support and colonists for the settlement he had decided to establish. In London he was successful in persuading a merchant named Ralph Merrifield to form a small syndicate to invest in his proposed colony. Towards the end of 1623 the *Marmaduke* set sail with a very small number of men. The actual number is uncertain, being given by various authorities as anything between fourteen and nine-teen men. With this small resolute band Warner landed on St Christopher on 28 January 1624. Two previous attempts at colonizing the islands had been made: that of the reinforcements for Charles Leigh's colony who had sailed past the Wiapoco and landed on St Lucia, and another venture of 1609 on Grenada, both of which had failed because of attacks by Caribs. There was every chance that the same fate might have overcome Warner's

forlorn hope had he not been a wakeful and ruthless man. His men had
settled close to a Carib village, where Warner had made friends with the
chief in 1622, but this time the Indians became suspicious as they saw the
Englishmen erecting a large wooden building which, they were told, was
being built 'that they might look after those fowles they had about their
houses'. Although ignorant of both forts and fowl-houses, the Caribs did
not like what they saw and planned to attack their visitors, but Warner got
his blow in first. The English destroyed the Carib village, massacring the
majority of the inhabitants. This would not have been the end of the Carib
menace, because there were other settlements on the island and on neighbouring islands within sight of St Kitts. Warner realized his appalling
weakness in numbers and so, when a French ship arrived carrying a crew
of adventurers under Pierre Belain d'Esnambuc, Thomas Warner invited
the Frenchman to join forces with him. There is no record of the number of
Frenchmen nor of the negotiations that took place, but the forceful
Englishman succeeded in persuading the French to accept the northern and
southern extremities of the island, leaving the English a consolidated holding in the middle. Amicable arrangements allowed members of each nation
to pass freely through the territory of the other and to use all rivers, salt
ponds, woods and mines in common. Most important, the colonists agreed
to observe strict neutrality if their home countries should go to war, and to
render each other aid in the event of Spanish or Carib attack. Thus in the
small island of St Christopher both England and France had the foundations of their West Indian empires laid for them by enterprising individuals
who were prepared to make common cause and forget national differences.
There was much co-operation among men of the north European nations
in the seventeenth century. Not long after the pact of Warner and
d'Esnambuc at St Kitts, other Frenchmen made an amicable division with
the Dutch of the island of St Martin, sixty miles to the north-west, which
has survived to the present day. Dutch and English made common ventures in Guiana and were to develop a mutually profitable sugar trade in
Barbados until the English government put a stop to it. Among the
Buccaneers, English, French and Dutch were all to fight together against
Spain. The point is that these friendships were formed not by governments
but by individual adventurers far away from the supervision of their home
authorities.

Fortified though they were against possible Carib or Spanish attack, the
French and English colonists could do little of mutual assistance when
nature struck against them with the first hurricane, which destroyed
Warner's first crop of tobacco. Hurricanes, occurring rarely south of latitude 10° North and therefore unknown in Guiana or on the Amazon, were
a new experience for Thomas Warner and one that he had to grow used to,

because in the Leeward Islands they come on an average once in five years. So the shattered colonists set to work replanting. By March 1625 they had raised another crop which created a good impression when it reached London on the *Hopewell* under Captain John Jeafferson.

Tobacco was the ideal crop for the pioneer colony of St Christopher because it was easy to grow. Half an ounce of seed produces between fifteen and twenty-five thousand plants which are ready for harvesting after four to six months, depending on the variety. The island was well watered and possessed of fertile soil. Lying across the direction of the north-east Trade Winds, its leeward coast provided sheltered anchorage. In England pipe-smoking was the social rage. Although Sir Walter Raleigh is popularly credited with the introduction of tobacco, there is no direct evidence that he was responsible, only that Ralph Lane, governor of the first attempted Virginia colony, presented his patron with an Indian pipe. By 1600 the smoking habit was widespread and by 1619 the Pipemakers'

St Christopher, showing the partition of 1627

Company of London was incorporated. Early pipe-smokers' equipment was cumbersome, consisting of tobacco-box, pipe, ember-box, priming flint and steel, but the 'noxious weed' was ridiculously cheap, selling in London for 1s 8d a pound.

Early in 1625 Warner and d'Esnambuc gave each other mutual support in driving off a massive Carib attack launched from neighbouring islands. It was estimated that nearly four thousand Indians descended on the struggling settlements. Shortly after this event there arrived an English ship homeward bound from Bahia in Brazil, under Captain Henry Powell. On the way Powell had found himself, more by accident than design, at the uninhabited island of Barbados. He may have heard of it previously because it had been visited in 1620 by Captain Simon Gordon, the first Englishman recorded to have seen it. Situated as it is eighty miles east of St Vincent, Barbados lies outside the chain of the archipelago and many ships sailing northwards missed it. The Spaniards knew of its existence but had shown no interest in it, although a beneficent Spanish captain had loosed some pigs ashore for which the early colonists were to be grateful. Henry Powell had been impressed with the island's potential. He took possession of it, setting up an inscription reading 'James, King of England and this island'. While he waited at St Christopher some of his sailors talked about it and Warner got to hear of it. Obviously the new island held a great advantage over St Kitts, for if it was uninhabited and well to windward of the other islands it should be spared the menace of Carib attacks. Warner filed the information in his retentive memory, doubtless labelled for urgent action, and then took himself home to England, possibly on Powell's ship, for apart from Powell's discovery it was time to seek official recognition for his own colony. Henry Powell must have later come to curse the fate that had led him to St Christopher, for out of his blabbing sailors' mouths arose calamitous troubles.

Once home Warner went quickly to work. Charles I had succeeded his father, James I, in February and was spoiling for war with Spain, so any planting enterprise in America was assured of royal favour. On 13 September 1625 a royal patent was issued authorizing Thomas Warner, Ralph Merrifield and others to plant and colonize the islands of St Christopher, Nevis, Barbados and Montserrat. Warner was appointed governor and John Jeafferson, captain of the *Hopewell*, his deputy. For some unknown reason Warner did not hurry back to St Kitts, but during his time in England further merchant backing was received, notably from Maurice Thompson of London and Thomas Combe of Southampton. Eventually it was with three ships belonging to them that he sailed in May 1626 with a hundred new colonists. On the way Warner acquired sixty negro slaves and reached St Christopher on 4 August. Next month another hurricane struck, destroying two of the ships, but the tobacco crop previously harvested was saved. In 1627 Combe and Thompson's surviving ship brought home thirty thousand pounds of tobacco. Their investment was beginning to pay quick returns.

At the same time Henry Powell had been busy. Looking for financial backing as all his fellow adventurers had to do, he found a prominent London merchant in the person of Sir William Courteen, the son of a Netherlands refugee in the reign of Elizabeth. Leaving Courteen to arrange for the necessary patent, Powell sailed with eighty colonists in a ship called the *William and John* and landed in Barbados on 20 February 1627, founding the second English colony in the West Indies. Because the island was uninhabited, however, Powell's first task was to ensure an adequate supply of provisions. To do this he sailed south to the Essequibo river in Guiana, where an Anglo-Dutch colony had been in existence since 1616 under a Captain Groenwegen. From this well-established settlement Henry Powell returned to Barbados with yams, cassava, maize and plantains to plant for feeding the colonists, and plants or seed of tobacco, cotton and annatto (a dye) for cash crops. To initiate his greenhorns into the secrets of tropical agriculture he brought between thirty and forty Arawak Indians and these unfortunates, instead of being repatriated as they had been promised, were later enslaved, though not by Powell. In May Henry's nephew John arrived from England with another ninety settlers, including the first women. The Arawaks also brought with them oranges, lemons, limes and pomegranates. In the meantime the colonists had been hunting the feral pigs.

The ham-shaped island of Barbados is bigger and less mountainous than St Kitts. Though both measure twenty miles from north to south, Barbados is more than twice as wide and rises to only 1,100 feet. Consisting mostly of limestone it has few rivers, so that water-supply was an early problem. In

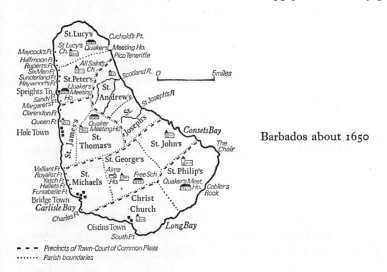

Barbados about 1650

- - - Precincts of Town-Court of Common Pleas
.... Parish boundaries

1627 it was covered with forest, full of 'Brazil-wood', the loose term used at the time to include various kinds of dye-wood. Until the forests were cleared the dye-wood provided a valuable trade item, for dyes were much in demand, especially in the Netherlands, where the first permanent black dye from logwood had been discovered in 1600. Neither island possessed a natural harbour, but there was good sheltered anchorage along the leeward shores. Hand-clearing of the forests was slow work. Because it was done by burning, the early farms were dotted with blackened tree stumps; it was a long time before the island assumed the neat garden-like appearance it presents today. In both Barbados and St Kitts immigrants began to arrive at an increasing rate. In 1627 St Kitts welcomed its first women colonists headed by Mistress Warner. By 1629 it was estimated that there were about three thousand colonists there, and between 1,600 and 1,800 at Barbados.

If the colonists had been left to develop their plantations in peace, economic prosperity might have climbed quickly to a high level, but considerations of government came to exercise a serious check. As it has been described, the first English colonies had come into existence by the enterprise of individual adventurers without any government initiative. There was therefore no government machinery in existence to deal with their regulation, and resort was made to two expedients: either a royal patent issued to an individual like Sir Humphrey Gilbert or Sir Walter Raleigh, or the incorporation of a chartered company like the East India, Virginia, or Amazon Companies. As far as purely trading ventures were concerned, the system worked conveniently because the governor and merchant members of the company were made responsible for the orderly conduct of their affairs and the discipline of their traders. If there were complaints the responsible officers were close at hand in the City of London. But when the same system came to be applied to colonies separated from London by four thousand miles of ocean and a round voyage of a minimum ten or twelve weeks, new problems were bound to arise. Irregularities in the colonies could develop into undesirable customs before anything could be done about them, while complaints of abuses made only a faint whisper in London. Not long after the first issue of Charles I's patent to Warner and Merrifield the King had second thoughts: he preferred to keep the control in the hands of courtiers who owed him feudal allegiance. Merchants, who owned the all-important money, found it necessary to seek a titled patron to deal in person with the King. So Merrifield, Combe and Thompson, joined by another merchant, Marmaduke (later Sir Marmaduke) Royden obtained the patronage of James Hay, first Earl of Carlisle, a jovial spendthrift who had come from Scotland under the wing of James I, and who was heavily in debt to Royden. On 2 July 1627 a royal patent was issued to Carlisle appointing him Lord Proprietor of the English Caribbee Islands, including St Christopher, 'Barbidas, Domenica, Mittalenea' [Martinique], St Lucia, St Vincent, Grenada, Montserrat, Antigua and others; in other words most of the Lesser Antilles.

Over six months later, on 25 February 1628, a royal patent was also issued to Philip Herbert, Earl of Montgomery (made Earl of Pembroke in 1630), as Lord Proprietor of the islands of 'Trinidado, Tabago, Barbudos, Fonseca alias St. Bernard'. That the last island was non-existent is immaterial; the important point is that both patents named Barbados. Pembroke was the patron of the Powells and Sir William Courteen. By the time the Pembroke patent was issued the Powells had already taken their colonists to Barbados. There then ensued a bitter quarrel behind the two patrons' backs between their merchant supporters. Trading on the existence of the island of Barbuda seventy miles north-east of St Kitts, Royden and his associates threw dust in the eyes of William Courteen and his brother that they were after this island and not Barbados; in the meantime Royden's friends gathered a batch of eighty colonists together and dispatched them to Barbados under Captain Charles Wolverston, appointed governor by Carlisle. About the time that this party sailed Carlisle obtained a revised patent in which pains were taken to leave no doubt at all about his intentions towards the island of Barbados. To cope with the spelling vagaries of his day the patent referred to the island of 'Barbadas alias Barbades alias Barbudos alias Barbadus'. There was no doubt which island was meant, but it is curious that none of the four versions coincides with the modern spelling. It was curious at the time, too, that the dispute that arose between Pembroke and Carlisle over their patents was settled in favour of Carlisle, not by the common law judges but by the King himself. Lord Keeper Coventry also spoke in favour of Carlisle; it is tempting to wonder what presents found their way into the royal purse.

In Barbados the quarrel nearly had disastrous results. Marmaduke Royden had prompted Carlisle to claim Barbados in the hope that he would be able to recover the large sums of money owed him by the Earl. Accordingly ten thousand acres of land were allocated to Royden and his London merchant associates. When Charles Wolverston arrived in June 1628 fighting between his men and the adherents of the Powells was averted only by the intervention of a clergyman named Kentlane who persuaded John Powell to surrender. In February 1629 the tables were turned when Henry Powell arrived, seized Wolverston and carried him off to England as his prisoner, at the same time helping himself to tobacco worth £12,000 belonging to Royden and Carlisle. He left John Powell as governor.

But not for long. Another character soon made his appearance, one of several colourful personalities in the early days of Barbados. This was an audacious and unscrupulous adventurer named Henry Hawley, who had received the appointment of governor from the Earl of Carlisle. Arriving on 9 August 1629, he found that Henry Powell was back from England, so he invited uncle and nephew to dinner on board his ship. There he seized them and kept them chained to the mainmast for a whole month. Another Courteen man, Sir William Tufton, was goaded into making a protest, arrested, put through a farce of a trial and shot. This time Courteen tobacco was seized. The strong-arm action of Henry Hawley brought the Carlisle party to victory but the quarrel was not over.

Among the colonists such violent quarrels between rival authorities had a serious demoralizing effect. Planting was neglected, food ran short, so that the years 1630 and 1631 became known as the 'Starving Time'. When Sir Henry Colt visited the island in the latter year he left a picture of overgrown farms and idle servants loafing in the sunshine and drowning their sorrows in poisonous drink.

Over in St Kitts there were no disputes over the proprietorship. In 1629 Thomas Warner paid a second visit to England during which he was knighted and appointed governor for life by the Earl of Carlisle, but on the island there occurred trouble of another kind. On 7 September 1629 the annual voyage of Spanish galleons, on its way to Darien, was diverted from its usual more southerly route and appeared at St Christopher. Its thirty-five galleons and merchant vessels must have been an awe-inspiring sight, for the colonists put up little resistance. Four hundred Frenchmen managed to escape across the sea to St Martin, and between two and three hundred English took to the woods in the high centre of the island, but seven hundred others were forced to surrender. Don Fadrique de Toledo, the Spanish admiral, was merciful. Although he destroyed the plantations and timber dwellings, he sent his prisoners back to England with the warning not to return on pain of death. As the Spanish ships sailed away, the refugees in the woods crept back to their ruined farms and started replanting. They had withstood two hurricanes and two Carib attacks and were not to be deterred by a Spanish armada. Sir Thomas Warner on his return in May 1630 soon had planting in full swing again, so much so that in that year the settlement of Antigua and Montserrat began with an overflow of colonists from St Kitts. Nevis, two miles from the southern tip of St Kitts, had received its first settlers in 1628 under Captain Anthony Hilton.

Details of the working of Carlisle's proprietary patent explain the reasons for the unpopularity of proprietary government among the colonists. Carlisle was vested with palatine powers, similar to those granted by William the Conqueror to the Bishop of Durham shortly after 1066 as an exceptional arrangement necessary to secure order in the remote north. Carlisle was therefore vested with king-like powers, including the right of life and death over his subjects. As Carlisle's appointed governor, Sir Thomas Warner sentenced a man to death for defaming Colonel Jeafferson, the deputy-governor. In keeping with feudal custom, Carlisle held his fief of the king by knight service and a quit rent of £100 per annum. He was authorized to set up courts, appoint judges and make laws with the assent of the freeholders. In return for these functions, Carlisle was granted the control of revenue by a seven years' exemption of customs duties, which he made the colonists pay and so derived an income of between £9,000 and £12,000 a year. In addition he took a levy of five per cent of the planters' produce in Barbados and forty pounds of tobacco per head, half of which went to the governor. In St Kitts there was no five-per-cent levy, but the colonists had to pay, in addition to the forty pounds of tobacco, another ten pounds for the upkeep of the church and minister, twenty pounds to the

Captain of the Train Bands and an extra tax of forty pounds for six years towards the cost of defence against the Caribs. Carlisle was also entitled to an anchorage fee of £1 on all foreign ships and seven per cent on all foreign goods landed. A further source of income in Barbados was a rent of twenty pounds of cotton on fifty acres of land for each person over the age of fourteen living on it. In 1632, however, Carlisle was granted a royal pension of £3,000 a year and the King took the customs duties. In Barbados the merchants made money by the acquisition of land which they had worked for them by indentured servants working under overseers. These white slaves were a demoralizing element in the population. There were fewer of them in St Kitts.

In return for all this taxation the colonists derived little benefit, except for the provision of rudimentary defence, a governor and tax-collectors they could well have done without, and a few ministers. Proprietary government was harsh and unsympathetic (frequent use was made of the pillory, whipping, branding, and the cutting off of ears) but it proved itself moderately efficient, for St Kitts and Barbados flourished, if not because of it, then in spite of it. Conditions were better than in the French parts of St Kitts, but this did not prevent the colonists from hating the system. Carlisle was not interested in their welfare, only in the money he could make out of them. The first earl died unmourned in 1636 and his son succeeded to the patent. The Civil War brought temporary relief, but in 1645 Carlisle's rights were restored. In 1647 he leased them to Lord Francis Willoughby for twenty-one years, but the arrangement came to an end soon after the Restoration when Charles ii assumed the proprietorship himself and so turned the islands into Crown colonies.

By 1631 St Kitts had recovered from the effects of the Spanish assault and Barbados saw the end of the 'Starving Time'. From that year there survives an account of a visit made to both islands by Sir Henry Colt, Knight, of Colt Hall in Suffolk. He spent a fortnight at Barbados before moving on to St Kitts and was the first visitor to start lecturing the colonists about how they should run their island after he had been ac-quainted with it for only a short time. Colt took no account of the facts that Barbados had been colonized for only four years when he arrived, and had suffered from the quarrels over government described above. Never-theless, reading between Colt's lines, it becomes obvious that much work had been done and enterprise displayed in the first four years for Colt described the following growing: cotton, vines, oranges, lemons, pome-granates, plantains, pineapples, Indian wheat red and white (maize), cassava for bread, peas, beans, water-melons and musk-melons. All these had been introduced from Guiana. In addition he saw turkeys, peacocks, hens, wild and English hogs, tame and wild pigeons, English cows 'whose milk tastes better than in England' and edible rats (probably agouti or coney). He ate turtle meat (which he thought tasted like a mixture of veal and fish) and commented on the abundance of fish in Carlisle Bay.

Sir Henry described how most of the first plantations had been made near the sea to make use of water-transport before there were any roads, but this exposed the crops to blasting winds off the sea and the attacks of possible marauders. In fact he thought the colonists were careless because no guards were set at night. Obviously he did not appreciate the advantage of the isolated position of Barbados. The ship's captain obliged him by moving the ship opposite the house of the governor – Henry Hawley – so that Sir Henry could entertain him to dinner. His description of this social event was sarcastic: 'The afternoon was spent by some in valiant exercises, according to custom, in drinking and quarrelling.' When Colt was entertained to supper by a Mr Futter the table was laid with pigs, capons, turkeys, chickens, Indian wheat, cassava and cabbages 'whose stem or stalk was two hundred feet long'. This must have been the top of the cabbage-palm.

Before they sailed with a cargo of fustic and tobacco, members of the crew ashore were summoned by the firing of a gun. As they sailed between 'Martinico' and Dominica Colt hoped that Caribs would come out to trade because he had promised a cousin to buy him a '*hammaca*'. He used one himself and describes how a fire was lit beneath it to keep mosquitoes off. Near Les Saintes, the islands between Guadeloupe and Dominica later to be made famous by Rodney, two Spanish ships gave them chase. In escaping this menace they were driven too far to leeward and took a long time beating up into the Trades until they reached St Kitts, where Colt landed on 26 July, twelve days after leaving Barbados. The first action taken by the ship's captain was to warn colonists on Nevis and across at St Martin of the proximity of the Spanish squadron, but it sailed away, missing a wonderful prize, for at St Martin there were no less than forty-eight Dutch vessels refitting with their sails ashore and no ballast aboard. This precious detail underlines the insecurity of life in the early West Indian colonies.

Although Sir Henry Colt landed on St Christopher seven years after the first settlers, his experiences were like those of the pioneers. He described how he ate his supper off the top of a chest in the moonlight, under a moon bright enough to read by and in the balmy open air where the lack of a roof was no hardship. Nevertheless, his first task was the building of a house. He chose a site between two streams, 'for water is to be prized above anything else', but this meant that it was 'far from timber and palmetto for roofing, so that all must be transported upon the shoulders of men', half a mile from the sea, all uphill. He had chosen an abandoned Indian plantation overgrown with plantains and sugar-canes, also annatto, 'that takes the place of fustic in Barbados'. St Kitts had a better soil and more water than Barbados, but 'Barbados has gnats, St Christopher's, rats! . . . They are both equal in squeaking of lizards and other crying creatures at night.' After a few days Sir Henry stopped building the house to plant provisions – maize, peas and potatoes – against 'next year's journey'. He was a restless man. After writing to his son to send him another forty men, he mentioned that the ship coming home was bringing a hundred tons of salt, about fifty tons of fustic and perhaps 100,000 weight [sic] of tobacco. He was sending pines, plantains, guavas, prickly pears, and pepper. 'I do them up in pitch, if they be not ripe hang them up. . . . I would have sent Jack a parrot but they be curst and biting.'

Before the end of 1631, Colt sailed away to Trinidad, where he started a small colony near Punta Galera, the north-east point. But it was attacked and destroyed by the Spanish governor of Margarita Island, whither the enterprising knight was taken and executed in 1632 – a sad ending to one of the earliest chroniclers of West Indian colonization.

After Sir Henry Colt there were few informants about St Kitts and the neighbouring islands until after the Restoration. It must be presumed that 'no news is good news', and this must have been largely due to the long governorship of Sir Thomas Warner, the founder of the colony, who remained in office until his death in 1649. In 1639 he was joined in the French part of the island by a notable Frenchman, the Chevalier Phillippe de Longvilliers de Poincy, who was appointed governor-general of all the French colonies which by then included Guadeloupe, Martinique and Tortuga. Warner and de Poincy were friendly to each other, which was well for the island as it was impossible to travel between English plantations on windward and leeward coasts without passing through the French parts of the island. De Poincy and Warner made a common agreement in 1639 to limit the further planting of tobacco to prevent a fall in price and a discouragement to other crops. In the hills above the future Basseterre de Poincy built himself a wonderful château which would have compared well with any small palace on the Loire. By 1700, however, it was in ruins, probably as a result of the serious earthquake of 1689, which proved the less pretentious wooden houses of the English planters to be more practicable. Warner the autocrat called no assembly in his day. His family was last heard of in the person of Pelham or 'Plum' Warner of cricketing fame in the 1920s.

Between 1630 and 1641 Barbados was kept in order by Henry Hawley, a man of obscure origin, iron determination and unscrupulous ambition. Not surprisingly he had no love for Warner, whom he refused to recognize as lieutenant-general of all the Caribbees, although he was appointed by

Carlisle. On his own island Hawley imposed tenure by feudal service on the earl's personal estates. He demanded labour as well as a poll-tax of twenty pounds of clean cotton or tobacco for each indentured servant. Ostensibly this was to pay for defence although there was scarcely a gun in any fort at the end of his term of office. He collected arbitrary fines for trivial offences and made an order that 'no strong beere should be sold but to the Governor and Councell and such as he pleased'. He demanded excessive fees for land transfers and imprisoned any man who protested. Perhaps he can hardly be blamed for taking a leaf out of Charles I's book of personal government at the same period of time.

For the days of slow communications in which he lived, Hawley kept himself remarkably up to date with events in England. In 1638 when the Earl of Warwick bought the Pembroke patent and reopened the quarrel with Carlisle, Hawley hurried over to make a pact with Warwick, posing in London as the governor of Barbados in spite of having had his commission recalled by Carlisle. Then he doubled back to the island in time to oppose the take-over by Carlisle's new appointee, Henry Huncks. This he effected by removing all officials likely to cause trouble and calling the colony's first assembly to win the support of the planters. They obligingly elected him governor because he posed as Warwick's nominee and they saw an opportunity to rid themselves of the hated proprietorship of Carlisle. When Henry Huncks arrived he was refused permission to land, in spite of holding the king's letter of approval for his appointment. But Hawley's gamble failed. Warwick lost his attempt to obtain the proprietary patent and four royal commissioners arrived to install Huncks and demand Hawley's surrender. In June 1640 he was taken home after his estates had been sequestrated, accused of thirteen charges. Among these were the purloining of 6,300 pounds of tobacco due to the earl in taxes, a threat to Peter Hay, the Receiver-General, 'that he should be served as Sir William Tufton with a Bullett in his bosome', and the boast 'that he had more authority with his staffe which hee bore in hand on ye way, than your master the Kinge of England'. The amazing thing is that after trial by the Privy Council he was reinstated in possession of his estates. He returned to the island in 1641 to take an active part in politics until he died in 1677 at the ripe old age of eighty, a testimony to the healthiness of the climate of Barbados.

4

PROVIDENCE

While the English colonists were still struggling to establish their plantations of St Christopher, Nevis and Barbados, another group directed their attention to a small island only 250 miles north of the strategic Spanish town of Porto Belo on the Isthmus of Darien. There at the end of May 1631, on the island known to the Spaniards as Santa Catalina, a band of ninety Englishmen landed to found the colony of Providence, or Old Providence as it came to be called to distinguish it from New Providence in the Bahamas, with which it is often confused, even by the few people who have ever heard of it.

As in the case of Barbados and the Leeward Islands, Providence was started through the co-operation of adventurous sailors and venturesome London merchants. Captain Daniel Elfrith had discovered the place and had found for his patron Robert Rich, Earl of Warwick, already known for his interest in the Somers Islands Company at Bermuda. A royal patent issued on 4 December 1630 had incorporated 'The Governor and Company of Adventurers of the City of Westminster for the Plantation of the Islands of Providence or Catalina, Henrietta or Andrea and the adjacent islands lying upon the coast of America', between latitudes 10° and 20° North. Following the pattern of previous patents, the Company was given the responsibility of running the colony, but with this difference: because of its proximity to Spanish lands the Providence Company was given the right to fit ships, furnish them with arms and ammunition and, in case of attack, to make reprisals against their assailants. In furtherance of this right the Company was granted permission by the Privy Council to purchase from the Crown twenty pieces of ordnance.

A less obvious difference emerges from a study of members of the Company. The first governor was Warwick's brother Henry, Earl of Holland, and among the rest were Lord Brooke, Lord Saye and Sele, and John Pym. They were all prominent Puritans. Their chief aim was to

39

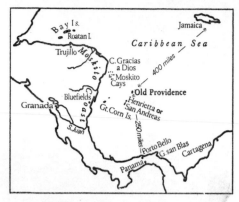

Providence shown in relation to Jamaica and central America

Providence

establish a model Puritan colony, not in the rigorous climate of New England but in the languid air of the Caribbean Sea. The experiment proved a failure. Experience was to show that rigid Puritan morals might survive in a rigorous climate, but languid air led to moral laxity. Although the colony survived for ten years, its Puritan character had disappeared in five.

To cynical twentieth-century ears Puritan morals and privateering sound strange companions, but there was nothing incongruous to Warwick and his friends in their double aim. The Catholic Church was the whore of Babylon that God wanted true Christians to destroy. Spain was the main support of Catholic idolatry: any blow struck against Spain was service to God and the true religion. No doubt the Company hoped to make a profit, but this was a secondary motive that was never achieved. Shareholders were called to 'sub up' on more than one occasion and did so cheerfully. In the end there were great losses. In 1649 Pym's estate alone was called upon for £1,740, Lord Saye and Sele for £1,190.

The two islands chosen for the main activities of the company possessed great attractions. Providence, six miles long and four miles wide, was fertile and well watered, with hills rising to nearly two thousand feet. The climate was equable and healthy, but its greatest asset was a ring of coral reef with hidden and intricate passages leading to a sheltered haven on the western side. San Andreas, sixty miles south-west, called Henrietta by the colonists no doubt in honour of the Queen, was lower, less fertile and less well protected. For this reason it was never permanently settled, but the woods that covered it gave rise to a small shipbuilding industry.

The Company searched for three classes of emigrants: first, labourers or planters who were to cultivate the crops of tobacco and cotton, sharing profits with the Company on a fifty-fifty basis; secondly, artificers to work on the same basis or to be full employees of the Company, in return for meat, drink and a wage of £5 per annum; and thirdly, apprentices or servants about fourteen years of age, to be indentured to other colonists for a term of two or three years in return for food, drink and clothing. This social order was based on the pattern of contemporary English society.

The first batch of emigrants contained no women. They were drawn from Essex, Northamptonshire, Oxfordshire, Cornwall, Devon and Wales, recruited by members of the Company in their home regions. A barber-surgeon was included to look after health, and Lewis Morgan, a young Welsh minister, was placed in charge of spiritual welfare. The whole band was committed to the command of Captain William Rudyerd, a man of some military experience. John Pym, now Company Treasurer, chartered a small vessel called *Seaflower* to take the expedition to their new home. Although he took personal charge of the accounts, there was trouble soon after sailing. The rations were inadequate and of poor quality because John Tanner, master of the *Seaflower*, withheld as much as he could to sell at journey's end. It was a common occurrence, as examples from other colonies have already shown, and not difficult to understand in the light of the low wage of £4 a month paid to the ships' captains of the day.

Also on board were Captain Philip Bell, the governor-designate, and Daniel Elfrith, the promoter, who was Bell's father-in-law. He held the appointment of admiral of the island. Philip Bell had been governor of Bermuda. His detailed instructions nominated a council of six to advise him. The all-male fraternity was divided into 'families' of six or seven persons with one as head to take care 'that he with his whole family, besides public duties, do daily, morning and evening, pray together unto God that his blessing may be upon them and the whole island'. Stores were to be issued to each *paterfamilias* on credit against crop. As in Virginia and Massachusetts, each family was responsible for the good behaviour of its members.

The *Seaflower* sailed at the end of February 1631 and took three months to reach Providence, after collecting a few people at Bermuda on the way. On arrival little time was wasted. The ground was cleared and maize, which was to be the staple diet, was planted before tobacco, the cash crop. Fortune smiled and the first planting was a success. Daniel Elfrith, following his instructions, went off in search of plants: sugar-cane, figs and oranges. Best of all the translucent sea abounded in fish of many varieties. Fresh turtle meat became a mainstay of the colonists' diet.

Not long after the first settlement was made on Providence, the Company extended its interests to another strategic island seven hundred miles to the north-east: Tortuga, on the north-west coast of Hispaniola, controlling the Windward Passage. It is doubtful whether Pym and his colleagues realized that it was already the home of the Buccaneers. However, they were persuaded to adopt it by that plausible rogue, Anthony Hilton, who had moved from St Christopher across to Nevis to escape from Thomas Warner, and then, after quarrelling with the Earl of Carlisle, had taken himself away to the Buccaneer stronghold just as they were settling there. In May 1631 while the *Seaflower* was approaching Providence, Hilton persuaded the Company to include Tortuga in their patent and appoint him governor.

The Company called their new colony Association, and the first thing they did, significantly, was to purchase six pieces of ordnance and a magazine for its defence. Next they chartered the *Little Hopewell* of sixty tons and seven guns, of which Matthew Harbottle was master. Among its passengers sailed Anthony Hilton, Captain Christopher Wormeley, deputy-governor, and a council of six, as arranged for Providence. Unlike Providence, however, the Company did not dispatch a carefully chosen Puritan community. Instead Hilton was instructed to recruit his colonists in the Indies. He knew they were already waiting for him there, for what Hilton had achieved was an official cloak for the settlement of his Buccaneer friends. There is no evidence why the colony was named Association, but a strange association it certainly was of godly Puritan capitalists and irreligious desperadoes, effectively united by their common hatred of Spain.

The Buccaneers hated Spain because that proud country's claims to exclusive rights in the Americas had prompted the Spanish authorities to attempt the extermination of small settlements of squatters or beachcombers thrown up by the sea on the deserted north coast of Hispaniola. Here they had made a precarious living from hunting the wild cattle and pigs that had spread across the large island from abandoned Spanish *hatos* around the administrative headquarters of Santo Domingo. These men, who referred to themselves as Brethren of the Coast, prepared dried meat by smoking it over a slow fire on a wooden grill called a *boucan*. It was from this that the word *boucanier* or *buccaneer* derived. The surplus of their meat and the hides they sold to passing ships in exchange for the bare necessities of their trade: guns, powder, shot, knives and a minimum of clothing, for along the tropical coast of Hispaniola few clothes are needed even to this day. They cut their own shoes, and, according to the Abbé du Tertre, their most treasured item of clothing was a sack which they wore round their waists in daylight and used as a primitive mosquito net at night. There were many nationalities among their numbers, but the majority were English, French and Dutch.

In 1629 and 1630 the Buccaneers moved across the narrow strait to the island of Tortuga, where a good harbour made a convenient centre for their trade in *biltong* and hides. It was these cattle-hunters that Hilton had joined.

On 23 July 1631 the *Little Hopewell* left England for Association, sailed on to Providence, returned to Association and was back in London in April the next year. Hilton's instructions were to grow cotton, maize and tobacco and cut dye-woods on the mainland. This he arranged for Dutch and Frenchmen to do, but it was not long before this strenuous labour – dye-woods are some of the hardest trees to cut – was delegated to Negro slaves. Details are lacking, but for a time Tortuga gave shelter to the ill-matched groups of planters and cowkillers. In 1632 a minister named Key was appointed. He stayed for two years, after which he was transferred to Providence at his own request to escape from a recalcitrant flock.

It was not long before the Company came to have doubts about their governor at Association. They received no returns on their capital because Hilton seized all the tobacco for his own profit and failed to pay for the stores they had supplied. Debts incurred during his time on St Christopher and Nevis were still unsettled. It was decided to dismiss him, but he died before he was superseded, and Captain Wormeley automatically succeeded to the command.

Whatever the Providence Company knew or did not know about their colony of Association, to the Spaniards it was a pestilential pirate nest. In January 1635 they exterminated it, executing and hanging all their captives. This really marked the end of the English colony of Tortuga. Although some attempts were made to revive it, and Pym seriously considered going out himself to settle the problems of Association on the spot, the English lost control of the island to the French.

The Spanish attack was a turning point in the history of the Buccaneers. The few survivors returned to the ruined settlement vowing to take revenge for the Spaniards' brutality. Taking to the sea, they started a long series of attacks on Spanish shipping. Before long their numbers were swollen with new recruits enabling them to attack Spanish towns and spread chaos and terror throughout the Caribbean. The Spaniards had stirred up a hornets' nest at the very centre of their American empire; they would have done better to ignore Association. This was not apparent in 1635 for the Buccaneer movement did not reach full strength until twenty-five years later.

Down at Providence development was steady. In 1632 eighty colonists arrived from Bermuda and a hundred and fifty from England on the *Charity* of two hundred tons, including women and children. In spite of Pym's precautions the master, Thomas Punt, treated his passengers as scurvily as John Tanner on the *Seaflower*. They were issued with short rations, and, being all good Puritans, were horrified at the brutality with which Punt treated his seamen. This humanitarian streak in the Puritan character is worth noting. Samuel Rishworth, who was in charge of this contingent, found himself odd man out when in the following year he protested against the introduction of negro slaves. So strong were his convictions that he assisted a number of them to escape. The members of the Company, however, had no hesitation in rebuking him 'for groundless opinion that Christians may not lawfully keep such persons in a state of servitude *during their strangeness to Christianity*'. They were enslaved not because they were Negroes but because they were heathen. Nevertheless a protest had been made. Although his fellow Puritans did not agree with Rishworth, it was from their theological successors, the Evangelicals, that the most telling opposition to slavery eventually arose.

The runaway slaves took refuge in the 'Palmetto Grove' in the south-east of the island, where they led a precarious existence similar to the later Maroons in Jamaica. Hunts were organized to catch them.

Although tobacco and cotton proved to be the most successful crops, the Company encouraged experiments with new plants. In fact the Puritan conscience was not too happy about the encouragement to smoking that their importation of tobacco was causing in England. They referred to the plant as 'the noxious weed'. Madder and indigo were planted, for dyes were in great demand, as well as potatoes, cassava, plantains, pineapples, oranges, bananas and melons. Figs and vines proved unsuccessful. Few cattle were kept because of a lack of fences.

It was obvious that much hard work was done in the first three years. Doubtless because of this some of the planters began to complain of the fifty-per-cent share of profits taken by the Company, the members of which they accused of being solely and covetously desirous of profit. In defence the Company pointed out that each investor had subscribed at least £600, more than ten times the capital outlay in other colonies. The planters, they said, lived well and had 'likewise means to do God and their country-men great service in spreading Religion and advancing the honour of the English name in those little known parts of the world'. They were horrified at reports of drunkenness and ordered Governor Bell to confiscate and destroy all cards and dice. Chess and shooting, on the other hand, were approved. To encourage a better level of moral behaviour the Company sent out three new ministers to replace Lewis Morgan, who had proved unsatisfactory, but their intentions were defeated. One man died soon after arrival; the second returned, accused of an excess of levity in that he and others used to sing on the Sabbath day 'songs that were not divine'. The third, Hope Sherrard, remained to become an unpopular theocrat who came to consider it within his province to admonish the governor. Yet Governor Bell was strict himself: he forbade mixed dancing. It was not long before quarrels became frequent between tolerant and narrow-minded circles. Local justices of the peace were appointed in 1633 and found their office no sinecure.

Shortly after extending his interests to Association, John Pym cast his eyes on the Moskito Coast, 150 miles to the west, as a possible area where trade might be developed. In April 1633 two pinnaces, the *Elizabeth* and the *Pole* sailed from Dartmouth with forty-two passengers (half of them indentured servants) for Association, St Christopher (where they were to buy cotton seed) and Providence. From there they were to proceed to the Gulf of Darien to explore the chances of trade with the Indians, renewing friendship with them 'as favourers of the English nation and especially of Don Francisco Draco (whose name they seem to honour) . . . to labour to possess them with the natural goodness of the English nation'. The captains were to restrain any boisterous carriage to the women, particularly 'mocking, pointing or laughing at their nakedness'. To ensure that this condition was carried out, none of the seamen was to be allowed any dealings with the Indians. Unfortunately these plans came to nothing because three Dutch ships had attacked and alienated the Indians before the sober Englishmen arrived.

A second attempt was made with the *Golden Falcon* pinnace in the region of Cape Gracias a Dios further north. After leaving a group of strong Puritans at Providence – incidentally the last of such persuasion to arrive – Captain Sussex Camock crossed to the mainland and established friendly relations with the Moskito Indians, which led to the English protectorate over the coast that existed until 1900. The happy relations between the English and the Moskito Indians were based on the instructions issued by John Pym: 'You are to endear yourselves with the Indians and we conjure you to be friendly and cause no jealousy.' The Indians were not to be enslaved – or allowed the use of gunpowder: Pym was a man of great wisdom. Nearly two hundred years later Lady Nugent, wife of the governor of Jamaica, had the doubtful pleasure of entertaining the Moskito king. Pym also wanted missionary efforts made to convert them to Christianity.

So successful were the efforts of Sussex Camock and Samuel Axe, who accompanied him, that Pym and the company decided to apply for a separate patent to cover the Moskito trade. This was issued in March 1635, incorporating 'The Governor and Company of Adventurers of the City of London for a trade upon the coast and islands of divers parts of America'.

They were granted the monopoly of trade with the *heathen*. The articles of trade listed are interesting, some of them being completely fictitious: tree-gum, silk-grass, lignum vitae, annatto, skins of fur, cassia fistula, sarsaparilla, 'contra-yerba' (an antidote for snake-bite and poisoned arrows) and 'the bezar stone, the manatee stone, and the stone in the alligator's head'.

Silk-grass, also referred to as 'Camock's flax', is thought by one authority to have been sisal, although the name hardly fits that spiky cactus-like plant. Whatever it was, Camock's flax remained undeveloped. This curious list is a testimony to the lively interest taken by our seventeenth-century ancestors in the products of the tropical world, which was so new to them. The sailors' trade in monkeys and parrots was discouraged for no obvious reason unless it was to reduce their chances of encounter with the Indians and their lightly-clad belles.

In spite of this considerable enterprise, by 1635 the affairs of Providence Island were giving the Company cause for concern. The *Long Robert* of three hundred tons and two smaller vessels that sailed for the colony in September 1634 made a loss of £1,300 on the round voyage. There were few passengers because of reports of the high-handed bearing of the governor and council and the restraints placed upon behaviour by Minister Hope Sherrard. The *Long Robert* had found little produce to bring home largely on account of calls made by Dutch interlopers. The shareholders put their hands in their pockets and paid for the loss.

In 1635 there were on the island five hundred white men, forty women and a few children, and ninety Negroes. The little settlement of New Westminster contained thirty well-built houses only, because the planters lived in timber houses on their farms. Most of the town houses were also built of timber but the governor's house and the church were brick buildings. Once a week the men and their servants were mustered to do military drill, for everybody knew that they must be ready to meet a Spanish attack sooner or later. There were forty pieces of ordnance on the island but they were scattered among no less than thirteen forts. This was bad strategy for it meant that the small defence force was scattered instead of being concentrated on a strong point. Professional gunners, employed by the Company on salaries varying between £20 and £40 per annum, plus land, were in charge of the principal forts and gave training in musketry. There were twelve shallops, built on Henrietta, which acted as scouts and messengers.

It was well that the colonists were prepared. On 2 July 1635 Don Nicholas de Judice, governor of Cartagena, appeared off the island with three ships and four shallops from which he landed three hundred men. The colonists beat off all attacks and after seven days the Spaniards withdrew. It was not until December that the Company heard of the attack.

Probably they were expecting it, for they wasted little time in applying to King Charles for permission to exercise their right of reprisal. This was readily granted and they conducted the necessary measures as a financial investment. It was decided to raise £10,000 in twenty shares of £500, to be subscribed individually or in syndicates. Pym put up £500. It was almost as if this was the chance the Company had been waiting for, because they reorganized their business principally as a privateering enterprise.

With the change of emphasis the occasion was judged ripe for the relief of Governor Bell and his succession by Captain Robert Hunt. Hunt sailed on 28 March 1636 on peculiar terms : the Company paid for the transportation of himself, his wife and three children, and two maids. He was to have a hundred acres of land and twenty servants to work it, but no salary. A sergeant gunner and three trained soldiers accompanied the new governor. At the same time the Company changed the unpopular system of sharing half profits and instituted a system of rents.

A further change, and one that reads peculiarly, was the Company's renunciation of their responsibility for defence. This was thrown on the colonists who were obviously expected to pay for it out of the profits of the privateering they were to be encouraged to pursue, and by way of a licence the Company was to be paid one-fifth of the value of all prizes. Sailors were to receive a share of the plunder instead of wages. It was a simple system that saved a great deal of accounting — in London. Accounting would still be required in Providence, otherwise how would the Company be guaranteed their rake-off? This was the weakness of the arrangement. It is obvious from facts revealed in Spanish sources about the end of the colony that the colonists had been retaining more than their share of the plunder.

Governor Hunt reached Providence in May 1636 with three ships, the *Blessing*, the *Expectation* and the *Hopewell*, all significantly optimistic names. Soon after arrival, following Company instructions Captain William Rous, previously a fort commander at Providence, led the *Blessing* and the *Expectation* in an attack on Santa Marta, but he found his men greatly outnumbered and was forced into an ignominious surrender. The prisoners were sent to Spain where they were imprisoned or sent to the galleys, but Rous eventually bribed his way out of prison and reached England towards the end of 1639.

Records are far from complete. There must have been less ambitious cruises and numerous short pounces by island shallops on passing Spanish coasting vessels. In 1638 Captain Nathaniel Butler, a former governor of Bermuda from 1619 to 1622, arrived at Providence to relieve Governor Hunt. In October Butler sailed away in company with some Dutch rovers and captured the small town of Truxillo in Honduras, extracting a ransom of 16,000 pieces of eight (about £4,000). Robert Hunt had been a strict

Puritan, but opposition to the Puritan element had been steadily growing, led by Daniel Elfrith, the original promoter of the colony. Butler turned against the Puritans, but he spent little time at his island base. When he sailed back to England in 1640, he left as deputy-governor Captain Andrew Carter, a man with no Puritan sympathies at all. He arrested the formidable minister, Hope Sherrard, and a new minister named Leverton, newly arrived from Barbados, and dispatched them in chains to England together with Richard Lane and Henry Halhead, who had come out with Samuel Rishworth, the protester against slavery. Carter evidently imagined he had settled their Puritan activities for a long time, for he consigned them to the tender mercy of Archbishop Laud with the information that they were disaffected to the liturgy and ritual of England. Fortunately for his victims his plans miscarried because they arrived in England after Laud had gone to the Tower. The Puritans in control of London received them kindly.

On Providence, although privateering distracted attention from planting, the Company strove to maintain the two activities side by side. One of the spoils of privateering was Negro slaves. As their numbers increased they threatened internal security. Orders were made in vain to keep their numbers to less than half the white population. Planters were taxed forty pounds of tobacco for each Negro they kept and it was required that they should be used for public works on sixteen days every year. In 1638 these fears were justified when there was a rebellion that was suppressed with difficulty. By no means all Negroes captured from Spanish ships were kept on the island, for numbers were sold to Virginia and New England.

In England, after John Hampden lost the Ship Money Case in 1637, Warwick and Saye and Sele were so discouraged by the turn of affairs that they decided to emigrate to Providence. In 1638 they asked the king for permission to leave, but when Charles became involved with the Scots in the serious religious trouble that led to the First Bishops' War, they decided to stay. It is fascinating to watch how the tiny island of Providence was so closely linked to the mighty political struggle developing in England. During the years of the king's supremacy in the early thirties, Pym and his friends were grateful for the distraction afforded by the business of their little colony, but as the king became entangled in his difficulties in Ireland and Scotland the directors of the Providence Company, who were also the leaders of the Puritan opposition in England, found most of their attention riveted to home affairs. With the opening of the Short Parliament John Pym handed over the management of the Company to Lord Mandeville and Lord Saye and Sele.

By 1640 the tempo of events was also rising on Providence. Goaded by increasing attacks on Spanish ships and settlements, the governor of Cartagena, Don Antonio Maldonado y Tejada, appeared off the island with a fleet of six small frigates and a galleon. He landed eight hundred soldiers and two hundred Negro militiamen. Fierce fighting ensued round the principal forts until a rising gale forced the Spaniards to withdraw after suffering more than a hundred casualties. Governor Carter marred his victory by executing his prisoners in spite of promising their lives when they surrendered. This brutality caused great indignation in Cartagena and brought retribution in due course. It was the protest against Carter's inhumanity by Sherrard, Leverton, Halhead and Lane that led to their deportation in irons. Over in Cartagena the defeated Spaniards arrived at the same time as the galleons from Spain. The admiral of this fleet, Don Francisco Diaz de Pimienta, was so incensed at the dishonour to the arms of Spain that he determined to avenge it. Yet so centralized was the government of the Spanish Empire that Don Francisco deemed it expedient to return to Spain and obtain his royal master's approval. He returned from his seven-thousand-mile round journey at the end of the year and settled down to the elaborate preparations for what he insisted was going to be the end of the English plague-spot at the heart of the Spanish Caribbean.

First, the admiral gathered all available information. Spanish pilots who had visited Providence advised him that there were on the island six hundred men under arms. There were fourteen forts defended by fifty-six great guns and 148 smaller pieces of ordnance. Don Francisco drilled his men strenuously. On 6 May 1641 when all his preparations were complete he sailed from Cartagena with two thousand men in a fleet of twelve ships. On 17 May the armada appeared off the island. Don Francisco was in no hurry. He probed the passages for a week and landed his men at the south-east corner of the island. Marching over the 1,150-feet-high pass, the Spaniards took New Westminster from its undefended rear and laid siege to the church and governor's house, the only substantial buildings in the place. Surprisingly the colonists made little resistance. After two days, on promise of their lives, Governor Carter and his men surrendered. The Puritan survivors of the colony had the mortifying experience of having to watch the celebration of a High Mass and the singing of a Te Deum in the ruined town square of New Westminster.

Surprisingly the Spaniards were merciful. The sixty women and the small number of children were placed aboard an English ship and sent back to England. The men were taken to Spain for a long captivity. For once the tables were turned for the Spaniards reaped a booty of gold, indigo, cochineal and six hundred Negroes, in all worth half a million ducats. This is also an indication of the extent to which the islanders had been cheating the Company. Not all the men were captured. The hardier individuals escaped in small craft to Henrietta and the Moskito Coast, turning up eventually at Tortuga, Barbados or St Kitts to continue their carefree careers. Don Francisco, leaving a strong garrison to prevent the island from becoming reinfested, sailed to a hero's welcome in Cartagena and Spain. In England the arrival of the refugees in March 1642 was greeted with protests of indignation, but the more momentous chain of events leading to the outbreak of the Civil War distracted attention from the fate of the tiny colony.

Although the colony was finished, the Company continued to issue privateering commissions. In July 1642 Captain William Jackson sailed from St Kitts with Samuel Axe, formerly on the Moskito Coast, as his vice-admiral. At Barbados they found willing volunteers and left there with seven ships and 1,100 men to rampage round the Caribbean for three years. Captain William Rous, ex-Providence islander and leader of the ignominious attack on Santa Marta, was in command of the soldiers. After attacking Margarita, Maracaibo and New Granada, and landing on Hispaniola, on 5 March 1643 Jackson captured St Jago de la Vega, the Spanish capital of Jamaica; but he was able to extract for it only the miserable ransom of seven thousand pieces of eight, a measure of its neglect under the Spaniards. Completing the circuit of the Caribbean and Gulf of Mexico, Jackson returned to England in March 1645 leaving an uproar behind him. Ten years after his raids the full Puritan reply to the Spanish capture of Providence took shape in Cromwell's Western Design.

The main reasons for the failure of the Providence colony become clearly apparent from this detailed account of its brief history. Its size was too small and its position too precarious to give it any hope of survival. Insolently placed in the track of the treasure galleons, it was never strong enough to attack the great ships. Even if there had been no privateering and the colonists had confined themselves to peaceful planting, the Spaniards would not have tolerated their presence any more than they were to welcome William Patterson and his Scottish colonists at Darien sixty years later. That the Spanish government took so long to stamp out the settlement is due to their distraction by the attacks of the Dutch, who had settled on Curaçao in 1634 and successfully resisted all Spanish attempts to throw them out. At the same time the French appeared on Martinique and Guadeloupe. Internally the colony was bedevilled by quarrels between privateer and planter, Puritan and pirate, colonist and Company. Nevertheless there had been no hurricanes and no serious sickness. Valuable experience had been gained which was to be remembered in the early days of Jamaica.

Regardless of its failure the colony of Providence provided a link between all the main trends of early English colonial activity. Its Puritanism formed a link with New England and gave rise to trade; its planting activities were similar to those of Barbados and the Leeward Islands; it relied on privateering as much as early English Jamaica was to do; and its connection with the Moskito Coast and the Bay Islands linked it to the future colony of British Honduras. Today the island belongs to Colombia and forms a popular holiday resort.

5

BARBADOS AND THE
CARIBBEES, 1642-88

There is no record of how the news was received in the West Indies when the Civil War broke out in England in the summer of 1642. It is doubtful if anybody could have foreseen the important changes it was to cause in the island colonies. Its effects were greatest in Barbados. In St Kitts uneventful progress continued under Sir Thomas Warner until his death in 1649. Some time in 1641 Philip Bell, the former governor of Providence, arrived in Barbados to settle. The next year he became deputy-governor and in 1645 governor, although it is not clear from whom he held his commission. Both King and Parliament attempted to exercise control in the colonies, but while they were fighting in England they could spare nobody to enforce their claims. Parliament appointed Robert Rich Earl of Warwick, their most experienced supporter in colonial affairs, as governor-in-chief and Lord High Admiral of all islands and plantations in America, and he and Bell knew each other well. But Philip Bell steered a neutral course. He wrote to Warwick that the Barbados colonists wished to remain impartial. They had not accepted the King's commissioner, the Earl of Marlborough, and they welcomed all merchants and seamen arriving from Parliamentary ports as their livelihood depended on maintaining trade. In 1646, after Carlisle had had his overseas estates restored to him by the remnant of the House of Lords on payment of a fine of £800, Warwick wrote again to Bell commanding him to declare his allegiance both to the Earl and to Parliament. Bell and the council framed a diplomatic reply. They wished, they wrote, to be serviceable to the kingdom, to honour Parliament and to keep their allegiance to the King, but they were less able to submit any more than before as the inhabitants had passed a resolution 'not to receive any Alteration of Government until God should be so merciful unto us as to unite the King and the Parliament'.

On the island the planters practised what they preached. An unwritten law required that anyone 'whoever named the word "Roundhead" or

"Cavalier" should give to all those who heard him a shoat [young pig] and a Turkey, to be eaten at his house that made the forfeit'. But as the war swung more and more in Parliament's favour it became difficult to maintain neutrality. After 1646 an increasing stream of Royalist refugees began to arrive in the islands; and some Royalist prisoners were given the option of imprisonment in the Tower or transportation to Barbados and were glad to accept the latter. By 1650 it was estimated that there were more than thirty thousand white people in Barbados. Under the leadership of Colonel Humphrey Walrond and his brother Edward the Royalists planned to seize control and Governor Bell's careful nurture of neutrality was shaken. First, the Walronds rid themselves of a rival Royalist, Colonel Guy Molesworth, by accusing him of plotting to confiscate all Round-head estates. This gave them the support of Colonel James Drax, the Roundhead leader. Molesworth was imprisoned and then banished. As he left he was seized by a pirate and ruined for life. Next, the Walronds attempted to cause a division over religious policy. This prompted Drax to demand an election for a new assembly. Bell was placed in a quandary: to oppose the Walronds meant trouble; to give way to them would mean civil war, so he issued writs for a new assembly. The infuriated Walronds then denounced the governor as a Roundhead. A pamphlet war broke out and young Cavaliers gathered in the parish of St Philip ready to fight. Bell issued a stern proclamation, forbidding anyone to take up arms and ordered Colonel Drax to raise the militia. Just as a thoroughly ugly situation was developing, a ship arrived in Carlisle Bay carrying Francis Lord Willoughby of Parham, who was possessed of two commissions, one from the Earl of Carlisle appointing him lieutenant-general in the Caribbees, and the other from the exiled Charles II appointing him governor. The date was 5 May 1650.

Francis Willoughby was a man of the stamp of Gilbert and Raleigh, a dreamer of idealistic dreams and a man of action to carry them out. Like many of the nobility he found himself torn between allegiance to the King and the support of the liberties of Parliament. He started as a Parliamentarian and, while he was such, leased Carlisle's proprietary patent in 1647 for a period of twenty-one years. Shortly afterwards he became disgusted with the extremists on the Parliamentary side and changed sides to become vice-admiral of Prince Rupert's fleet based in Holland. His arrival in Barbados as a Royalist governor put an end to the island's neutrality and took the wind temporarily out of the Walronds' sails. But they were by no means finished. They persuaded the assembly to suspend Willoughby's recognition for three months. While Willoughby was waiting at St Kitts, they made use of the time to ruin the Roundhead planters so that Willoughby would become dependent on their own faction. About one hundred of their victims returned to England where they complained to Parliament and obtained retribution in due course.

Meanwhile Willoughby had made contact with a recently arrived planter who had already embarked on an influential career in the West Indies that was to carry him to the top of the tree. This was Colonel Thomas Modyford, a Royalist from Exeter who had emigrated to Barbados in 1647 about the age of twenty-seven. Already he had played a mediating part between the Walrond firebrands and Governor Bell. Now with other men of moderate views, Modyford gave Willoughby the support that enabled him to deprive Humphrey Walrond of all his official appointments and reverse the measures against the Roundhead planters who had remained in the island.

At home in England Parliament had decided to take measures to end the Royalist support in Virginia, Bermuda, Antigua and Barbados. On 15 October 1651 there appeared a small but strong squadron of seven ships and 820 men under the command of Sir George Ayscue. After it had ended in England, the Civil War had now come to Barbados. Willoughby had warning that Ayscue was coming. With the support of the assembly he decided to fight. Anticipating the sentiments that prompted the American Declaration of Independence in the following century, the Barbadian assemblymen passed a resolution in which they said: 'Shall we be bound to the government and lordship of a Parliament in which we have no representatives? . . . In truth, this would be a slavery far exceeding all that the English nation hath yet suffered.' They ordered every freeman to go before a justice of the peace and declare his intention to defend the government of Lord Willoughby. Any man refusing to subscribe to 'The Engagement', as this declaration was called, had his property confiscated. A standing force of militia was raised and placed on monthly pay, for which a levy was imposed, falling hardest on those suspected of Parliamentary sympathies. The forts were put in readiness and every ship in the roadstead was required to contribute one or two pieces of ordnance. Morale was boosted by the report that Prince Rupert was on his way with a fleet to defend the island.

When Ayscue arrived, therefore, Barbados was ready to resist. Willoughby had a force of six thousand foot and four hundred mounted men under his command, far outnumbering the men who had come with Ayscue. An exchange of fire with the forts was marked more by the enthusiasm of the defenders than the accuracy of their fire. Ayscue settled down to blockade the island into surrender, but not without letting Willoughby know news of Cromwell's final victory at Worcester and the hopelessness of the Royalist cause. Willoughby's reply was as noble as his title: 'I have never served the Kinge in Expectaĉon soe much of his Pros-

perous Condiĉon as in consideraĉon of my Dutye. And if it have pleased
God to add this sadd affliccon to his former I will not be a means of increasing
it by deliveringe this place to your keepinge.' So Ayscue waited. Scurvy
appeared among his men and he was forced to take action. On 22 November
a Captain Morris led a night raid with two hundred men on 'the Hole'.
Four guns were spiked and thirty prisoners taken without loss. On
1 December another Parliamentary squadron arrived, bound for Virginia.
On 7 December a larger night raid by four hundred men drove a force of
twelve hundred Barbadians inland with the loss of a hundred men killed
and sixty prisoners taken. Only eight raiders were lost. Already moderate
Cavaliers were beginning to have second thoughts about resistance. Ayscue
worked on their misgivings to drive a wedge between them and Willoughby's
die-hards. Once again Modyford assumed his moderating guise. On 6
January 1652, he went over to Ayscue with his whole militia regiment
solidly behind him. Ayscue landed and preparations for a local Marston
Moor were made. Ayscue and Modyford's two thousand men were drawn
up facing three thousand men under Willoughby, but the Royalists were
beginning to waver and Willoughby withdrew. Then the heavens opened
and three days of tropical rain cooled the defenders' ardour. Willoughby
wisely submitted.

Ayscue's terms were generous. The colony's constitutional privileges
were confirmed; no taxes were to be imposed without consent of the
assembly; Roundheads' estates were to be restored, and in return the
Royalists were to receive back their sequestrated estates in England,
Scotland and Ireland; Willoughby was guaranteed all his estates in
England, the West Indies and Guiana, where he had recently founded a
colony on the Surinam river; Barbados was to be allowed free trade with
all countries at peace with England; but the forts were to be handed over
to Ayscue and the militia was to pass under his orders. In August Parliament ratified the terms. Once in control, Ayscue banished the Walrond
brothers for a year. Willoughby sailed to England via Surinam. Leaving a
Parliamentary governor, Daniel Searle, in charge, Ayscue moved on to
St Kitts and the Leeward Islands to settle affairs there.

More important than any military or political events of the Civil War,
however, had been the economic revolution that had quietly taken place in
Barbados during the eight years of virtual self-government enjoyed by the
colonists. As trade with England declined they came to rely increasingly on
New England for their provisions and other products of temperate lands,
and on the Dutch with whom they had long had friendly associations for
goods of all kinds. In 1624 the Dutch had captured the Portuguese colony
of Bahia or San Salvador in Brazil and had there developed the planting
of sugar-cane. At an unrecorded date they persuaded the English planters

on Barbados to plant cane. Coming at a time when the tobacco market was glutted and planting on Barbados was in the doldrums, the Dutch suggestion was received with interest. Among the first to experiment were Colonel Holdip and James Drax, the Roundhead. At first the planting did not go well, but the Dutch took Holdip and others south to Bahia and demonstrated the successful methods followed there. Richard Ligon, who left a detailed description of sugar-planting, arrived in Barbados in 1647 with Thomas Modyford and stayed for three years, during which, he said, he saw methods greatly improved. In early days, apparently, the planters had reaped the canes after twelve months instead of leaving them for fifteen, and they had planted the shoots supplied by the Dutch upright in holes instead of laying them flat in trenches from which new ratoon canes would shoot for several years.

Cotton and tobacco had been ideal crops for the pioneer days because they were easy to grow and required no great labour force, but sugar-cane was much more demanding. It took twice as long to grow; it needed more labour to harvest it and a carefully laid-out works to manufacture the sugar from the cane-juice. All this demanded capital. The obliging Dutchmen offered loans. They also supplied the boiling pans, the cooling pots and pipes for the works. Labour? Negroes from Africa, advised the Dutch, and they could supply them too. Markets? The Dutch carried away all the sugar the island could produce. When Ayscue reached Barbados in 1651 there were fifteen Dutch vessels anchored in Carlisle Bay.

The introduction of sugar-planting had enormous economic and social effects. It turned the small island from a struggling community into the most prosperous English colony. John Scott, writing in 1666, reckoned that Barbados was then seventeen times richer than it had been before the coming of sugar. Richard Ligon stated that Major Hilliard's property had been worth £400 before he planted cane, but he was able to sell half of it to Thomas Modyford for £7,000 in 1648, and Colonel Drax, whom Ligon knew as one of the wealthy planters, was reputed to have arrived in the island with a capital of only £300. Modyford, Ligon wrote, hoped to make a fortune of £100,000. If some planters went up in the world, however, others went down. While ambitious, energetic men with initiative made fortunes, the indolent and unimaginative tobacco planter was ruined. He sold his land to the rising sugar man and became dependent on him for employment. For the more efficient there were openings, but for the poorest class of white colonists there was little demand, for their place was taken by Negro slaves. According to Ligon, on a five-hundred-acre plantation there were needed one 'Prime' overseer at £50 per annum – 'a man that the master may allow sometimes to sit at his own table' – five assistant overseers, thirty white servants, one third of them women, and a hundred slaves of both sexes. Ligon reckoned that for a capital outlay of £14,000 on such an estate an investor could expect a net profit of £7,500 per annum, i.e. more than fifty per cent. For the ruined and dispossessed smallholder there were no prospects and Barbados was faced with the first 'poor whites' problem. Some migrated to Antigua and Nevis. In 1651 some went to colonize Willoughby's new plantation in Surinam. In 1655 no less than four thousand joined Penn and Venables's expedition that captured Jamaica, and in 1664 when Thomas Modyford moved there he took eight hundred Barbadians with him. In the continuous ebb and flow of population and the absence of any reliable statistics, it is difficult to say how many people there were on Barbados during the Civil War. For 1636 a figure of 6,000 whites is given; for 1643, 37,200 whites and 6,000 slaves, which must have been a gross exaggeration ; in 1655, more than 25,000 whites and 20,000 blacks. Not until 1673 was an official census taken and then there were 21,309 whites and 33,184 black slaves.

The landowning pattern also changed from a large number of small estates to a small number of large plantations. On Old Providence it had been calculated that fifty acres would support the owner and fourteen white servants growing tobacco. In early Barbados one white servant was thought to be able to look after one acre and cure, cut and roll the 2,500 pounds of leaf that could be expected from it, as well as growing his own provisions.

But the most important result of the switch to sugar was the arrival of large numbers of African slaves. For their first fifteen or twenty years Barbados and the Leeward Islands had been white communities which, except for the presence of a few Negro and Indian servants or slaves, had been close reproductions of the English social order in seventeenth-century villages at home. In the fifth decade of that century the islands became tropical plantations based on slavery and sugar, a bitter-sweet mixture of wealth and degradation that made them no longer comparable to the home scene.

In this economic and social revolution the Dutch had played the leading part and reaped handsome profits, while their English competitors had been restricted in their trading during the Civil War. Even before the end of the last fighting in 1651, London merchants brought pressure to bear on the victorious Parliament to take measures against the Dutch. The result was the Navigation Act of 1651 and the beginning of mercantilism: the insistence that colonies existed for the benefit of their mother-country and were to be debarred from trade with foreign countries. Coming as the Navigation Act did after ten years of virtual independence and free trade, it was bitterly hated in the colonies. Their easiest and most effective reply was to ignore it and continue to trade with their Dutch friends as before.

Even Governor Searle countenanced the presence of Dutch ships. During the First Anglo-Dutch War that followed from 1652 to 1654 Barbadian juries refused to find Dutch captains guilty of contravening the act. When Penn and Venables arrived in 1655 in command of Cromwell's Western Design they found no less than fifteen Dutch ships in Carlisle Bay and captured the lot; but unless ships of the English navy were about the Dutch interlopers continued their trade. The colonists had no love for the London merchants, whose prices were higher than those of the Dutch.

Meanwhile the routine of sugar-planting and manufacture had been worked out. Because of the fifteen-month growing period canes were planted at all seasons in fields of ten or twelve acres. A bell at 6 am roused the slaves and indentured servants and sent them off without delay under their overseers into the cane-fields. At 11 am another bell was the signal for a two-hour break in which they were given their dinner, usually 'loblolly' (a flat cake made from maize flour and baked on a tray, served cold), bonavist (a kind of kidney bean) and potatoes. At 1 pm they returned to the fields and worked till 6 pm. Supper was a repeat of dinner and eaten in the twilight. The long night was their own. At crop-time Ligon described how the canes were cut with little hand-bills, tied in bundles after stripping and de-heading and loaded on to the backs of donkeys which carried the canes to the works and returned for more without a guide.

The manufacture of sugar consists of three processes: the extraction of the juice from the canes; the reduction of the juice to a syrup by boiling; and the separation of the sugar crystals from the thick syrupy molasses. A modern sugar factory is highly technical, with its series of rollers, its vacuum-pans and centrifugals, but until the latter half of the nineteenth century when modern methods were introduced the manufacturing process was simple and crude. Instead of a few large central factories dealing with the canes of a wide area, each early sugar estate had its own works. The ruins of these old buildings are still to be seen on many estates, half demolished for the building of houses and newer works, covered with creepers and half-buried in the earth. Sugar produced by the crude early methods was known as Muscovado, a word derived from the Spanish *mascabado* meaning lowest quality. Very rarely today in remote country parts of some of the islands little shops may be found selling 'head sugar', the product of small patches of cane, squeezed between the wooden rollers of a donkey mill and boiled down in the simplest way. This is the nearest approach to Muscovado sugar that can be found today.

The ideal site for a factory was not the level ground chosen today, but the gently sloping spur of a hill on which the different parts of the works could be arranged to make use of the force of gravity. The cane was unloaded from the donkeys' backs on to a barbecue or stone platform adjoining the mill-house. Clumsy hardwood rollers at the centre were turned by cogs attached to a vertical axle rotated by long sweeps yoked to half a dozen horses and/or oxen trudging round inside the low walls. Two Negroes fed the canes between the rollers, passing them to and fro and then dropping them for women and girls to carry away as trash to fire the boilers. The juice was drained out of the tray into which it fell by an underground pipe leading into the collecting cistern in the boiling-house. From there it was piped again into the first or clarifying copper and the boiling commenced.

This was the anxious time, when the rising scum was skimmed off and the boiling juice removed by ladles from one copper to the next. The scum from the first and second coppers was thrown away as unfit for further use, but that from the remainder was piped down to the still-house where it played an important role in the manufacture of rum. Meanwhile in the sweltering boiling-house the steady ladling went on, day and night, strenuous work that required even slaves to be relieved by new shifts every four hours. Gradually the juice thickened into a syrup, until in the fifth copper, encouraged by the addition of the temper (water and ashes) that had been made in the preceding three, the juice was ready for crystaliza-tion. Over this last copper, distinguished from the rest as the tach or tatch, presided the sugar-boiler, eyeing the bubbling liquid until his experience told him that it was ready. At his order the heavy syrup was transferred in great two-handled ladles to the cooling-tank where the crystals formed.

Only on Sundays were the fires put out, a risky gesture to religious convention since unboiled juice would barely keep a day. At one o'clock on Monday morning the work restarted, to continue relentlessly till the following Saturday midnight.

When the liquid mixture of crystals and molasses was luke-warm it was ladled from the cooling cistern into tapering wooden pots, sixteen inches square at the top and twenty-six or twenty-eight inches deep. The pots were left to cool for two days in the filling-room, at the end of which time they were rapped to test for sound sugar which gave out a ringing sound, while bad sugar sounded dead. Having passed this test, the pots were then carried to the curing-house. Now the curing-house was a necessary but wasteful adjunct to a Muscovado factory, because no way other than slow draining was known for the separation of the crystals from the molasses. In the place of the modern centrifugals, a great building and hundreds of wooden pots were needed to perform the same function in thirty days that the modern machines speed through in half that number of minutes. Ligon's curing-house was a two-storeyed building, a hundred feet long by forty broad, the top floor covered with the sugar pots fitted close together between strong wooden stanchions and draining the molasses into hollowed wooden gutters on the floor beneath, at the corners of which lay four large collecting tanks. The curing-house was rendered gloomy by the almost total absence of windows 'for the moyst ayer is an enemy to the cure of suger', so much so that in rainy weather pans of well-kindled coals were stood about in the lanes between the pots.

After the pots had drained for a month they were carried down to the knocking-room, where they were turned upside down and sharply dropped on the floor, when the sugar came out, a pyramid two feet high weighing approximately thirty pounds, varying in colour from light yellow at the base to deep brown at the apex. A good sugar planter knocked off top and bottom for reboiling with the molasses to make Penneles sugar, a grade slightly inferior to the second best Muscovado, but according to Ligon the majority of Barbadian planters did not go to this trouble.

The good Muscovado, 'of a bright colour, dry and sweet', was shipped away in casks or chests, or kept for further treatment to make white sugar, a long process that consisted of covering the top of the pot with a mixture of clay and water and leaving it for four months, at the end of which the water was found to have drained off many of the impurities, leaving the middle white and 'excellent lump sugar', sold in London for the good price of 20d a pound.

The manufacture of rum in the seventeenth century was less an art than an elementary process. Molasses and the skimmings from the coppers worked together to produce a fermenting liquor which was distilled only twice. Ligon's description of the finished product is vivid: 'so strong a Spirit, as a candle being brought a near distance to the bung of a Hogshead or But, where it is kept, the Spirits will flie to it, and taking hold of it, bring the fire down to the vessell, and set all afire, which immediately breakes the vessell, and becomes a flame, burning all about that is combustible matter.' Rather a long-winded way of describing an explosion! Ligon never uses the word rum: he refers to the spirit as 'kill-devil'.

The Anglo-Dutch War of 1652–4 had little effect in the Caribbees. The Royalist exiles in Holland made the most of it and Prince Rupert sailed to the Caribbean with a squadron in 1652, but his navigator missed Barbados, and in the Leewards he received no support. Finally his ships were dispersed by a hurricane, in which his brother, Prince Maurice, was drowned. Rupert limped back to Holland with nothing achieved. A more momentous occasion was the arrival at the end of January 1655 of Cromwell's 'Western Design'. National aggrandizement, Puritan hatred of Catholic Spain, and private revenge for losses incurred at the Spanish capture of Providence in 1641 all played their part among the motives behind the expedition. The ethical excuse given in the Protector's instructions was to release the natives of the Indies from 'the Miserable Thraldome and bondage both Spirituall and Civill' of the King of Spain; and to spread the true (Protestant) religion. But the main object was 'to gain an interest' in the West Indies anywhere between Hispaniola and the Orinoco. The exact locality was left to the decision of the leaders after their arrival at Barbados.

With the Western Design, Oliver Cromwell started a tradition of badly organized expeditions to the West Indies that was to last England for much too long. The veterans of the New Model Army were not to be spared for such a venture. Volunteers were called for, and, it was later alleged, no officer let any but his worst men go. The paper strength of the land forces was supposed to be three thousand but only 2,500 men sailed, many of them without military experience, pressed into the service and hurried on board without even a parade. With only fifteen rounds of ammunition per man, muskets shipped without their wooden stocks, and pikes left to follow in storeships that never sailed from Deptford, the expedition sailed from Portsmouth on Christmas Day 1654 — 'a sad day for the married men and the young men in love', as one account puts it. The naval element was better. There were no fewer than thirty-eight ships in all, led by the *Swiftsure*, a second-rate frigate of sixty-four guns, but the seamen were too contemptuous of the soldiers to co-operate with them.

To lead this ill-planned and ill-found expedition Cromwell had appointed two leaders of indifferent quality. General Robert Venables was a man of forty-one when he sailed from Portsmouth. He had served in the Parliamentary army during the Civil War and had spent the last five years in Ireland, where he was not without popularity. A man of honest intentions, he proved himself incompetent, dilatory when quick decisions were needed, and guilty of cowardice if accusations from more than one quarter are to be believed.

Admiral William Penn was a very different personality. Eight years younger than Venables, he had served with distinction under Blake in the Mediterranean, but he was a careerist in touch with the exiled Charles II at The Hague. In 1660 it was his ship that brought Charles back to England, a service for which he was knighted, but for his performance of duty on the Western Design he received nothing but reprobation and disgrace. Yet it was his son, William Penn the younger, who founded the Quaker colony of Pennsylvania.

With an incompetent and a careerist in command, it was not surprising that they quarrelled, but they were encouraged to do so by the wording of their commission which in the preamble named Venables before Penn, while in the body of the document Penn's name was written before Venables's. In addition there were three other commissioners: Edward Winslow, a former governor of New Plymouth and one of the original

Pilgrim Fathers; Daniel Searle, the governor of Barbados, who did valuable service in recruitment there but never left his island; and Gregory Butler, a man of West Indian experience probably connected with Providence. As Searle stayed at Barbados, Winslow died before reaching Jamaica, and Butler sailed home from there as fast as he could, they need not concern the story further. As the ships of the Western Design sailed into Carlisle Bay, they received a warm welcome from many of the colonists who sailed out in small boats to meet them, but it was not long before many of the leading planters turned against the expedition. As recruitment started they found their indentured servants missing; they had to find billets for the soldiers, and rations, and muskets, and discovered that Venables had been authorized by Cromwell to use two-thirds of the island duties towards the cost of the expedition, which was tantamount to imposing an extra tax. Worst of all, fifteen ships of their Dutch friends found trading in the bay were captured and their cargoes confiscated for contravention of the 1651 Navigation Act. It became apparent that a secondary object of the Western Design was to enforce that unpopular trading restriction. The sighs of relief when Penn and Venables sailed on must have filled their sails. Thomas Modyford had given his support to the enterprise and had made himself unpopular as a result. Writing to his brother shortly after its departure he commented on 'such strange cursinge and raylinge at these men after they were gone, that it would have troubled your ears to have heard it'. He lost his assembly seat at the next election.

The fate of Penn and Venables's expedition will be described in the next chapter. When it became apparent in Barbados that it had conquered Jamaica and brought a new English colony into being, the Barbados planters feared its competition and resented attempts to find more recruits for it. At the same time the Barbadian leaders expressed concern at the increasing number of rebels, pirates and criminals that Cromwell was having transported to their island home. The start of the evil system of transportation must be laid at Oliver's door.

The Western Design marked the peak of Cromwell's colonial activity. He showed himself reasonable when the Barbadians petitioned him to change the duties on colonial produce from a levy on weight to an impost *ad valorem* and reduced the export duty on horses, but he did not favour the original suggestion of Thomas Modyford that Barbados should be allowed to send two representatives to Parliament at Westminster. It was not such an impracticable idea as it might at first have sounded, for colonists did make visits to England and London merchants were in direct contact with the island. Perhaps if Modyford's suggestion had been adopted and applied to all colonies, there might have been no American War of Independence; but such idealism was not to be. Thomas Modyford had other ideas too: later he suggested that the English nobility should be required to help in the settlement of colonies and that assisted passages should be provided for poorer emigrants. Modyford had started as a barrister before the Civil War took him soldiering. In spite of the service he had given to Ayscue that had resulted in Willoughby's wise decision to make a peaceful surrender, Governor Searle accused him of Royalist sympathies. Modyford's vehement protest was recorded: 'I doe in ye Presence of ye all seeing God from ye bottome of my heart, abhorre and abjure ye said Interest of ye Stuarts, as inconsistent with ye Peace and Happiness of our Nation, and shall with my life and fortune Defend ye Present Government.' Cromwell restored him to the command of the militia regiment of which Searle had thought fit to deprive him.

After the death of Oliver in 1658 and the failure of Richard Cromwell to prove himself a chip of the old block, there was much speculation about the future government of England and her colonies. On 11 December 1659 representatives of the people of Barbados laid a petition before Parliament asking for self-government, the appointment of their own governor and the minting of their own money. The Council of State went a long way to meet this request by appointing Modyford governor of Barbados. Then the King was restored to his throne. Lord Willoughby was compensated for the loss of his proprietary rights by being appointed governor and Modyford's doom was certain. Willoughby had not forgiven him for deserting him in 1651 and Modyford's protestation above should have brought his fall. Yet he survived. Willoughby wrote appointing Humphrey Walrond as his deputy until his arrival and Walrond had Modyford arrested and accused of high treason, but there was no evidence and Walrond had to watch Modyford released. Charles II had decided he was a good man at heart. Writing to the Earl of Clarendon he spoke of Modyford, 'of whom I have heretofore had a very good opinion, that I will pardon and forgett all that is done amisse.' The reason behind this curious survival is that George Monk, who had brought about the restoration of the King, and had been created Duke of Albemarle for his services, was a cousin or close kinsman of Thomas Modyford and looked after his interests at court. He was to do so again on a later occasion. In 1661 an order came from the Privy Council 'that the said Colonel Thomas Modyford bee not disturbed or further persecuted for anything he had formerly acted, but that he be permitted to enjoy the full benefitt of His Majesty's Gracious Act of Oblivion'. Shortly afterwards he was elected Speaker of the Barbados assembly. Willoughby delayed his arrival in Barbados until August 1663 and Thomas Modyford moved away six months afterwards to Jamaica where he was appointed governor. By then he was a baronet – one of thirteen Barbadians made baronets in 1661 – and when he sailed he took eight hundred settlers with him. Lady Modyford followed a little later with the remainder of the eighty persons of his private household. He must have achieved the aim Richard Ligon said he had formed on arrival to make a fortune in Barbados.

One of Willoughby's first acts as royal governor was to persuade the Barbados assembly to pass an act establishing a permanent revenue by imposing a tax of four and a half per cent on all exports from the colony. It was of course intended to pay for the expenses of government and replaced various levies that the proprietors had made at their discretion, but for two hundred years the four and a half per cent duty became the biggest bone of contention between Barbados and the home government. At times the tax was used for other expenses and the assembly was called upon to vote supplementary supplies. In 1669 Charles II farmed the duty to Sir Charles Wheler and three associates for a fixed payment of £7,000 per annum. Two years later Sir Charles Wheler was appointed governor of the Leeward Islands and so the highly unsatisfactory situation arose of the governor of one colony farming the taxes of another.

Willoughby discovered that before his arrival, his appointed deputy, Humphrey Walrond, had been acting in his typically high-handed manner, levying illegal imposts and looking after his own interests. Walrond calmly admitted helping himself to £1,000, promised to hand it over and then failed to do so. When the Provost Marshal attempted to recover the sum from Walrond's estates he organized an armed rebellion and slipped away to England before he could be arrested. There he brazenly appealed to the Privy Council, but justice caught up with him and he was consigned to the Fleet Prison. In most of the references to him Humphrey Walrond appears as a swashbuckling adventurer, yet he had a better side, for Richard Ligon spoke well of him for looking after the welfare of his indentured servants and kindness to Ligon when he fell ill.

In November 1664 Lord Willoughby sailed off to inspect the colony he had founded in 1651 on the Surinam river in Guiana. He had had much trouble in England over the recognition of his title to the colony and had to remain satisfied with a half-share, his co-proprietor being Lawrence Hyde, the second son of the Earl of Clarendon. Little is known about events in the colony before 1660, except that it enjoyed even more independence than Barbados had done in the preceding decade. The colonists elected an assembly that elected a governor and he appointed his own advisory council. It is likely that few people in England knew of its existence. When Willoughby arrived on 18 November 1664, he found the colony in a thriving condition. It may seem curious that what today appears a far from interesting country should have proved so attractive to seventeenth-century English colonists. The main reason was the advantages offered by a navigable river. As in the colonies attempted on the Amazon and Wiapoco earlier on, Surinam possessed in its river a natural highway and an abundant water supply. Fifteen miles from the mouth, the English founded the small settlement of Pramorabo, but the capital, Torarica, with its church and one hundred houses, was sixty miles upstream. As far as that and for thirty miles beyond the river was navigable to ships of three hundred tons, the size of the largest merchant ships visiting the West Indies. Along the river were five hundred estates, of which between forty and fifty had profitable sugar works. Defended by a fort at Pramorabo and spared the ravages of hurricanes that damaged crops so frequently in the Caribbees, Lord Willoughby's river colony appeared to have a bright future before it. There were approximately four thousand inhabitants, both white and black. Health had been good from the early days. Most of the planters had come from Barbados and constituted a representative cross-section of that island community. Governor William Byam would have been a credit to any colony, but there were also some Walrond-like types. Before Willoughby's arrival, Byam had locked in the Torarica gaol for stealing a Dutch sloop Colonel Robert Sanford, who 'vomited forth such pickled language as exceeded the Rhetoric of Belingsgate', reported Byam. When he had cooled down Sanford admitted: 'Granted that I railed in the idiom of an oyster wench, it can be at worst but an incivility.' He was fined five thousand pounds of sugar, banished to England and kept in irons until he sailed.

Another colonist of like disposition nearly put an end to the career of Lord Willoughby. This was John Allen, who had been in Surinam since 1657. He visited Willoughby at Christmas and complained that he had been the victim of slanderers: he had been tried for blasphemy and duelling. Willoughby promised to investigate. But Allen was impatient. On 4 January he burst into the council chamber and attacked his Proprietor with a cutlass. He stabbed himself and later took poison, but Willoughby nearly died and was incapacitated for several months. It was 9 May 1665, when he finally left for Barbados.

By then the Second Dutch War had started. The West Indian colonies, which had suffered little from the First Dutch War, were seriously affected by the second. In St Kitts the treaty of neutrality was forgotten when France joined the Dutch against England. The French overran the English plantations and drove many of the colonists to seek refuge in Virginia. They captured Antigua and Montserrat. Although they burnt most of the houses, they treated their English captives with civility, but they let loose their Carib allies on Antigua in an orgy of pillage and rape. The redoubtable Dutch admiral de Ruyter attacked Barbados but was repelled by fire from the forts, and three Barbadians were killed in the engagement. Then

Francis Willoughby struck back and tragedy followed. In July 1666 after being repelled in an attack on Martinique his ships were struck by a hurricane and Lord Francis Willoughby was drowned. The only trace of him was a couch known to have belonged to him that was washed ashore with parts of a ship on Montserrat.

This tragedy did not have the serious effect it might have had. Willoughby had left Barbados in charge of his two nephews, old Henry Hawley and another settler named Samuel Barwick. When news of his disappearance reached London, the King appointed his brother William to take his place as governor. Lord William reached Barbados in April 1667 with a force of eight hundred soldiers under the command of Sir Tobias Bridge. Too precipitately, William Willoughby attempted to recapture St Kitts and was repelled before the arrival of a strong squadron which he knew was coming under Sir John Harman. All this time little Nevis had remained in English hands. After relieving the pressure there, Harman sailed to Martinique where in a week's protracted action he destroyed the French fleet.

Meanwhile down in Guiana the Dutch had captured Surinam. Governor Byam had made a spirited resistance but had received poor support from the colonists. On 6 March 1667, he surrendered to Abraham Crynsens, who gave him generous terms: equality of status with Dutch planters and security of estates, liberty of conscience, and freedom to sell and remove elsewhere later, if they wished it. On 8 October Surinam was recaptured by Sir John Harman, but it was too late, for on 21 July peace had been signed between England and the Netherlands at Breda. According to the terms of the treaty all possessions were to remain in the hands of the nation that held them on 21 May. So Surinam was handed over to the Dutch in exchange for their colony of New Amsterdam at the mouth of the Hudson river, which was destined to grow into the great state and city of New York. Few English people remember that there was once an English colony at Surinam. Yet it was remarkable in producing the first English woman novelist, Mrs Aphra Benn, whose book, *Oroonoko, or the Royal Slave* was well received by the contemporaries of John Dryden. She is also credited with the introduction of milk punch into England. After a few years of Dutch rule, the colonists decided to move. Some went with William Byam to Antigua, where his family was prominent until well into the nineteenth century, and others under James Bannister went to Jamaica, where they were granted land in the west of the island in a region known as Surinam Quarters to this day.

At the Peace of Breda, the French handed back the English portion of St Kitts, in return for the recognition of their rights in Acadia, Nova Scotia. It was a sad end to what had started as international co-operation. With the more serious wars to follow all hope of *condominium* was ended and the

French finally gave up their share of the little island at the Treaty of Utrecht in 1713.

The Second Dutch War had placed a strain on the Caribbee Islands that Barbados alone was financially capable of bearing. It was reckoned that the wealthy sugar colony had contributed £100,000 to the cost of the war. In consequence demands for self-government were revived. When William Willoughby went home in 1669 on government business, he left as deputy-governor Christopher Codrington, a second-generation planter who was only twenty-nine. In spite of his comparative youth he managed affairs with efficiency, but was shabbily dismissed when Willoughby belatedly returned in October 1672. Deprived also of his seat in the council, Codrington stood for election to the assembly and such was the esteem in which his fellow planters held him that he was elected Speaker nine times between 1674 and 1682. In the meantime William Willoughby made almost as dramatic an exit as his brother: in April 1673 he fell ill and died after a short illness. He and his brother Francis had been good governors, being both planters themselves and therefore having a stake in the island, and peers of the realm at the same time, able to speak to the King with the experience and facility of courtiers. The next permanent appointment was a courtier and not a planter. Nevertheless, Sir Jonathan Atkins came to identify himself with the planters' interests so much that the Lords of Trade and Plantations complained to Charles II: 'He doth labour with more arguments than ye Inhabitants themselves.' He strongly resisted the appointment of courtiers to the various patent offices in the island, because they leased their patents to inefficient and grasping deputies. As an example of his cool attitude to home authority, when asked to supply a map of Barbados he regretted that it was impossible as the only competent draughtsman was a Quaker, whose religious principles forbade him to mark on it anything as warlike as forts and coast defences. When he was recalled in 1680 at the age of seventy – with a deputy-governor of twenty-nine and a governor of seventy Charles II's governments were delightfully free of colonial regulations – Sir Jonathan Atkins had won two points. He had stopped the abuse of the patent offices and won the principle that laws passed by the Barbados assembly would be permanent, unless specifically disallowed by the English government, and not be required to be renewed every two years.

Atkins's successor, Sir Richard Dutton, was a very different type. He was an adventurer who came to advance his fortune. At first the Lords of Trade thought they had found a good man, but as time went on complaints about his high-handed and unjust behaviour found their way home and in 1685 he was recalled in disgrace.

6

THE CAPTURE AND SETTLEMENT OF JAMAICA

After clearing from Barbados on 31 March 1655, the fleet of Penn and Venables made its way to St Christopher and picked up Gregory Butler and the recruits he had managed to collect among the Leeward Islands. The army on board then numbered approximately eight thousand men, more than half of them colonials. In spite of the non-arrival of the vital store-ships, it was decided to make a landing at the Rio de la Hina, ten miles west of Santo Domingo on the island of Hispaniola. Assuming that Penn had his Dutch prizes included in his fleet, the approach of the fifty-four ships under his command must have made an impressive sight. But the Spaniards had received word of the English approach. As in England in 1588, alarm beacons ashore carried the news to the capital. Although the Spaniards had only one-third of Venables' numbers, the English put up one of the most abjectly miserable showings of any of the many unsuccessful expeditions sent out from our shores. For the three weeks ashore in Hispaniola, the accounts are full of stories of mismanagement, disobeyed orders, rank cowardice and leaders' quarrels. Provisions ran short, men broke ranks to chase stray cattle and fell into ambushes laid by small forces of Negroes and mulattos. Dysentery appeared. Many suffered from thirst, for they had landed on a dry coast where the Spaniards had blocked up all the wells. The better equipped English soldiers fell victims to heat, because many wore thick jerkins or light armour. To add to their miseries it rained. In all, two attempts were made to reach the city, but because the landings had been made forty (instead of the intended ten) miles from it, the walls were never reached. No sortie was required to drive the attackers away, so frightened were they of their own shadows. For this all four leaders agreed in blaming the colonial troops. Writing to Governor Searle, Venables said, 'To say the truth, your men and the men of St Christopher's lead all the disorder and confusion.' When the last miserable soldiers were re-embarked it was calculated that a thousand had perished ashore.

Drifting westwards on the Trade Wind, Venables suggested they had better make an attempt to capture Jamaica as something to show to Cromwell on their return. So on 10 May 1655, a landing was made at Passage Fort, at the extreme western end of the present Kingston Harbour. The Spanish resistance was so feeble that not a man was lost. Next day the English marched to Villa de la Vega through a fine savanna and invested the Spanish capital. Showing no initiative, here Venables sat him down in a comfortable billet, while the Spanish governor, under pretence of studying the terms of surrender, used the time to evacuate the few colonists and their cattle over a rough track to the north side of the island, where they were to hold out for five years.

On 21 May Penn sailed off to England with two-thirds of the fleet, leaving Venables ill with dysentery. As soon as he was well enough he followed the admiral, going, so he said, at the request of the army to represent their conditions to the Protector. When Cromwell asked him if he had ever read of any general that had left his army, Venables had the temerity to quote the Earl of Essex. 'A sad example', said Oliver drily and committed him to the Tower to keep company with Penn, but six weeks later they were released, never to receive another commission under the Commonwealth; treatment which in their eyes justified intrigue with the Royalists in Holland and the enjoyment of some favour at the Restoration.

Such is the unprepossessing story of the capture of Jamaica, taken as a sop to appease Oliver Cromwell. In the long run it proved a more practical proposition than the seven times greater island of Hispaniola, which would have been found too large for the available forces and immigrants to occupy. As it was, it called for considerable effort to hold Jamaica. If it had not been taken at a time when Spain was terribly weakened, it could not have been held at all. Blake's destruction of the Spanish fleet at Santa Cruz in the Canary Islands in 1657 still further reduced the chances of Spanish retribution.

The damage to their national prestige was more serious to the Spanish government than the loss of their colony. Spain had not developed the island at all: at the time of the English descent it is estimated that there were no more than 1,500 Spaniards and an equal number of Negro slaves. They grew a little cocoa, indigo, sugar-cane and citrus fruit, all of which they had introduced to the island, and their slaves raised cassava, corn, potatoes, cotton and tobacco, the crops which the Spaniards had found the Arawak Indians growing. These peaceful and friendly people had been exterminated by the time the English arrived. But the most important product of the Spanish colony was beef and pork, supplied by half-wild herds that were hunted when meat was required.

The chief Spanish settlement had been at Spanish Town, known to its founders as Villa de la Vega, but called Santiago de la Vega by the English, and then merely St Jago, a name to be still seen on a few old milestones. Venables's rabble destroyed many of the two thousand houses the town contained, but there were still five hundred standing in 1661. Over on the north coast near the present St Ann's Bay, the original Spanish settlement of Sevilla was mostly in ruins and other settlements were quite unimportant. The English therefore gained little from the Spanish owners and were faced with a virtually uninhabited island; but the Spaniards contested possession until 1660.

The great difference between the start of the English colony in Jamaica and that of Barbados and the Caribbees was the government enterprise that lay behind its capture. Once the news reached England, Cromwell made up for the indifferent quality of the original expeditionaries by sending out Major-General Robert Sedgwick and eight hundred picked soldiers of the New Model Army. In December 1656 another thousand arrived under General William Brayne, but these reinforcements were seriously infected with sickness that carried off many other ranks and both the newly arrived commanders. In September 1657 there succeeded to the command Colonel Edward D'Oyley, who was to become the real conqueror of Jamaica.

Edward D'Oyley had come out with Venables and attended his councils of war. It was in his family's tradition to administer a newly conquered land, for his ancestor, Robert D'Oilli, had come over to England with William the Conqueror. For one of his manors the original D'Oyley had been required to provide the King with two fine linen tablecloths a year. These had been made by the women of the household, who developed over the centuries a name for decorative embroidery that has come down to the present day in the table-mats or doyleys that so many people use without any idea of their feudal origin. There was little table service for Edward D'Oyley, however. In 1657 and again in 1658 he took a force of seven hundred soldiers by ship round to the north side where they engaged the surviving Spaniards in two sharp actions. On the latter occasion at the Rio Nuevo three hundred Spaniards were killed for the loss of twenty-eight English. This broke the back of Spanish resistance. On 9 May 1660, the last Spaniards sailed away to Cuba from the spot traditionally marked as the pleasant swimming beach of Runaway Bay.

By 1660 D'Oyley was faced with another serious problem: would Charles II recognize the conquest of the usurper Cromwell? With less than two thousand soldiers remaining and no men-of-war, the situation was critical. It was therefore a great relief when in June 1661 Charles sent D'Oyley his commission appointing him governor. This marked the beginning of civil government in Jamaica, which until then had been under martial law. When D'Oyley left the island the next year and went home, he received no reward for his excellent service and led an uneventful life until his death in 1675.

Charles II did little to encourage the development of Jamaica beyond making the appointment of Thomas, Lord Windsor, as governor of the colony. As a peer, it was thought he would enhance the reputation of the island, but Windsor spent only ten weeks in Jamaica before sailing home again. All he did was to disband the last of the soldiers and authorize the formation of five regiments of militia. He also published a proclamation which promised to every person taking up residence in the island within the next two years thirty acres of land in return for armed service when called upon; and declared that all children born in Jamaica of English subjects were to be free denizens of England. This was a very small inducement to immigration. In fact thirty acres was a very mean offer, for in Jamaica England had acquired an island over twenty-five times the size of Barbados. In consequence few settlers arrived from England, where the end of the Civil War and republican government had removed the main causes of emigration. For its first settlers Jamaica drew upon Barbados and the Leeward Islands. Once fighting was over, the miserable soldiers from those colonies proved themselves useful planters. In 1656 Luke Stokes, the elderly governor of Nevis, had transferred himself to Jamaica with 1,600 people. It was unfortunate, however, that they chose to settle in the Morant Bay area which was to prove so unhealthy: within a year Luke Stokes and two-thirds of his companions had died, but the rest survived to form a prosperous settlement. The death of these people from Nevis and the high mortality among the soldiers gave Jamaica an unfortunate early reputation that took time to dispel.

In the same way that confusion over the early government in Barbados had discouraged settlement and produced the 'Starving Time', early changes of governor in Jamaica had a like effect. Sir Charles Lyttelton, who had taken over from Windsor, called the first assembly, but in two years he had had enough and returned to England in May 1664. A month afterwards Sir Thomas Modyford arrived from Barbados to fill the dual role of planter and governor and bring the stability at the helm which the young colony sorely needed. His term of office lasted seven years. One set of figures indicates his important influence: when he arrived there were less than five thousand inhabitants; when he left there were over fifteen thousand.

English government policy over the appointment of governors was to vary considerably for the rest of the seventeenth century. Of the sixteen men who administered the government between 1660 and 1700, five were peers of the realm, four were soldiers, one was a merchant and six were planters. With the exception of the Earl of Carlisle (no relation of the

Proprietor) none of the peers was a success. In 1692 Samuel Bernard, Speaker of the assembly and a considerable planter, wrote to the secretary of the Lords of Trade that there was need of a governor whose quality 'is not too much above ours, and who will not, like Lord Inchiquin, devote all his words and actions to the heaping up of money'. But the office did call for a man of some wealth and considerable public spirit. The salary during this period was never more than £2,000 per annum, more often than not paid far in arrears. This was the main cause for Lyttelton's departure. He complained that he had been granted no salary and his table alone cost him £600 a year. Later when Sir Henry Morgan was in command he reported that during the seven months' session of the assembly he had spent £1,000 on entertainment as 'Governors at such times are forced to keep open house'. The most successful governors were Modyford, Sir Thomas Lynch and Sir William Beeston, all of them considerable planters.

As in Barbados, however, local residents showed a tendency to quarrel. There was little love lost between Lynch and Modyford. It began with a well-intentioned attempt by Modyford to make an administrative improvement. Thomas Lynch had arrived with Penn and Venables, holding a life patent for the office of Provost Marshal. Because this was a military appointment, Modyford suggested that it would be more appropriate if the name of the office were changed to Sheriff, but Lynch objected to such an extent that he returned to England and stayed there for the whole of Modyford's term as governor. Then in 1671 he returned, knighted, with a lieutenant-governor's commission and took satisfaction from having Modyford arrested and sent home in disgrace as a result of Morgan's sack of Panama. Shortly afterwards Morgan suffered the same experience at his hands. Understandably, when Morgan and Modyford returned to the island restored to favour in 1675, Lynch returned to reside in England until 1682, when he returned as full governor. By then Modyford was dead, but Lynch had Morgan's commission as lieutenant-governor revoked and shortly afterwards had him dismissed from the council. Reporting this to the Lords of Trade Lynch said: 'Sir Henry Morgan and Captain Morgan (his cousin) have set up a special club, frequented by only five or six more, where (especially when the members are drunk) the dissenters are cursed and damned. The whole country was provoked by their taking the name of the Loyal Club, and the people began to take notice that it looked as if he hoped to be thought head of the Tories; consequently I must be of the Whigs.' At a time when in England the Whigs had earned a traitorous reputation over the Exclusion Bills and the Rye House plot, Lynch's anxiety to clear his name may be appreciated. It is also an interesting proof of the way the leading colonists kept in touch with current English politics. Morgan and his friends did not take their defeat lying down. The quarrel continued until the death of Sir Thomas Lynch in 1684. Even then Morgan found his guns spiked, for Lynch had arranged for a dormant commission as lieutenant-governor to be given to Colonel Hender Molesworth, one of his close supporters, and so defeated Morgan's hopes of securing the position for himself.

Although the early Jamaicans had never experienced the virtual independence that Barbadians had enjoyed during the Civil War, they were no less determined to reduce the interference in their affairs by the home government to a minimum. Between 1672 and 1677 the assembly, which Modyford had called only once and then dispensed with, made itself notorious for high-handed and unconstitutional behaviour. They passed an act suppressing lawyers; they had the Receiver-General imprisoned, and interfered in the course of justice by ordering a stay of execution in the case of a man convicted of privateering. The Lords of Trade and Plantations decided that the reins of government needed tightening. This was warrantable, because the Jamaica assembly was showing signs of autocracy comparable to the notorious 'Rump' that Cromwell had turned out, and it was threatening individual liberty. But it was extraordinary that the English authorities could think of no other model for their measures than Poynings's Law, which had been applied to the Irish Parliament in 1494. This provided that the Irish Parliament could be summoned only with the approval of the King's Council in England. To apply such a measure to a dependency not a few days' journey away but lying across four thousand miles of ocean was absurd. It also disregarded all the constitutional changes that had occurred in England during the 184 intervening years. By 1678 the English Parliament was no longer a servile, tax-voting, law-endorsing body. When Charles II was restored to the throne, the House of Commons feared nobody; they held him by the purse-strings, initiating legislation as well as considering royal bills, and had laid down the law that three years should not elapse between the dissolution of one Parliament and the election of the next. The Jamaica assemblymen knew their recent history and were determined that they were going to exercise the same rights and enjoy the same liberties as the English House of Commons. So when the Earl of Carlisle arrived as governor on 18 July 1678, battle was soon joined. In addition to Poynings's Law Carlisle had been instructed to persuade the assembly to pass a permanent revenue on the Barbados model. He proved himself a good diplomat, often showing his sympathy with the assembly as he said 'to quiet the minds of the inhabitants of His Majesty's most promising plantation'. In the end a deputation led by Samuel Long, the Chief Justice, went home to present their case before the Lords of Trade. Fortunately reason prevailed and a compromise was reached: in return for granting a Seven Years' Revenue, the Jamaica assembly was to be allowed to initiate legislation, but such laws would require not only the consent of the governor and council but the King's assent as well. As in Barbados all the royal revenue was to be devoted to the expenses of island government, but the home authorities took the opportunity to withdraw the former subventions that had been made for the salaries of the governor and other officials and threw this on to the shoulders of the Jamaica assembly. If they wanted more control over their country's affairs they would have to pay for it. In this way the system of government was hammered out that lasted for the better part of two hundred years until it was suspended after the Morant Bay Rebellion of 1865. In modern parlance it was representative, not responsible, government and with it the planters remained content.

Carlisle, who had accompanied the deputation home, never returned to Jamaica. For Sir Henry Morgan, who had taken over as lieutenant-governor, he made an interesting plea that represents the greatest compliment ever received by that controversial figure. In the list of salaries for the officials the English authorities expected the Jamaica assembly to pay, there was no provision for the deputy-governor. Writing to the secretary of the Lords of Trade and Plantations Carlisle said, 'Sir H. Morgan will do his best to get a compliance with what his Majesty and the Lords expect, but I find there will be a difficulty to get the Revenue Bill perpetual. I heartily desire you would move the King to give his part of the prize taken by Captain Heywood to Sir H.M. You know there is taken from him £600 per annum payable here, and his company of foot, so that this gift will hardly recompense the loss of the other this year, and the place he lives in is so chargeable that with his generous humour I know he will be a beggar, although I also allow him £600 per annum out of what you have left me.'

DEFENCE BY BUCCANEERS

Among the many problems with which the early governors of Jamaica were faced, the greatest was the question of defence; if the colony was insecure nobody could be encouraged to plant. For an offensive anti-Spanish policy its situation was excellent, 'the key to the Caribbean'. The King of Spain was expected to attempt its recapture, lying as it did, to quote one contemporary observer, 'within his Bowels and in the heart of his trade'. But an offensive policy was expensive. Cromwell soon found himself in financial difficulties and Charles II was always short of money. Without a naval squadron Jamaica's position was extremely vulnerable, 'circled with the enemy's countries'. It was a repetition of the situation at Providence on a bigger scale. Barbados and the Caribbees were too far away to render assistance if Jamaica were attacked. Although it took only a week from east to west, a voyage eastwards from Jamaica to Barbados in the teeth of the

Trade Wind usually took seven or eight weeks. A realistic governor soon came to realize that he must rely on his own resources.

To begin with there had been sufficient ships of the English navy to pursue an offensive policy in the Drake tradition. After Penn and the dross of his fleet had left, Vice-Admiral William Goodson on 31 July 1655 sailed to the Spanish Main and sacked Santa Marta. The next year he went to Rio de la Hacha. He was a staunch Puritan and this was godly work. About the same time a small force reoccupied Anthony Hilton's old haunt at Tortuga. Here the Buccaneers had continued their activities since the end of their occupation of Providence, largely under French protection, until in 1653 the Spaniards had once more recaptured it. For four years it remained in English hands. Then in 1659 it was relinquished to the French to become the base from which they occupied the western half of Hispaniola, as the great colony of Saint Domingue. But those four years of English occupation were important, for it was then that contact was made with the Buccaneers and their association with Jamaica began. Goodson's successor, Captain Christopher Myngs, made use of them in a joint expedition to the Main in 1659, when the capture of the towns of Coro and Comina yielded a booty of over £200,000.

The arrival of the Buccaneers at Jamaica gave rise to the town of Port Royal, built at the western extremity of the Palisadoes, the nine-mile-long sandspit that serves as a breakwater for the magnificent natural harbour of modern Kingston. The Spaniards had never occupied the site. Their nearest settlement had been at Caguaya, where the English landed and

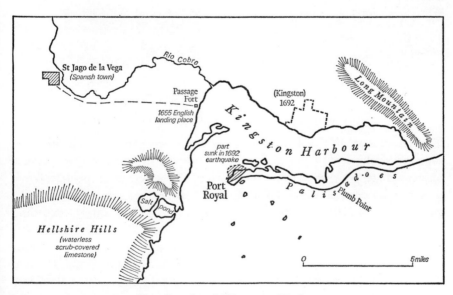

Port Royal and Kingston Harbour

which they called Passage or Passage Fort, using the anglicized name Cagway for the harbour and Point Cagway for the beginnings of Port Royal. The first mention of a town there was made by General Brayne in July 1657: 'There is the fair beginning of a towne upon the poynt of this harbour, which with a little chardge will be made past the Spaniards gaining.' A fort had already been started there and by 1661 there were five hundred houses in the town, chiefly for the accommodation of seamen, especially, wrote Hickeringill (in *Jamaica Viewed*) 'the Privateers, who are their best customers'. The general kept his official residence there, together with a small number of merchants and manufacturers. Shortly after this the name was changed to Port Royal. Already it had superseded the old Spanish capital in importance.

During their years of independence between the fall of Providence and the capture of Jamaica, the Buccaneers had evolved their own rules of war. A day of embarkation was first advertised when all joined in a common council to decide first of all on a place to collect provisions and, secondly, what objective to attack. Meat was their main diet, and pork their favourite meat. After hunting the feral cattle and pigs and 'boucaning' the meat they sailed away to the town chosen as their bloodthirsty destination. Although ruthless to their Spanish enemies, the Buccaneers observed a strict code of honour among themselves. Articles were drawn up for each venture. The chief was the principle of 'No Prey, No Pay', but once a booty was obtained it was divided according to a recognized scale:

First of all, to the wounded:

for the loss of a right arm	600 pieces of eight or	
	6 slaves (£150 approx.)	
left arm	500 pieces or 5 slaves	
right leg	500 pieces or 5 slaves	
left leg	400 pieces or 4 slaves	
an eye	100 pieces or 1 slave	
a finger	100 pieces or 1 slave	

The remainder of the booty was then divided among the company, captains of ships receiving five or six times the ordinary man's share, a master's mate two shares, other officers and carpenters in proportion down to boys who received only half a share. Buccaneering sometimes brought good returns but never great wealth, the ordinary share rarely exceeding £30; frequently it was less.

Back in port booty was quickly spent, by the more prudent in maintaining their ships, but by the majority in drinking, gambling and women. They were never mean. It was nothing to spend two or three thousand pieces of eight in one night's debauchery. One man was recorded as paying a strumpet five hundred pieces of eight for stripping before the company; another would stand in the street with a pipe of wine (105 gallons) and insist on every passer-by drinking with him on threat of being pistolled for refusal. The taverns of Port Royal did a roaring trade, and not only the taverns, for there was a constant demand for arms and ammunition, provisions, and work for skilled men on the ships. There were valuable plate, costly materials and slaves to buy from the returning captains. Port Royal prospered and its streets were lined with three-storeyed houses that were likened to Cheapside. Port Royal also suffered disorders, but the law was easy in the town – the price Jamaica had to pay for such protection.

Yet there were misgivings expressed about privateering. Major-General Sedgwick said of his fellow-commissioner Goodson's sack of Santa Marta, 'I must say I think this kind of marooning cruising West India trade of plundering and burning towns, though it hath been long practised in these parts, yet is not honourable for a princely navy.' In 1664 Thomas Lynch when acting governor admitted that 'the Spaniards call all rogues in these seas, of what nation soever, English.'

Although considerate for one another, the Buccaneers showed no mercy to their Spanish enemies, usually because they offered fierce resistance but often for the only reason that they were Spaniards. All the hatred of the unoffending Haitian cowkiller for the proud Dons who would not leave him alone, the hatred of the Puritan for the Catholic derived from Providence, and the national hatreds of the northern European countries for the arrogant Spaniard who refused them trade, were pent up in the fury of the Buccaneers. At the news of their approach Spanish colonists hastened to the nearest castle or into the densest woods, carrying with them what possessions they could. After a hard battle the Buccaneers would find a town empty of people and treasure. A furious hunt for prisoners followed. Men, women and children were tortured to discover the whereabouts of hidden treasure with all the revolting methods of those times which discounted human suffering: the rack, twisted cords, burning matches between fingers, plain beating, hanging by the toes and other extremities – all were used to extort confession. In the debauches that followed the capture of a town women were raped, children left in churches to starve, and men, if they were fortunate, quickly dispatched as an example to others of what happened when treasure was concealed. The chivalrous treatment of prisoners that had characterized the privateering exploits of Sir Francis Drake had long been forgotten. The seamy side of the Buccaneers' character was inherited by the eighteenth-century pirates.

But it is important not to dismiss the Buccaneers as pirates. Buccaneers were the local West Indian cowkillers who had taken to the sea to revenge themselves on the Spaniards for unwarrantable attacks on their peaceful cattle-hunting. Pirates were the enemies of all nations and attacked their own nation's shipping as much as any other's. The word 'Buccaneer' is not used in the official correspondence of the time relating to Jamaica. They are always referred to as 'privateers', but a clear distinction was always made between them and common pirates. The government of Charles II was hesitant about using them. Thus both Windsor and Modyford were instructed to call in all commissions and endeavour to establish a peaceful trade with the Spanish colonies. When the Spanish authorities refused, Windsor made a declaration of war and unleashed Myngs, who sacked Santiago de Cuba and San Francisco de Campeche. In 1663 occurs the first official mention of the privateers in the *Calendar of State Papers*: '11 frigates and brigantines belonging to Jamaica with 740 men and 81 guns, under the command of Captains Sir Thomas Whetstone, . . . Swart, Morris and Mansfeld, manned with English, Dutch and Indians.' As soon as orders were received to call in commissions, the privateers moved away to other havens. In June 1664 Colonel Edward Morgan, Modyford's deputy, wrote: '*Pirates* appear to be increasing with the recent inhibition of *privateers*.' He said there were fourteen or fifteen sail of them with between two and three thousand men and there was a danger that they might be tempted to attack Jamaica. In 1665 Modyford reported that fourteen *pirates* had been tried and condemned to death. Then he went on to express the hope that all *privateers* would come in and take commissions against the Dutch, as the Second Dutch War had started. Piracy was never countenanced. A privateer was officially appointed with a governor's commission for which a fee of £20 was charged. It is perhaps worth mentioning that Sir Thomas Whetstone or Whitstones, the privateer captain above, was also the Speaker of the first Jamaica assembly.

Once ensconced at Port Royal, however, the privateers were difficult to dislodge, as Thomas Lynch explained to Sir Henry Bennet: 'The calling in of the privateers will be but a remote and hazardous expedient and can never be effectually done without five or six men-of-war . . . Naked orders to restrain or call them in will teach them only to keep out of this port and force them to prey on us as well as the Spaniards.' England would receive no thanks from Spain, 'though we live tamely at Jamaica and sit still and see the French made rich by prizes, and the Dutch by the trade of the West Indies'. Lynch was being realistic, because he had no love for privateering himself.

Shortly afterwards, in June 1664, Modyford arrived as governor. By then Myngs had been recalled to England with all naval ships, leaving Jamaica defenceless, so that it was not long before Modyford was authorized to grant commissions officially on the occasion of the start of the Second Dutch War in March 1665. Once again a semi-official expedition was organized under the command of Deputy-Governor Colonel Edward Morgan, with the Dutch colonies of Curaçao, Saba and St Eustatius as its objective. The corpulent colonel, however, died of a heat-stroke during the landing on St Eustatius and the venture proved a failure. The Buccaneers had no particular interest in plundering the Dutch: their avowed enemy was Spain, and many of them were French, so that it was not long before Modyford and his council were passing a resolution, on 22 February 1666, that it was in the interest of the island to grant letters of marque against the Spaniards, and they set down their reasons without one moral justification among them. First of all, attacks on the Spaniards furnished the island with many useful commodities at easy rates. Privateering brought in coin, bullion, cocoa, logwood, hides, tallow, indigo, cochineal; it attracted an exchange of trade with New England, and filled Port Royal with merchants. The poorer planters got sale for their provisions; the richer planters were able to buy slaves. It attracted from the Caribbees English, French and Dutchmen, many of whom turned planters. It was the only means of keeping the Buccaneers on Hispaniola, Tortuga, and the Cays of Cuba from being enemies and attacking Jamaican plantations. The ships of the privateers intercepted Spanish advices and kept the governor of Jamaica well informed. The King received his fifteenths, the Duke of York (as Lord High Admiral) his tenths of the booty. Artificers at Port Royal were kept in work. The more sober kind spent their takings in strengthening their ships. (Nothing was said how the other kind spent their gains.) The privateers were of great reputation to the island and of terror to the Spaniard, and kept up a high and military spirit in the inhabitants. Finally, the council argued, 'As the old ways of kindness have been unsuccessful in gaining free trade with the Spaniard, who when all old commissions were called in and many prizes restored, continued taking our ships and murdering our people, this new way may gain free trade.' Modyford himself stated that he had been against employing the privateers while in Barbados, but had seen his error in the decay of the forts and wealth in Jamaica. As soon as they were invited back the recovery of Port Royal was astonishing. With the war in progress he received official permission to employ them from the King, the Earl of Clarendon and the Duke of Albemarle, his especial patron. The five boom years of privateering from Jamaica had been officially initiated.

It is at this time that the name of Henry Morgan first appears in the annals of the Buccaneers, a name that has suffered too long as the pirate-governor of Jamaica, the terror of the taverns of Port Royal, the richest and wickedest city in the world. The origin of the infamous legend probably goes back to the well-known book about the Buccaneers of America by the Dutchman, Johan Esquimeling. This was first published in Holland in

1678 under the title *De Americaensche Zeerovers*. In 1681 it was translated into Spanish as, significantly, *Piratas de la America*, and into English in 1684 as *The Buccaneers of America*. Because the English version was made from the Spanish it is understandable how the use of the word 'pirate' has come in. Henry Morgan disapproved of the book so strongly that he brought a libel action against the English publisher and was awarded £210 damages – disappointing, for he had demanded £10,000.

Henry Morgan's origin is obscure. Esquimeling said he went to Barbados as an indentured servant, served his time, and moved on to Jamaica where he took up privateering. This is supported by an entry in the Bristol archives dated 9 February 1656, in a list of indentured labourers transported voluntarily to Barbados: 'Henry Morgan of Abergavenny in the county of Monmouth, labourer, bound to Timothy Tounsend of Bristol, cutler, for three years to serve in the Barbadoes in the like condicions.'

The late Frank Cundall, however, in his *Governors of Jamaica in the Seventeenth Century* wrote that he was usually said to have been the eldest son of Robert Morgan of Llanrumney in Glamorgan, or a son of Thomas Morgan, a yeoman-farmer of Pencarn, near St Mellons close by. Both are near Cardiff. Now Henry Morgan married his first cousin Mary Elizabeth Morgan, the second daughter of Colonel Edward Morgan, the deputy-governor who died at St Eustatius, and his wife who was the daughter of a Saxon nobleman, Johann Georg, Baron von Pölnitz. After fighting on the Royalist side in the Civil War, Edward Morgan took refuge with his in-laws, and is mentioned in their rent rolls as 'Edward Morgan of Landumenij', which Mr Cundall took for the germanized form of Llanrumney. In the course of time Henry Morgan became the owner of several estates in Jamaica, one of which he named Llanrumney near Port Maria, and another, Penkarne, in the old parish of St George. As these two names are associated with the Morgans of Glamorgan, perhaps it is reasonable to conclude that Henry Morgan named Penkarne after his own birthplace and Llanrumney to commemorate the origin of his wife's family; and if he was the Henry Morgan mentioned in the Bristol archives, perhaps he gave his origin as Abergavenny because he had run away from home: he mentioned having left school very young. He was born about 1635 for in an affidavit dated 2 December 1671, he gave his age as 'thirty-six years or thereabouts'.

An interesting question follows: in Barbados did he not know Modyford who was sugar-farming there? The date he went on to Jamaica is unknown, but it was probably around 1658. Modyford first mentioned him in a report to Albemarle in August 1665 recounting the adventures of a party of Jamaica privateers who had sailed from Jamaica in 1663 with commissions from Lord Windsor under Captains Jackman, Henry Morgan and John Morris. During twenty-two months they rampaged over four thousand

Buccaneers, Pirates and Sailors

A cattle hunter in Hispaniola. Before 1630 these men led a carefree life hunting the cattle and pigs which had escaped from Spanish ranches and gone wild. They dried the meat on wooden frames called 'boucans' over slow fires, hence their name of 'boucanier' or 'buccaneer'. They sold their meat to passing ships in exchange for guns, powder and lead. This was their only contact with the sea until the Spanish authorities decided to exterminate them. In retaliation they became corsairs, sworn to eternal war against Spain.

Above The capture and sack of
Puerto Principe, Cuba, by the
Buccaneers in 1667, under
Morgan's leadership. He showed
a preference for inland towns
which had not previously been
attacked.

Right Sir Henry Morgan as
depicted in Esquimeling's
Buccaneers of America.

After the official encouragement to the Buccaneers ended, some like Morgan took up planting while others turned pirates, attacking the ships of all countries. Among the most colourful were the women captains Mary Read (*top*) and Anne Bonny (*bottom*). Sentenced to death at Jamaica in 1721, they escaped the noose by convenient pregnancies.

The notorious pirate, Edward Teach, or 'Blackbeard', hanged at Jamaica in 1718.

Above, left Young Horatio Nelson, a portrait by J. F. Rigaud begun in 1777 when he was commissioned and finished four years later when he was a Captain.

Above, top Admiral John Benbow, who died at Port Royal from wounds received in an engagement with the French off Santa Marta in 1702. His tomb is in the Kingston Parish Church.

Above, middle Admiral Vernon, 'Old Grog' to his men, from his grograin cloak, from which was derived the sailor's grog – a dilution of his rum ration with water, introduced by Vernon to reduce drunkenness.

Above, bottom Rodney.

Left Sir Thomas Picton, first British Governor of Trinidad before the Peninsular War, where he distinguished himself. He was killed at Waterloo.

Below The Old Naval Hospital, Port Royal, built in the mid-nineteenth century. It has deteriorated since the Royal Navy left Port Royal, but there are plans to restore it as a tourist attraction.

The British capture of Trinidad from the Spanish, 1797. The Spanish Admiral burnt his four ships without fighting the seventeen British ships under Rear Admiral Henry Harvey. General Ralph Abercromby commanded the army contingents.

The fort on Brimstone Hill, St Kitts.

On deck off Port Royal.
Note the awning and the
live animals carried for
fresh meat.

A West Indiaman getting
under way at the Needles,
Isle of Wight.

miles of sea, land, river and lake from Jamaica to Campeche and Tabasco, back round Cape Catoche to Truxillo on the Gulf of Honduras (where they sacked the town first attacked from Providence twenty-five years before), down the Moskito Coast to the San Juan river, up the river in canoes to Lake Nicaragua to sack the sheltered town of Gran Granada, 150 miles from the Caribbean Sea, then back to Jamaica. It was a rollicking adventure, dear to Morgan's heart, for he showed a liking for inland towns that had not been previously sacked.

Modyford regarded the venture as an important reconnaissance, for he concluded his report: 'I have represented this matter to your Grace, being convinced that if ever reasons of State at home require any attempt on the Spanish Indies this is the properest place and the most probable to lay a foundation for the conquest of the whole.'

Morgan's first exploits, 1663-5

It was at the conclusion of this long expedition that Henry Morgan was married. Not long afterwards he was at sea again, sailing as captain of a ship under Edward Mansvelt, the Dutch Buccaneer admiral. When Mansvelt was killed at Providence Morgan succeeded to the command. He then led his five hundred men towards Cuba, where the sack of the inland town of Puerto Principe yielded a booty of fifty thousand pieces of eight.

In 1668 Morgan led four hundred men to Darien for an attack on Porto Bello, the strongest fortress in the Indies after Havana and Cartagena. When his men grumbled that they had insufficient numbers to attack such a strong city, Morgan won them over by saying, 'If our numbers are small, our hearts are great. And the fewer persons we are, the more union and better shares we shall have in the spoil.' So against Porto Bello with its two almost 'inexpugnable' forts Morgan led his desperate band, stealing along

G   81

the coast in a flotilla of canoes at dead of night, as Drake had done nearly a century before at Nombre de Dios nearby. Surprise carried the Buccaneers into the first fort, which was blown up to persuade the defenders of the second of their enemies' ruthless determination. But the Spanish governor was equally determined. When Morgan tried the ruse of driving before his men a screen of captured monks and nuns, the governor did not hesitate to fire on them, but sheer desperation carried the attackers into the fort. The governor refused to surrender, and was summarily shot. According to Esquimeling, prisoners were tortured to discover where their wealth was hidden. Morgan always denied such charges, but whatever the truth a ransom of a hundred thousand pieces of eight was demanded to save the town from being fired. This was to be Morgan's most lucrative raid, the individual share of booty working out at £60 a man. Morgan's share was probably not more than £400. Only eighteen of his force had been killed and thirty-two wounded. It had been a notable military success. The Spaniards were rudely shaken and Morgan's name was made.

Modyford, however, reproved Morgan for attacking the towns of Puerto Principe and Porto Bello when he had been issued with a commission against ships alone. Yet in his official report home the governor said:

It is certain that the Spaniards had full intention to attempt this island but could not get men: and they still hold the same minds, and therefore I cannot but presume to say that it is very unequal that we should in any measure be restrained while they are at liberty to act as they please upon us, *from which we shall never be secure until the King of Spain acknowledges this island to be His Majesty's and so include it by name in the capitulations.**

It is difficult to determine how genuine was this expressed fear of Spanish attack, or whether it was the excuse for Modyford's official support of privateering. In December 1668 Richard Browne, a ship's surgeon who sailed with Morgan, wrote to Secretary Williamson: 'This island is in a very thriving condition and grows rich by privateering and the produce of the country, and the Governor has the character of a prudent and obliging person.' He was certainly obliging to the Buccaneers, and it was prudent to employ them as long as the capture of Jamaica was not recognized by Spain.

Early in 1669 Morgan sailed to a rendezvous at the Isle la Vache off the south-west peninsula of Haiti. This time his flagship was HMS *Oxford*, a frigate sent to Jamaica on the understanding that she was locally paid and victualled. There were high hopes of an even greater exploit than Porto Bello: Cartagena was rumoured as Morgan's objective, but an appalling disaster forced him to modify his plan. While he was at dinner with his

* Author's italics.

captains the *Oxford*'s magazine blew up killing nearly the whole two hundred of her crew. Instead of Cartagena, Morgan sailed into the land-locked Gulf of Maracaibo. The profits of the raid were disappointing because the region had been plundered only three years before by French Buccaneers from Tortuga under the cruel François L'Ollonais. After collecting booty which gave an individual share of only £30 a man, Morgan's men found the narrow exit of the lake blocked by three Spanish warships of forty, thirty and twenty-four guns. Calling a common council in traditional Buccaneer fashion, Morgan asked for suggestions. The out-come was a fireship, cunningly disguised with logs covered with clothes and hats to simulate a crew. Led by their disguised hulk of gunpowder, the Buccaneers approached the exit. Everything went better than they could have expected. The fireship succeeded in grappling with the forty-gun Spaniard and destroyed her. In a panic the enemy sank their second ship to prevent its capture while the third fell easily into the Buccaneers' hands. Overbold from this success, they swarmed ashore to capture the fort, only to be thrown back in confusion. They returned to Maracaibo town to think again.

On their second appearance before the fort, the Spaniards were deceived into preparing for a land attack again. Boatloads of Buccaneers were seen being rowed ashore before dusk. The heavy guns of the fort were slewed round to meet the expected night attack. It never came. Morgan's men had all returned on board, stretched out flat in the bottom of their boats. With sails still furled the Buccaneer ships slipped silently towards the fort on the ebbing tide. They were in front of it before they were spotted. As the alarm went up the sails were spread. Desperately the Spaniards worked to bring their guns round to bear, but their targets were out of effective range before the guns were laid. Morgan fired seven great guns as a parting signal, but the dumbfounded Spaniards could not reply with a single musket shot. Morgan had executed one of the neatest manœuvres of extrication ever performed at sea. The gullibility of the Spanish commander, Don Alonso del Campo y Espinosa, is astounding. He had actually received information about the fireship but refused to believe the Buccaneers had the wit or the resources to build one. He was one of many Spanish commanders defeated by unorthodox tactics.

Once again Morgan found himself reproved for attacking towns when only commissioned against ships, and it is evident that Modyford recalled all commissions for a while. As a result he was able to report that some of the privateers were buying plantations and others were trading with the Indians in hides, tallow, turtleshell and logwood. But even so there was one voice raised in alarm at their ungodly influence. In January 1670 one John Style, an Englishman who had arrived recently to plant, wrote home complaining that tippling houses averaged one to every ten inhabitants while sugar and rum works sold without licence. 'The worst of Sodom or the Jews that crucified our Saviour might here behold themselves matched, if not outdone, in all evil and wickedness by those who call themselves Christians.' But the age was a coarse one, and no notice was taken of his complaint.

For the better part of a year Sir Thomas Modyford issued no privateering commissions. Then the time lag, as much as anything, between Europe and America caused by slow communications was responsible for the resumption of hostilities. The Queen Regent of Spain had issued commissions of reprisal following Morgan's sack of Porto Bello, and these started to take effect just as the Jamaica privateers were called in. In March 1670 Modyford complained to Lord Arlington of Spanish attacks. In April his brother, Sir James, wrote to Lynch in England: 'This war, our making a blind peace, no frigates, nor orders coming, gives us cruel apprehensions.' In April Sir Thomas asked for approval to retaliate against the Spaniards if they attempted to attack Jamaica. At the end of June the council of Jamaica decided to take action. In a lengthy minute dated 29 June 1670, after citing advice received from the governor of Curaçao of the Queen of Spain's instructions to her governors to make open war against English subjects, and the quotation of certain minor Spanish attacks that had actually been made, the council resolved,

That a Commission be granted to Admiral Henry Morgan to be Admiral and Commander-in-Chief of all the ships of war belonging to this harbour, and all the officers, soldiers and seamen belonging to them, requiring him with all possible speed to draw them into one fleet, and with them to put to sea for the security of the coasts of this island and of the merchant ships and other vessels trading to and about the same; and to attack, seize, and destroy all the enemy's vessels that come within his reach; and also for destroying the stores and magazines laid up for this war . . . that he have power to land in the enemy's country as many of his men as he shall judge needful, and with them to march out to such places as he shall be informed the said magazines and forces are; and then accordingly take, destroy and disperse, and finally do all manner of exploits which may tend to the preservation and quiet of this island, being his Majesty's chief interest in the Indies; and that for the better Government of the said fleet, officers, soldiers and seamen he have power to exercise martial law . . . and it is further ordained that in regard there is no pay for the encouragement of the said fleet that they shall have all the goods, merchandises, &c, that can be got in their expedition to be divided amongst them according to their usual rules. . . .

Here was the *carte blanche* that Morgan needed for his long-treasured ambition to cross the Isthmus of Darien and sack the city of Panama, 'the greatest Mart for silver and gold in the whole world'.

About this time the following written challenge was found nailed to a tree in the west of the island:

I, Captain Manuel Rivero Pardal, to the chief of the squadron of privateers in Jamaica. I am he who this year have done that which follows: – I went on shore at Caimanes, and burnt twenty houses, and fought with Captain Ary and took from him a catch laden with provisions and a canoa. And I am he who took Captain Baines, and did carry the prize to Carthagena, and now am arrived to this coast and have burnt it. And I am come to seek General Morgan, with two ships of twenty guns, and having seen this, I crave he would come out upon the coast and seek me, that he might see the valour of the Spaniards. And because I had no time I did not come to the mouth of Port Royal to speak by word of mouth in the name of my King, whom God preserve. Dated the 5th of July 1670.

Morgan evidently thought it beneath his dignity to take notice of this challenge. At the end of September one of his captains ran into Pardal at the east end of Cuba and killed 'the vapouring Admiral of St Jago'.

The day after Morgan's fleet sailed from Port Royal an ominous dispatch arrived from Arlington, ordering the suppression of the privateers as the King was negotiating for peace with Spain. As for Modyford's complaints about Spanish aggression: 'The Spanish men-of-war attacking English ships is not to be wondered at after such hostilities as your men have acted upon their territories . . . this way of warring is neither honourable nor profitable to His Majesty.' Charles II had at last made up his mind on the question of privateering because although it had never been honourable, it had ceased to be profitable. The extraordinary thing is that neither Modyford nor Morgan thought it advisable to cancel the expedition. Instead Modyford glibly reported that Morgan had sailed to his rendezvous, 'where they expect him to be in a better posture than ever any fleet that went out of this island, those rugged fellows having submitted to a stricter discipline than they could ever be brought to'. And Richard Browne, in another report to Arlington, said there were rumours that Prince Rupert was coming at the head of twenty-five ships and five thousand men, 'but without Admiral Morgan and his old privateers things cannot be as successful as expected; for they know every creek and the Spaniards' way of fighting . . . Admiral Morgan has been in the Indies these eleven or twelve years, and from a private gentleman by his valour has raised himself to now what he is, and no one can give so clear an account of a Spanish force.' Nobody at Jamaica took Arlington's dispatch seriously.

Morgan made his way in leisurely fashion to Darien. In December 1670 he captured Providence from its Spanish garrison, whence he dispatched a vanguard of four hundred men to take the fort at the mouth of the Chagres river. They had a desperate fight to win it, but Morgan kept their numbers small to avoid causing too great an alarm. Out of the Spanish garrison of over three hundred only thirty men survived, but a handful escaped to bring warning to the President of Panama, who had already assembled a defence force of three thousand men. Morgan wasted little time at Chagres. Leaving a garrison of five hundred men and another hundred and fifty to guard his ships, he set off along the river with between twelve and fifteen hundred men, five boats carrying artillery and a flotilla of thirty-two canoes. Thinking they would be able to live off the country, the Buccaneers took very little food. It was a serious miscalculation, for the Spaniards took great pains to remove all supplies from their enemies' route. On the fourth evening, exhausted from cutting their way through a tropical jungle and dragging canoes up a river with little water, Morgan's men fell to eating leather bags. These they sliced into thin strips, beat them to a pulp, boiled them and washed them down with gulps of water. The next day they came upon two sacks of meal, two jars of wine and some plantains. Morgan had them reserved for the weakest men. So the gruelling march went on until on the ninth day they caught their first sight of the Pacific. That evening they caught some cattle, upon which they fell with animal eagerness, hardly stopping to cook the meat, 'the blood many times running down their beards unto the middle of their bodies', according to Esquimeling. That evening they greeted the first glimpse of Panama with great halloos of joy, hat-throwing, and the sounding of drums and trumpets.

So far the Spanish plan had worked well. The Buccaneers were tired and they had taken no prisoners to give them information. In the open savanna leading to the city the President had thrown up earthworks and batteries behind which his main force was drawn up: six hundred horsemen, two thousand foot and, curiously, a great herd of wild bulls. Morgan's forces were no more than fourteen hundred. His unkempt and ragged army, however, was full of desperate courage, whereas the majority of the Spaniards opposed to them had seen little fighting, living as they did upon the shore of the Peaceful Ocean, and used at most to the opposition of ill-equipped Indians. As a mark of their lack of martial exercise they failed to take advantage of their own known ground, while the idea of driving bulls against Buccaneers was as stupid as trying to frighten American cowboys with a great drove of steers. As soon as he saw the barricades and batteries, Morgan made a detour through the woods – his men were used to them by then – and came out upon the Spaniards' flank. A vanguard of nearly three hundred men composed of his best marksmen were quickly sent forward to deal with the Spanish cavalry, rendered inoffensive by a marsh. The Spanish horse withdrew and became separated from their infantry. Then the Spaniards drove in the two thousand bulls, but these had no success at all beyond tearing the English colours before they stampeded from the field. After two hours the Spanish cavalry followed the bulls and in another hour the infantry had followed the cavalry. The way to Panama lay open, but the Buccaneers found the city burning. According to Esquimeling this was done at Morgan's order. Morgan emphatically denied it and is supported by the report of the President of Panama, Don Perez de Guzman, later sent home to his King. He described how the Buccaneers entered the city, 'to which the slaves and owners of the houses had set fire and being all of boards and timbers was most of it quickly burnt . . . at which they say the enemy fretted much.'

Old Panama contained seven monasteries, a nunnery, two churches and a hospital. The richer inhabitants lived in two thousand cedar houses of magnificent and prodigious building, and there were five thousand smaller houses besides. The whole city was surrounded by pleasant gardens and plantations; the Genoese merchants kept a great slave-warehouse there and there were many stables for the mule trains that continually crossed the isthmus to Chagres and Porto Bello. But of treasure the Buccaneers found little. The news of their coming had given the inhabitants ample time to remove and hide their valuables, the bulk of the treasure having been sent away on a galleon, together with the inmates of the nunnery. After three weeks the disappointed adventurers assembled for the return march across the isthmus. Morgan had every man including himself searched for concealed treasure for he knew that with a share of only £10 a man there would be bitter murmuring. Even Richard Browne joined Esquimeling in accusing Morgan of absconding with more than his share of the treasure. Browne estimated the total value at £70,000 but John Peake, Morgan's secretary, put it at £30,000 and no proof has ever been produced that it was more. Morgan's greatest military exploit had proved the least profitable of all.

The return across the isthmus was uneventful, good order being kept throughout. On 31 May 1671, Morgan attended a meeting of the council of Jamaica, where, according to the minutes, the council 'gave him many thanks for the execution of his late Commission, and approved very well of his acting.' The attack on Panama was the last of Henry Morgan's expeditions. Although the booty was disappointing, it had been a considerable military exploit. He kept better discipline than any other Buccaneer leader and both at Panama and Maracaibo showed outstanding generalship. Long before the news of Panama reached Europe the Treaty of Madrid had been signed, so it cannot be said that it was Morgan who forced Charles II of Spain to make belated recognition of the capture of Jamaica by England. Yet in Jamaica nobody had any doubts about their debt to the Buccaneers. Confidence in the future of the island became assured and planting increased.

Although the articles of the Treaty of Madrid allowed twelve months' grace before its terms were carried into effect, the capture of Panama was embarrassing to Charles II's government. As an earnest of English good intentions Modyford, replaced as governor by Lynch, was sent home under arrest in June 1671 'for making depredations and hostilities against the subjects of His Majesty's good brother, the Catholic King'. For two years he was imprisoned in the Tower until the Spanish racket had died down. Morgan's return home was delayed by sickness. In fairness to Lynch, he gave both his prisoners good characters. Of Henry Morgan he said: 'To speak the truth of him he's an honest brave fellow, and hath both Sir T.M.'s and the Council's commission and instructions, which they thought he obeyed and followed so well they gave him public thanks.' Morgan was sent home in April 1672. He never went to the Tower. When John Evelyn met him in 1674 he was still cursing the warning that had allowed the President of Panama to save the bulk of the treasure. By then Morgan was being lionized in London. In November of that year he was knighted and appointed deputy-governor to Lord Vaughan. When they sailed for Jamaica early in 1675, Sir Thomas Modyford went with them. Apart from a short spell as Chief Justice, Modyford took no part in public affairs until his death in 1679. He spent his time developing his properties and setting a good example as an improving landlord. He was long remembered not only for encouraging the Buccaneers but for the lead he gave to the development of planting.

THE SUPPRESSION OF PRIVATEERING

With the removal of Modyford and Morgan the situation developed exactly as Modyford had warned. With English commissions withdrawn, a few privateers took up Lynch's offers of land, a considerable number went logwood-cutting in Campeche, and the rest transferred their headquarters to Tortuga whence they continued their attacks. The Spaniards continued to issue privateering commissions in breach of the Treaty of Madrid and Jamaica ships began to suffer from serious interference. The Spanish governors regarded the logwood-cutters as thieves of Spanish property and still held to their exclusive claims. English prisoners who escaped from Spain described how they had been told in Cadiz that it was a crime for them to sail to the Indies. In 1672 Lynch complained: 'We have lost in this year of peace by these kinds of seizures twice as much as in Sir T.M.'s three years of war.' By 1678, when a petition for a reissue of commissions was addressed to the King by certain Jamaica merchants, it was stated that since the Treaty of Madrid the Spaniards had destroyed or captured seventy sail and a thousand mariners from Jamaica. Some of the crews made their way home with harrowing stories. For instance John Channon, master of the *Rebecca*, had his ship taken by Spaniards at Cape San Antonio, the extreme western point of Cuba. For thirty-one days he and his eight men travelled without meeting an inhabitant, with no food but wild cabbage, three snakes and two crabs. After two months they reached Havana, where they were seized and sent to Spain for seven months until the English ambassador secured their release. Throughout 1673 Lynch's troubles grew: 'Here is a vast country to be kept by a few men; a port to be defended with no ships; a town without fortifications; ammunition, guns, carriages, fireships, platforms etc., to be had and made without money.' Without ever saying it, he must have regretted the ban on privateering. Charles II, as short of money as ever, could send no ships, wanted as they were in the Third Dutch War, but he found an expedient that helped without costing him a penny: the news of the appointment of Sir Henry Morgan as deputy-governor caused the Spanish authorities to start repairing their defences on the Pacific.

Although Morgan never went cruising again the ship carrying him and Modyford mysteriously got separated from that carrying Lord Vaughan on the voyage out to Jamaica. When Vaughan reached Port Royal on 15 March 1675, it was to find that Morgan had been there a week after suffering shipwreck at his old buccaneering haunt of the Isle la Vache. Later Vaughan openly accused Morgan of setting up privateering and asked for his removal from the council, but Secretary Williamson urged him to make up his quarrel. In 1677 Vaughan complained: 'All local men in authority have interests in privateering and therefore will not co-operate in suppressing it.' In March 1678 Vaughan demitted office to Morgan and went home. He had achieved little.

In his four months in command of Jamaica before the arrival of Carlisle, Henry Morgan had two new batteries built at Port Royal and christened them the Rupert and the Carlisle. He was regarded as the local expert on defence. On his arrival in 1675 the assembly voted him a salary of £600 per annum as lieutenant-governor 'but to none of his successors'. Carlisle and Morgan got on well together. Shortly after the governor's arrival privateering commissions were issued again, under which a notorious expedition was launched led by a Captain Coxon which followed Morgan's route to Panama and then circumnavigated South America, leisurely plundering Spanish settlements until they reached Barbados in 1682, where they were refused permission to land.

When Carlisle left Morgan in command in 1680, the former Buccaneer bent all his energies to the suppression of the followers of his former profession. His dispatches home read strangely: 'Privateering is a temptation to the necessitous and unfortunate – I spare no care to put down this growing evil. These privateers discourage Spaniards from private trade with us.' Some he brought to trial but withheld sentence of death, 'lest it should scare all others abroad from returning to their allegiance'. When some adventurers were captured he showed remorse at the measures he was forced to take: 'I abhor bloodshed, and am greatly dissatisfied that in my short government I have been so often compelled to punish criminals with death.' He claimed to have received thanks from Spanish governors on the Main for exerting so much care and vigilance in the suppression of privateers.

Then in May 1682 Lynch arrived as governor with the revocation of Morgan's seven-year-old commission as deputy. It must have been a bitter pill, for no reasons were given. For a time he continued to serve on the council, but Lynch eventually had him dismissed together with his brother-in-law, Colonel Robert Byndloss. His cousin Charles Morgan lost his command of the Port Royal forts and a new friend, Roger Elletson, was debarred from his legal practice. Their appeals to England were of no avail. 'In his drink,' Lynch reported, 'Sir Henry reflects on the government, swears, damns and curses most extravagantly.' He and his friends had been enjoying wild carousals in Port Royal. After his dismissal from office Morgan retired to his plantations, whence he continued to give trouble to the governor. Lynch died in 1684 and demitted office to Colonel Hender Molesworth, who continued the complaints against Morgan. It is evident that he took to drink. In 1687 when he was living at Llanrumney close to Port Maria he was described as entertaining the captain of an interloping ship and feasting with him on fat guinea goat. In 1688, Sir Hans Sloane, who came to Jamaica as private physician to Christopher, second Duke of Albemarle, the son of Modyford's patron, described a visit he paid to Sir Henry, whom he found ' . . . lean, sallow coloured, his eyes a little yellowish, and belly a little jutting out or prominent. Not being able to abstain from company, much given to drinking and sitting up late'. A month before he died James II authorized his restitution to the council, but it was too late to help him mend his ways. A terse entry in the log of the *Assistance* frigate describes his end:

August 1688. Saturday 25th. This day about eleven hours noone Sir Harry Morgan died. On the 26th was brought over from Passage fort to the King's House at Port Royall, from thence to the Church, and after a sermon was carried to the Palisadoes and there buried. All the forts fired an equal number of guns. We fired two and twenty, and after we and the Drake had fired, all the merchantmen fired.

So Harry Morgan was buried, but not to be left in peace. Four years later his grave accompanied the King's House where he had resided and the taverns which had echoed to his laugh and his extravagant swearing into the waters of the harbour in the great earthquake.

When Henry Morgan came to his sad end English privateering was over and he, the Prince of Buccaneers, had done much to suppress it. About that time, too, the French withdrew their recognition and Tortuga became a sleepy island off the coast of Saint Domingue, the principal French colony in the West Indies. The remnant of the Buccaneers passed north into Carolina and the Bahamas, where New Providence was founded in memory of Old, and where they degenerated into common pirates.

Their enthralling history did not end before providing its comic relief. In 1686 a Captain Bear, one of Governor Stapleton's officers in the Leeward Islands, turned pirate with considerable success, robbing ships from Jamaica, Ireland and New England. He then appeared at Havana, where he was accorded a ceremonial wedding. In honour of his bride, introduced by Bear as a noblewoman, the governor and leading citizens attended and the fort fired a salute. Governor Molesworth at Jamaica knew better: 'The nobleman's daughter is a strumpet that he used to carry about with him in man's apparel, and is the daughter of a rum-punch-woman of Port Royal.' He sent to Havana to demand Bear's extradition as a pirate, but – perhaps to conceal his *faux pas* – the Spanish governor took Bear into Spanish service. No more was heard of his lady.

The Buccaneers dominated the waters of the Caribbean for more than fifty years and gave it a chapter of history all its own. Their depredations seriously weakened the hold of Spain, affording the needed protection to the English at Jamaica, the Dutch at Curaçao, and the French in Haiti, as the early colonies of the northern nations challenged the Spanish claims to the exclusive monopoly of the region. Then they made way for the naval squadrons of Britain and France to fight the Spanish and each other throughout the eighteenth century, when strategy became worldwide and no longer recognized the principle of 'no peace beyond the line'. In the general weakening of the Spanish hold on the Caribbean the Buccaneers indirectly assured the continuance of the settlement of Barbados and the Caribbees, though their ships were rarely seen so far to windward. It was Jamaica that owed them most. Yet because of the 1692 earthquake there are no permanent remains. Modern skindivers may find fragments from the old town. They can scarcely hope to find much more. When future tourists gape at the treasures of old Port Royal it is perhaps too much to hope that they will be told that the Buccaneers were not pirates and Jamaica was never ruled by a pirate governor.

7
THE SEVENTEENTH-CENTURY WEST INDIAN LIVING PATTERN

The early years of the first English colonies in the Caribbean established a way of life and an outlook that became typical of the West Indies until the abolition of slavery. Some of the characteristics still apply today. First, in the Leeward Islands and Barbados, they were small communities settled on small islands by individual enterprise in days of slow communications. This fact has produced in each island an intense individuality, jealous of its neighbours, extremely sensitive about its independence, and hopelessly suspicious of any attempts to effect union or federation. All the time politics have lain on or very close to the surface of social life, and dominating personalities have exerted a powerful influence on their contemporaries, and sometimes on succeeding generations.

Then there is the geographical environment. For ninety-nine days out of a hundred the islands are an earthly paradise, with luxuriant vegetation clothing beautiful hillslopes which rise from a translucent, cobalt sea. In many there are rivers and streams as clear and cascading as any salmon stream in Wales or Scotland. In most the soil is so abundantly fertile that any seed falling into it, let alone any plant cultivated, will grow. But on occasions there are days when all hell is let loose. The dreaded hurricanes come; flood rains follow long parching droughts; unpredictable earthquakes shatter buildings and kill people. On ninety-nine days out of a hundred the sun shines out of a clear sky, tempered by sea-breezes that protect the islands from extremes of temperature and justify advertising slogans in the United States to the effect that 'the tropics are cooler'. All this common knowledge of today had to be discovered by the pioneers. In St Kitts they had their first hurricane before a year had passed; in Jamaica there was no hurricane for fifty years and colonists began to think they would never have one. The set-backs imposed by nature on the Caribbean are frightening experiences. The best answer to them is to forget about them and live from day to day.

In the Leeward Islands there were other preoccupations: attacks from Caribs and Spaniards that made security a primary consideration and focused attention on the organization of a militia and the erection of forts. In Barbados, a more isolated windward position protected it from interference; the first time the militia went into action was in the pursuit of the English Civil War when Sir George Ayscue arrived in 1651. The first foreign attack on Barbados did not occur until 1665 when de Ruyter appeared. In Jamaica, its military conquest left a military tradition, fanned by its association with the Buccaneers and maintained against possible Spanish attack which never materialized and later French threats which did.

As the products of private enterprise, Barbados and the Caribbees were subjected to the bare minimum of government machinery; proprietary government had been a mere projection of the squirearchy of rural England, with a small assembly added for short sessions between crops. In St Kitts Governor Sir Thomas Warner had been in effect no more than a benevolently despotic squire. He never called an assembly. In Barbados the early disputes between quarrelling proprietors had bred a factious tradition fanned by Roundheads and Cavaliers (during the Civil War and the decade of unofficial self-government which marked that uncertain time) into an antagonism to authority which was to cause incessant headaches to later home-appointed governors. Under the hot sun tempers flared to unusual heights and words were hurled between opponents with hurricane force.

But the main business of these early colonies was agriculture. English gentlemen and yeomen farmers had transferred themselves to a strange environment to make a living by growing strange crops for sale in distant markets. For their prosperity they came to rely on the seamen who carried away their produce and the merchants whose business it was to sell it when it arrived at London, Bristol or Southampton. The Civil War had let in the Dutch who had proved themselves better businessmen than their English rivals. When the English government tried to exclude the Dutch the first political differences appeared and West Indian politics came to adopt a bread-and-butter economic character, never idealistic and quite distinct from Whig and Tory policies at home.

Socially the men who founded the colonies of St Kitts and Barbados were to some extent a representative cross-section of English rural society at the beginning of Charles 1's reign. English manors of that time were largely self-supporting and living conditions were uncomfortable. Emigration to a new country, therefore, did not entail the great differences that later colonists from England's overcrowded towns were to experience in countries like Australia. Country gentlemen like Thomas Warner, Sir

Henry Colt and the first Christopher Codrington brought their own servants with them or men from neighbouring villages. Their main motive was to better themselves and to acquire land of which there was a shortage in England. Unlike the New Englanders and those who went to Providence, these colonists were not Puritans, but the majority were religious: one of the earliest buildings to be erected was a church. They took their relations with them, as Robert Harcourt had done to Guiana. Thomas Warner and Sir Henry Colt sent for their sons; Anthony Hilton, Henry Powell, Lord Willoughby and Thomas Modyford brought their brothers. The first shiploads contained no women, but they followed within two or three years. Jamaica started on a bigger scale. Although Venables was accompanied by his wife, she must have been an exception. The first Englishwomen to reach Jamaica were probably among the Nevis islanders who accompanied Luke Stokes in 1656. It is unfortunate that the experiences of the pioneer women went completely unrecorded.

For the first few years in each colony the manual labour was done mostly by English labourers brought out from their villages to continue their long hours of toil under a tropic sky. It was here that the first disagreeable lesson was learnt: the sun was too hot for white labour. The Spaniards, coming from their Mediterranean homeland, knew about the power of the sun and brought their siesta habit with them. The Dutch, from a similar climate to the English, soon learnt to avoid heavy work and leave it first to native Indians and later to Negro slaves. But the English habit of rushing out in the midday sun is proverbial. When Henry Powell fetched the forty Arawaks from the Essequibo it was not to supply labour, but to show the Englishmen how to plant cassava and maize and tobacco. Even after Negro slaves had been introduced white labourers worked in the canefields, as an observer recorded in 1667: 'I have seene thirty sometimes forty Christians, English, Scotch, and Irish at worke in the parching sun without shoe or stockin, while their negroes have been at worke at their respective trades in a good condition.'

Once the colonies had been established the maintenance of the labour supply depended on the efforts of merchants in England who drew up contracts of indenture with poor people anxious to emigrate. In return for passage, clothing, keep and lodging, the servant contracted his labour for periods varying between three and nine years, at the end of which he would get a few acres of land or a cash payment. Both men and women were sent out. During their period of indenture they became the absolute chattels of their owners, as the following (undated) example shows: 'I, William Marshall, of the island aforesaid [Barbados], Merchant, do by these presents assign, sett, and order all my right, title and interest of one Maide Servant, by name Alice Skinner, for the full term of four years from ye day of her arrival in this island, unto Mr Richard Davis or his assigns. . . .'

On arrival in Barbados servants were sold to the planters. Their first task was to build themselves cabins of sticks bound together with creepers and roofed with plantain fronds. Until these rude shelters were ready they slept outside. Inside they slept on bare boards or in hammocks. During the rains they were faced with a quandary over wet clothes. 'If they put off their cloaths [sic],' said Ligon, 'the cold of the night will strike into them; and if they be not strong men this ill-lodging will put them into a sickness; if they complain they are beaten by the Overseer; if they resist their time is doubled.' Ligon saw 'such cruelty done to servants, as I did not think one Christian could have done to another. . . . I have seen an Overseer beat a Servant with a cane about the head till the blood has flowed for an offence that is not worth speaking of.' By law a servant could complain to the justices of the peace, but as they were planters much sympathy could not be expected. The council, however, ordered punishment of masters who had been cruel to their employees and later a law was passed forbidding the burial of a dead servant until the body had been viewed by a justice of the peace or a constable. Frivolous complaints, on the other hand, earned the maker thirteen lashes. Stealing was punished by an extension of the period of service. Pregnancy earned a woman another two years and the man responsible, a further three. Runaways had their heads shorn on recapture and had to serve a further three years. Nevertheless, numbers did run away. When Penn and Venables passed through Barbados some planters lost as many as ten servants. The women must have been a temptation in a community predominantly male. In 1640 one John Haddock who went off with Anne Mitchell, the servant of William Light, was forced to serve as his servant for the unexpired two years of the woman's four-year term.

When African slaves became numerous the lot of the white indentured servant became more precarious, for a slave remained his master's property for life and was worth keeping alive, but the white labourer was often worked to death. It is not surprising that in 1649 a rebellion of white servants in Barbados was discovered just before breaking out. Eighteen ringleaders were hanged. In spite of these terrible conditions poor white colonists sometimes signed themselves into virtual slavery to pay their debts.

An important source of white labour in the colonies came from the transportation of lawbreakers in Britain. Cromwell started it with the transportation of prisoners of war, including Irish after Drogheda and Wexford, and Scots after Dunbar and Worcester. Large numbers of Irish came to be concentrated on the island of Montserrat. After the Restoration the supply of Scotsmen stopped, for that country returned to its pre-Civil War separate government, and trade between Scotland and the English colonies was contrary to the Navigation Acts. Governor William Willoughby in 1668 greatly regretted the ban, for the Scots 'made brave Servants and faithfull Subjects, as by experience they have been found'. The Irish he had found worthless. In 1664 the king issued a circular announcing the grant of a five years' licence to Sir James Modyford to take all felons convicted in their circuits and at the Old Bailey and afterwards reprieved for transportation, and to transport them to Sir Thomas Modyford, governor of Jamaica. As the number of Negro slaves increased the supply of white servants assumed a significant importance, for colonial laws required a plantation owner to keep one white servant for every ten slaves. Servants formed the rank and file of the militia and one of the principal functions of the militia was defence, not only against foreign attack, but against slave rebellions.

By 1647 there was no more land available in Barbados for allocation to time-expired servants. Offers were made to them in Antigua, but many remained in Barbados as 'poor whites' or 'red-shanks'. The transportation of unfortunates, sometimes through kidnapping, added a word to the English language: 'to barbados' someone meant the same as 'to shanghai' in a later age. It was from these time-expired servants and the numbers still serving who managed to escape that General Venables drew most of his colonial recruits at Barbados and St Kitts. That they proved unsatisfactory soldiers was not due to the degrading influence of the tropical climate, as Professor Newton alleged, but to the degrading social conditions under which they had lived for so long.

It was not surprising that, as a result of the ruin of the small farmer caused by the introduction of cane-farming and the shortage of land, Barbados was comparatively early faced with the problems of unemployment and poor relief. Parish vestries in the Restoration period found themselves having to provide almshouses, pesthouses and overseers of the poor. In 1663 a rope-maker named Bragge made an offer to the Vestry of St Michael's Parish to employ several poor persons picking oakum, which was an important material used in the caulking of boats, and this became the standard form of employment for inmates of the parish almshouse. For vagabonds a cage was built in 1668. Eight years later it had to be reconstructed and the churchwardens were required to erect 'a polstocke Whipping Post, with a Pillory upon the Cage . . . also to build a Ducking Stool at the Indian Bridge in St Michael's Town'. All the institutions and paraphernalia of Merrie England were transported to Barbados as well as the convicts.

At no time during the seventeenth century did the total white population

The Sugar Industry

'King Sugar' was introduced to the English colonies by the Dutch during the Civil War. It became the main industry in every colony. From sugar planting and the slave trade, which was its vital adjunct, many personal fortunes were made. A large labour force was necessary, organized in gangs of up to seventy, the strongest or 'great gang' being used for the strenuous work of ground clearance and hole digging. In this picture of holeing a cane-piece in Antigua, note the meticulous lay-out, the use of the hoe, the mixture of men and women, and the employment of boys for doing the light work like carrying sticks.

The second process was planting the canes, two cuttings to each hole. In the windy Leeward Islands windmills were used to the maximum for grinding the canes.

After twelve to fifteen months the canes were ready for cutting. This strenuous work was done by men, while women collected the cut canes and children the trash for carrying to the factory for fuel. The mounted figure is either the owner or manager talking to a driver. The well-clothed labourers date these last three pictures to the nineteenth century. Earlier, the slaves worked nearly naked.

An early nineteenth-century sugar mill, worked by a water wheel.

A rum distillery in Antigua, early nineteenth century. Rum and molasses were the chief by-products of sugar manufacture.

Previous pages A diagram illustrating the two main processes of sugar manufacture, the crushing of the canes between wooden rollers rotated in this instance by cattle. The slope of the ground was used to convey the juice down to the boiling house where it passed through five boiling pans till the right mixture of crystals and molasses was transferred to pots or (later) hogsheads for draining in the curing house (upper right). The white overseer and the naked slaves assign this picture to the eighteenth century.

Many small estates shipped their sugar direct from the nearest beach.

Theſe are in all humility to satisfy [crossed out], That Wee whoſe names are hereunto ſubſcribed have lived in his Ma.tie Iſland of Jamaica & other places in the West Indies & ſtill trade thither, & do humbly Certify that Rum made in Jamaica is preferrd before Brandy brought thither from England. Witneſs our hands this Second day of November 1687.

Wm Daſton

Samll Barry.

Roger Elonatt

Richard Laycock.   Sam. Hempthorn

Phillip Daſsigny   John Benne

Henry Greenhill   Mat: Postley

Jn: Champneys   Browne

An early testimonial from Jamaica to the popularity of rum. In actual fact it was never popular with the gentry.

in the English West Indies exceed forty thousand. Of this number more than half were always in Barbados. Jamaica never had more than eight thousand; St Kitts, Nevis, Montserrat and Antigua varied above and below two thousand each. As the slave trade increased, the black population began to exceed the white with noticeable variation from island to island. In 1684 Barbados had 23,624 white and 46,502 black people, i.e. a proportion of one white to two black. In the Leewards in 1678, the nearest year for which figures are available for comparison, St Kitts had slightly more whites than blacks, in Nevis there were 2,379 whites and 3,849 blacks, and in Montserrat, 2,783 whites and only 992 blacks. In Jamaica in 1673 there were 18,000 people of whom 10,000 were Negroes; by the end of the century the total was 47,365, of whom 7,365 were whites. The largest island still had large areas of unoccupied land. Barbados and the Leeward Islands were full.

Of the crops grown on the rising plantations, sugar, tobacco and cotton have already been described. In Jamaica the first considerable export was cocoa from the 'walks' left by the Spaniards. These cocoa walks were extended. In 1668 Sir James Modyford sent Secretary Williamson a present of cocoa, 'the best commodity of this island, neither sugars nor indigo will turn to account nearly so well.' In 1670 there were forty-seven cocoa walks producing 188,000 pounds of beans. Then misfortune struck and Governor Lynch began reporting 'the blasting of the cocoa trees'. Production steadily declined until by 1727 it had ceased.

Another early Jamaican product was indigo. Possibly cultivated by the Spaniards, its expansion was due to the Barbadian immigrants. By 1670 there were forty-nine indigo works, and in 1692 seven-tenths of all the indigo imported in England came from Jamaica. It was one of the several dye-stuffs which were in great demand by the cloth manufacturers in Europe. Another cultivated plant was anatto, but the principal sources of dyes were the forest trees, fustic, Brazil-wood and logwood, which were cut all over the Caribbean. Dye-woods formed a useful early export from Barbados until the trees were all cut down, but the principal cutting area lay in Campeche along the southern shore of the Gulf of Mexico. Between thirty and forty ships were sailing there from Jamaica in 1670 and the annual number nearly doubled in the next six years. But the trouble was that Campeche was Spanish territory and English logwood cutters were unwelcome. At one time two hundred men lived permanently on shore there, from whom the seamen bought the chippings at £3 a ton. If they returned to Port Royal safely they could sell the logwood at double the price, but many were taken by Spanish *garda-costas* and privateers. Among these ex-buccaneers and adventurers went William Dampier, later to make his name in the Pacific. As a young man he went to Jamaica to seek his fortune. His book, *Two Voyages to Campeachy*, contains an interesting account of the life led by these restless men. In 1675, 'the logwood cutters were then about 250 men, most English, that had settled themselves in several places hereabouts. Our cargo to purchase logwood was rum and sugar: we took no money for it, nor expected any. The rate was £5 per ton to be paid at the place where they cut it . . . we were always very kindly entertained by them with pork and pease, or beef and doughboys.'

Of the cutting gang he wrote:

There were six in company, who had a hundred tons ready cut, logged and chipped, but not brought to the creek's side. . . . When I came thither they were beginning to bring it to the creek . . . and hired me to help them at the rate of a ton of wood [i.e. £5] a month, promising me that after this carriage was over I should strike in with them, for they were all obliged in bonds to procure one hundred tons jointly together. . . . The first thing we did was to bring it all to one place in the middle and from thence we cut a very large path to carry it to the creek's side. We laboured hard at this work five days in the week, and on Saturdays went into the savannahs and killed beaver. . . .

Many of the cutters being good marksmen thought it a dry business to toil at cutting wood and so took more delight in hunting. But neither of these employments affected them so much as privateering. Therefore they often made sallies out in small parties among the nearest Indian towns, where they plundered and brought away the Indian women to serve them at their huts, and sent their husbands to be sold at Jamaica. Besides they had not their old drinking bouts forgot, and would still spend £30 or £40 at a sitting aboard the ships that came thither from Jamaica, carousing and firing off guns three or four days together. And though afterwards many sober men came into the Bay to cut wood, yet by degrees the old standers so debauched them, that they could never settle themselves under a civil government.

So the buccaneering way of life was prolonged on the coasts of Central America. Not surprisingly the Spaniards resented the presence of the boisterous logwood-cutters. In 1716 they drove the Englishmen from Campeche but not from the region. Slipping round Cape Catoche, the cutters transferred their activities to the Bay of Honduras, where they joined forces with others who had earlier established themselves on the Belize river. Out of this casual and happy-go-lucky venture grew the future colony of British Honduras.

In 1715 logwood was planted in Jamaica but it was a long time before it became a notable industry there.

Another maritime occupation was turtle-fishing. Turtle flesh was fed to servants and slaves in Barbados and came from the Leeward Islands, pickled. Port Royal sloops also went turtle-fishing at the Cayman Islands and along the South Cays of Cuba. In 1684 when this trade was interrupted by pirate attacks Molesworth wrote: 'The turtling trade being lost for a while, Port Royal will suffer greatly. It is what masters of ships feed their men on in port and I believe that nearly 2,000 people, black and white, feed on it daily at the Port, to say nothing of what is sent inland.' Hans Sloane mentioned that forty sloops and 180 men were engaged in the trade. He also mentions 'manatee, taken chiefly by Indians, reckoned very good victuals'.

The local shipping trade was considerable. It went on quietly with few records kept. In 1682 Lynch reported:

We have much money and a great quantity of hides, cacao etc, imported by our trading sloops, numbering 20, from 15 to 45 tons, built here, admirable sailers, carrying 20 or 30 hands receiving 40 shillings a month. They carry from here some few negroes and dry goods of all sorts, and sell them in the islands and along the Main in bays, creeks and remote places, and sometimes where they are Governors as at St. Jago (de Cuba) and St. Domingo, for they are bold where they are poor.

The governor was glibly describing local smuggling. In 1685 Lynch's friend Molesworth, who owned some of these sloops, went further: 'Could English manufactures be exported as well as slaves?' he asked the Lords of Trade. There was a good market for English manufactured goods and a source of bullion in exchange. He described what went on: 'English manufactures are done up in small parcels to protect them from rain. They are landed near some wood near the port to which they are bound, left with a man in charge to watch them till nightfall and then brought into the town.' No reply to Lynch and Molesworth is extant, but in a letter written in 1694 Sir William Blathwayt, secretary to the Lords of Trade, made the following statement: 'The King recognises the importance of Jamaica for the value of its trade *and the underhand trade with the Spanish Colonies** as well as the Asiento.' Connived at but unrecognized, these West Indian sailors in their little ships led a precarious but happy existence, yet their illicit trade was not reciprocated: the moment foreign ships appeared at Jamaica the authorities seized them.

In Jamaica the livestock left by the Spaniards proved a valuable asset. Once the ill-disciplined soldiers had been forbidden their wanton slaughter of the cattle, a stock-rearing industry was built up. The large island had the space for this compared to Barbados, 'where a man cannot turn a horse out but he presently trespasseth on his neighbour'. The Spanish *hatos* had been in a woodier and smaller way more like the open ranches of Argentina and Texas than the fenced stock farms of modern Jamaica. When the cattle

* Author's italics.

were needed they were hunted by a handful of slaves. The hogs were con-trolled in an ingenious way. For a time they were kept and fed inside a wooden stockade, until, thoroughly accustomed to the spot and its associa-tion with food they were turned loose in the woods to return when needed at the sounding of a horn or conch. In this way as many as seven hundred pigs could be raised for no cost at all beyond the feeding of two or three slaves. The stockade was known as a 'crawle', a name that still appears in place-names of the map of Jamaica, although the method of pig-rearing died out long ago.

Salt-making was a minor but important local industry, using the coastal salt ponds that occur along West Indian shores. In St Kitts the salt ponds were shared in common by French and English. At Jamaica in 1670 Captain John Noye was running a salt works at the ponds on the edge of the Hellshire Hills opposite Port Royal. Its principal use was in the salting of beef both locally and for export to New England.

The cultivation of local foodstuffs or ground-provisions was an im-portant occupation on most properties. Maize, cassava, yams and plantains provided the chief rations for slaves and servants, but were little eaten by the planters and their families who preferred imported foods. Ligon remembered with delight the lines of Negro men and women issuing from a plantain grove, each heading a bunch of green plantains. The West Indies even from early days have always been famous for their luscious fruit. Pawpaw, guavas, pomegranates, custard apples, pineapples, water and ordinary melons, bananas and coconuts are mentioned by early writers, as well as avocados, cashew nuts, soursops, oranges, limes and lemons. Less well known today, prickly pears and 'prickell apples' are also mentioned. Great emphasis was laid on the medicinal value of certain roots and fruits, especially the tamarind and china root, which together with gum guaiac, lignum vitae and cassia were said to cure 'many hurts, ulcers and dis-tempers'. There was little growing that the early colonists did not try out; lives must have been lost in the cause of culinary experimentation.

When Thomas Modyford arrived in Barbados in 1647 with Richard Ligon he went looking for a plantation and bought a half-share of Major Hilliard's, three miles south-east of Bridgetown. On its five hundred odd acres there was

a fair dwelling house; an Ingenio [sugar-mill] placed in a room of 400 feet square; a boyling house, filling room, Cisterns and Still-House; with a Carding house, of 100 feet long and 40 feet broad; with stables, Smith's forge and rooms to lay provisions of Corn and Bonavist [a kind of kidney bean]; Houses for Negroes and Indian slaves, with 96 Negroes and three Indian women, with their children; 28 Christians, 45 cattle for work, 8 Milch Cows, a dozen Horses and Mares, 16 Assinigoes.

For his half-share Modyford paid £7,000, '£1,000 in hand, the rest £2,000 a time at six and six months', and he was to receive half the profits. Of the five hundred odd acres, two hundred were under cane, eighty were in pasture, 120 acres were woodland, thirty were growing tobacco, five in ginger, five in cotton and seventy were being used for provisions – maize, potatoes, plantains, cassava and bonavist, and there were fruit trees listed above producing fruit 'for the table'. Ligon lived on the estate for three years.

Over in St John's Parish on the east of Barbados, the Codrington family owned two adjoining estates amounting to 750 acres. The first of the three Christopher Codringtons arrived in Barbados in 1628. He called the higher plantation Didmartens after the manor in Gloucestershire from which he came. The lower and smaller estate was called Consetts and led to the small bay of that name from which the products of the estates were shipped to Bridgetown, to avoid the muddy fourteen-mile journey across the island. There were three windmills for grinding cane, a large boiling-house with seventeen coppers and a still-house containing four large rum stills. In 1682 there were 250 Negroes. On Didmartens there was a large two-storeyed house with a shingle roof. It contained large rooms with massive doors and panelled walls. When the third Christopher Codrington died in 1710 he left this valuable property for the foundation of the college which still bears the family name.

The earliest planters' houses were not built of stone but of wood with roofs so low, said Ligon, 'that I could hardly stand upright with my hat on' – a social custom of his day that has continued in America but has long died out in England and the West Indies. He found the Barbadian houses airless. They had all their windows on the west side and when the sun shone in the afternoons 'those little low-roofed rooms were like Stoves or heated Ovens. And truly, on a very hot day, it might raise a doubt whether so much heat without and so much Tobacco and Kill-devil within, might not set the house afire.' The colonists explained to him that glassless windows on the east or windward side let in the rain. Ligon wondered why they had no shutters and supposed that poverty and apathy bred by hard toil and privation were the cause of it. The houses were built of the local hardwoods which were difficult to work. Cedar was the best material and iron-wood was used for shingles. As prosperity spread with the growth of sugar-cane, the Barbadians discovered they had excellent building stone, for like Bath stone in England, the soft Barbados limestone can be cut with a saw.

Inside, the colonists had found that the interior hangings used in England were no use in Barbados because of the tropical humidity. Some were experimenting with gilded leather. Ligon drew plans for an ideal house. It was T-shaped. The top of the T, consisting of two storeys to provide shade from the afternoon sun, was arranged along the west side. It was ingenious, but no planter showed any interest. Some furniture came with its owners from England, but colonial craftsmen were not long in discovering the excellent furniture-woods growing in the Caribbean. When Englishmen first settled there it was customary to keep clothes in a 'press' and not a wardrobe; this word 'press' is still used in present-day Jamaica.

The oldest surviving house in Barbados is Fontabelle, built in 1648 in what is now a suburb of Bridgetown. In Jamaica there are no seventeenth-century houses still inhabited. That island always distinguished itself by keeping a 'King's House' instead of a Government House for the official residence of the governor. In the seventeenth century there were two King's Houses, one in St Jago and the other in Port Royal. Usually they were in a state of disrepair, sometimes so bad that new governors had to lodge with prominent citizens until their official residence could be put in order. Of course the serious earthquake of 1692 destroyed most of the early houses and discouraged the building of pretentious homes for some time to come. A tropical climate soon erodes ruins and much of historical interest has been lost. The slave cabins and the miserable servants' quarters crumbled away very soon, but on some present-day estates a field called 'nigra house' indicates where the slave-lines used to be situated.

French visitors were impressed with Barbados in the 1650s. They noticed a great number of fine houses, many built in English fashion; shops and storehouses filled with all kinds of merchandise, and handsome churches. But what drew their attention most was the number of taverns – over one hundred in Bridgetown. Ligon mentions two by name: Mr Jobson's and Joan Fuller's, where fish meals were served, 'well dress'd; for they were both my pupils'. In the 1670s the Barbados assembly used to meet in taverns and its members saw no reason to vote money for a special building. Jamaica was equally well provided. The drinking that went on at the taverns of Jamaica and Barbados was copious, varied and disastrous. Within four years of the foundation of Barbados Sir Henry Colt was commenting on the excessive drinking that he saw there. In 1639 a letter from Thomas Verney stated that drunkenness was so rife that people were commonly seen lying senseless on the roads, where some were bitten and even killed by land-crabs. The early appearance of such drunkenness suggests that the tropical climate was less to blame than the bad habits brought by the colonists from England. Similar comments came from Jamaica. Shortly after his arrival there, Sir Thomas Modyford blamed intemperance for much of the ill-health, particularly among the old army officers, 'who from strict saints are turned the most debauched devils.' To cap his opinion he continued, 'The Spaniards (who trade with the Royal African Company) at their first coming wondered much at the sickness of our people until they knew of the strength of their drinks, but then wondered more that they were not all dead.' Richard Ligon considered drink in moderation was necessary to remain healthy: 'Certainly strong drinks are very requisite where so much heat is; for the spirits being exhausted with much sweating, the inner parts are left cold and faint, and shall need comforting and reviving.' Possessed of a catholic palate, Ligon bravely tried most of the local concoctions – 'mobbie' made from potatoes, and 'perino' made from cassava root, chewed by old Indian women, which tasted most like English beer; 'beveridge', a mixture of spring-water, sugar and orange-juice was pleasant and wholesome, but pineapple juice was 'the Nectar which the Gods drunk'. English beer, French, Spanish and Madeira wines and French brandy were all imported.

The leading planters gave dinner parties as fine as any in Europe. Ligon describes the bill of fare at a feast given by Colonel Drax, 'who lives like a prince'. First of all there was beef, fattened on bonavist, a choice of various cuts; tongue and tripe 'minced for pies' seasoned with sweet herbs finely minced; other parts went into an *olia podrida* (a kind of stew). There were fourteen beef dishes in all. There followed potato pudding, a dish of Scotch collops of a leg of pork, a 'fricacy' of the same, a dish of boiled chickens, a shoulder of a young goat dressed with 'his Blood and Time', a kid with a pudding in his belly, a sucking pig,

which is there the fattest, whitest and sweetest in the world, with a poignant sauce of the Brains, Salt, Sage and Nutmeg done with Claret wine, a Shoulder of Mutton, which is there a rare dish, a Pasty of the side of a young Goat, and a side of a fat young Shot [shoat] upon it, well seasoned with pepper and salt and some Nutmeg; a Loyn of Veal, to which there wants no sauce being so well furnished with Oranges, Lemons and Lymes, 3 young turkies in a dish, 2 capons, 2 hens with eggs in a dish, 4 Ducklings, 8 Turtle doves, and 3 rabbits. For cold bak'd meats two Muscovia Ducks larded and seasoned well with pepper and salt. And these being taken off the table, another course is set on and that is of Westphalia or Spanish bacon, dried Neats tongues, Botargo, pickl'd Oysters, Caviare, Anchovies, Olives and (intermixt with these) Custards, Creams, some alone, some with preserves of Plantines, Bonanoes, Guavers . . . cheese-cakes, Puffes . . .

This was washed down with a selection of all the drinks described above and sherry. A similar menu at Colonel Walrond's, who lived on the coast, had fish dishes instead of Drax's beef. Inland estates like Drax Hall had a problem: wine spoilt, brought up on negroes' heads in the hot sun. Walrond had his unloading done at night. Unfortunately, Ligon gives no indication of the number of gentlemen who sat down at table with Colonel Drax, but he does mention that he suffered from a long illness during which Walrond looked after him; it is tempting to wonder if it was not overeating that laid him low.

Food and health were more closely connected than Ligon and his contemporaries realized. Slaves and servants saw little meat except when a cow or a horse died and it was fed to them. Water hygiene was not understood at all. In Barbados with its shortage of rivers the main water supply came from ponds in which cattle drank and Negroes washed, 'whose bodies have none of the sweetest savours'. But the planters assured Ligon that 'the Sun with his virtual heat draws up all noisome vapours, and so the waters become rarefied and pure again'. Perhaps it was well that so little water was drunk. Some houses had gutters that led rain water into cisterns. Bridgetown in its early days was low and swampy but nobody understood that mosquitoes carried fever; a few people slept under nets to escape from their irritation and so avoided infection, but most people went early to bed, partly because the day's work started at 6 am when the sun came up, and partly on account of the poor lighting after it went down soon after 6 pm. Gentlemen would sit up with a pipe and a flagon of madeira at their side, at which their womenfolk would leave them and retire to an early bed. Down in the slave-lines, after seeing to the creation of the next generation, there was nothing to do but sleep, with every door and chink of window blocked, not against draughts and mosquitoes but for fear of the 'duppies' that walked by night. And the indentured servant, less frightened of the ghostly creatures of the night, would sit out under the brilliant moon and stars, grumbling with his companions about the shortage of girls and the miseries of life, until he turned in to sleep in his hammock or on his hard wooden bed and dream of slipping away to join the Buccaneers in their rollicking life on the waves of the Caribbean.

Over in Jamaica the colonists had all unwittingly chosen a healthy situation for Port Royal. Surrounded on three sides by the sea at the end of the Palisadoes sandspit, and tempered by constant breezes, it was as good as being on an island. The only drawback was the water supply which had to be brought over in casks from the Rio Cobre across the harbour. In spite of the hard drinking that went on in its taverns no reports of sickness in the town were made until after the earthquake. In its prime Port Royal was a remarkable town. It contained three-storey houses in which its merchants dined off gold and silver plate; there were large warehouses, a fine church and no less than six forts.

The early sickness suffered by Venables' soldiery was not caused by germs or virus endemic in the island, but by heat-stroke brought on by wearing too much clothing, and dysentery from eating rotten rations and putrid meat. The Spaniards may have brought malaria with them, but it is certain that there was no yellow fever in the island during the seventeenth century. It followed the slaves from certain parts of West Africa and found the vector insects waiting to spread it through the Caribbean in the eighteenth century. Modyford said he found Jamaica 'as healthful as Cotsall [sic] in England'. What is the effect of the tropical sun? Even in the twentieth century opinions have changed: at the beginning solar topees were *de rigueur*, now they are rarely seen. The early colonists went to the West Indies in their woollen English clothes and suffered accordingly. Some learnt to wear linen and keep cool by frequent bathing, but in the West Indies there has always been a tendency to wear too many clothes, especially on formal occasions. Men in shorts and open-necked shirts are rarely seen in shops and offices even today.

It was not long before the colonists learnt from experience that the most unhealthy part of the year was from May until the end of November, when it was hot and rainy. Governors urged home authorities to arrange for ships to arrive in the early part of the year before the hot season began and mortality among the crews in port began to rise. When this happened captains were inclined to press men; useful artisans were removed and immigrants were not encouraged to come and replace them. Generally, however, the West Indian colonies in the seventeenth century were no more unhealthy than England with its attacks of smallpox and plague.

In 1675 Barbados suffered its first major hurricane. Houses, churches, sugar works and windmills were blown down. Canes were flattened and some were torn up by the roots. Ships were blown ashore. Many of the leading planters took to living in huts and hesitated to build tall houses for a long time. The damage was estimated at £200,000.

The gentlemen, their servants and the yeomen who came to the West Indies brought their institutions of local government with them. Justices of the peace and their quarter and petty sessions made an early appearance. In Barbados parishes were paired to form precincts, each with a Court of Common Pleas, while criminal cases were heard at Grand Sessions in Bridgetown three times a year. The governor in council acted when required as a Court of Appeal. A departure from the English system was the patent office of Provost Marshal, which existed both in Jamaica and Barbados. The quarrel between Modyford and Lynch about the office has already been described. It was equally unpopular in Barbados. In 1673 Edwin Stede appeared before the Court of Common Pleas at Austin's to present his royal warrant for appointment as Provost Marshal. The judge, Henry Walrond, son of the troublesome Humphrey, refused to admit him, maintaining that such appointments lay with the governor and a royal warrant was invalid. When he refused to have the warrant read aloud, Stede held it up for all the five hundred people present to see: a fact that testifies to the social occasion made of the meeting of the courts. Eventually Stede succeeded in being admitted to his office, but he met with opposition that made it impossible for him to carry out his duties: no money was voted for the repair of the prison, so that he had to keep constant watch over it, 'it being soe decayed and insufficient that the prisoner escapes out of it at mid-day.'

Another office that has survived to the present day was that of Custos Rotulorum, the head justice of the peace in each parish or legal precinct, and usually 'the richest and best gentleman' resident there. In addition to his legal duties – presiding at quarter sessions – he was usually colonel of the local regiment of militia.

Now the militia was a very important institution in the early colonies. Again, its organization was a copy of the English model, but it assumed an importance far greater than its English counterpart, for defence against enemies or rebellious slaves was a vital function. In the early days every male between the ages of twelve and sixty had to enlist in a regiment. Regiments were elastic units of no fixed establishment. Plantation owners usually came as mounted officers bringing with them their indentured servants as foot soldiers. As a general rule each regiment was divided into companies with a captain, a lieutenant and an ensign in each company and anything between five and ten companies to a regiment. Each company was usually divided into files of six men, but again this varied with the locality and the numbers available.

When martial law was declared the militia was called out. Few people ever objected to martial law, because it meant a suspension of civil courts and debtors breathed sighs of relief. Nevertheless on paper discipline was strict. Severe penalties, including the death sentence, could be incurred for failure to attend guard, for falling asleep or getting drunk on sentry duty, leaving the colours, striking a superior officer, plundering, mutiny and sedition, and for making known the watchword without order. In a peaceful year duties were easy; in a troubled year militiamen might find themselves called out for months. In this case they received pay. In Jamaica in 1685 when martial law was declared over a Negro rising in Guanaboa Vale, a force of 120 men was kept constantly on duty at 5s a day for an officer, 2s 6d for a sergeant and 1s 6d for a soldier, with a prize of £5 a head for every Negro captured or killed.

In each colony the militia was a reflection of the whole social order. A visitor to Jamaica in 1700 gained the impression that the people 'are all Colonels, Captains, Lieutenants and Ensigns, the two last being held in much disdain'. The colonels and majors were the big landowners from whom the governor's council was chosen; captains and below formed the core of the elected assemblymen. To start with the militiamen did not wear uniform, but in 1681 Governor Dutton started to equip the Barbados militia with black helmets and red coats. About the same time the Jamaica militia began to wear uniform too. There is a brief description of the celebration of the king's birthday on 14 October 1686, when Colonel Hender Molesworth was governor:

The Governor reviewed the Regiment, many of whom were in scarlet, which they had provided expressly for the day. The Governor entertained all the gentlemen and officers with a very sumptuous dinner; and in the evening the Governor's lady, being waited on by all the gentlewomen of quality, gave them a very fine treat, and afterwards entertained them at a ball, composed of a suitable number of masqueraders, very cunningly habited, and a variety of music, all managed with that admirable order as gave great beauty and grace to it. They continued dancing very late, but the streets shone with bonfires to light them home.

In a pioneer community ceremonial is a precious relief to the dull tedium of daily routine. When Governor Lord William Willoughby died in Barbados in 1673, his body was conveyed on board ship for England with full military honours to the accompaniment of muffled drums. At the funeral ten years later of his sister-in-law, the Dowager Baroness Willoughby of Parham, there was trouble over protocol. Sir Martin Bentley allowed his coach to precede that of Colonel Newton who claimed seniority of rank. Newton complained to the council and Sir Martin was required to apologize. As the incident appeared closed, Sir Timothy Thornhill, a wealthy and influential planter, claimed that he should have had precedence as a baronet – Charles II created no less than thirteen baronetcies in Barbados – and when the council did not agree he sent in his resignation in disgust.

In Jamaica the arrival of a new governor was always made a social occasion. When Lord Vaughan arrived in 1675 he was, wrote Sir Henry Morgan, 'received with all respect imaginable, the forts firing many guns', and he was entertained at King's House in Port Royal to a splendid supper. Next day the new governor's commission was read by Peter Beckford, the island Secretary, and he was nobly entertained by the Commander of the Forts. On the third day Vaughan went to St Jago, 'attended by most of the gentry in their coaches, and was treated to a most splendid dinner by Sir Thomas Modyford.' Similarly the Duke of Albemarle was greeted with three days' entertainment at the public expense, a welcome that pleased His Grace to write to the Lords of Trade that he was 'kindly received by the Lieutenant-Governor and people'.

The West Indian colonies were founded in an age which accorded great importance to religion. In Barbados churches were built early in each parish. Under Governor Bell, whose Puritan persuasion has been noted in Providence, ministers were appointed and dismissed by parish Vestries, and their stipends were produced by a levy of one pound of tobacco per acre owned by each planter. In 1647 a law was passed by the assembly condemning unorthodox conventicles and calling on all people to 'conform to the government and discipline of the Church of England'. Schismatics were publicly whipped. Religious observance was strictly enforced. Family prayers were said morning and evening and attendance at church twice on Sunday was required from every colonist living within two miles. Those living further away were expected to attend at least twice a month. Absence was punished by heavy fines, and constables and churchwardens were expected, sometimes during service, 'to walk and search taverns, alehouses, victualling houses, or other houses where they doe suspect lewd and debauched company to frequent. And if they shall find any drinking, swearing, gameing or otherwise misdemeaning themselves, that forthwith they shall apprehend such Persons, and bring them to the Stocks, there to be imprisoned the Space of Four Hours.'

Soon after Governor Searle assumed command after Ayscue's descent upon the island, there was a row over the abolition of the Prayer Book. Parson Charles Robson of All Saints refused to surrender his copy. When he was arrested he was set free by a crowd of supporters in a near riot, which Searle firmly suppressed. In 1661 the Vestry of St Michael's commissioned Captain Robert Gullimore to build a church for 250,000 pounds of sugar (equivalent to £1,250 then), payable in three instalments. In 1663 Lord Francis Willoughby presented the Rev. William Frith MA as minister for St Michael's and the Vestry agreed to pay him twenty thousand pounds of 'Muskovady Sugar' per annum. They also provided him with a horse 'for his riding as a gentleman'. Fifteen years later Governor Sir Jonathan Atkins held a church visitation, and William Frith lost his living on account of the many complaints against him. Another visitation conducted by Sir Richard Dutton in 1681 discovered that a Mr Grey had been holding a living for twenty-four years without ever having been ordained in Anglican orders.

In Jamaica a more tolerant regime in church affairs prevailed. The first church dedicated was the old Spanish church in St Jago. Lord Windsor brought out five ministers with him in 1662 and a royal grant of £100 a year was made for each. Two years later, however, the royal grant had given out and they were thrown on the charity of their parishioners. When Modyford arrived there was still only one church, so that there had developed the custom of 'meeting alternately at each other's houses as the primitive Christians did, there to pray, read a chapter, sing a psalm and home again'. The custom of burials round houses too far removed from churchyards started at this time. The two oldest churches in Jamaica at Alley in Vere and Yallahs in St Thomas were started in 1671 and 1675 respectively. In 1681 Morgan wrote home pretentiously from Port Royal, 'This Government . . . is much countenanced from a graceful digestion of a full auditorie in a new church which we entered into on last New Year's

Day, to the great satisfaction of the inhabitants as well as strangers.' This Port Royal church, described by Lynch as 'the best English Church in America', went down in the earthquake with the grave of the ex-Buccaneer governor, who had reported its completion only ten years before.

The most noteworthy religious feature of early Jamaica, however, was the enjoyment of religious toleration before people in England were allowed it. In 1670 when Lynch received his instructions as lieutenant-governor he was told 'to give all possible encouragement to persons of different opinions in religion, but the Governor must be a Protestant even as His Majesty is'. While freedom of worship was allowed, however, there was considerable prejudice against Nonconformists in public life. Thus Quakers were required to pay *three* able and efficient soldiers to serve in the militia in their place. In 1680 Carlisle reported the dismissal of two assistant judges of the Supreme Court, Captain Sam Bache, 'an enemy to the Church and a supporter of conventicles in his own house', and Colonel Sam Barry, 'a stiff member of the Assembly'. The point in this case is not that they were dismissed for these reasons but that they had ever been appointed, in the days of the Clarendon Code. Papists were not encouraged. Under James II three had been appointed to commissions in the militia but resigned of their own volition as soon as news of the Revolution reached Jamaica. The Jewish community, which had survived from Spanish days, had its own synagogue, but they too found themselves in trouble for objecting to attending militia parades on their sabbath, while on Sundays they were suspected of receiving stolen goods from the Negroes while good Christian gentlemen were attending church.

Little attention was given to education in this early period. A free school is shown on the map of Barbados in St George's parish and there is a disapproving mention of schoolmasters who were found to have Quakers and Anabaptists among their numbers. The Quakers in fact were well represented in the island for they had no fewer than four meeting houses. These and the parish churches must have been used for schools, as in the case of Mr Heynes, Schoolmaster, who was licensed to teach in the parish church in 1662. The clergy held classes and took private pupils. For example, Christopher Codrington III was taught by the Rector of St John's until his parents sent him to school in England at the age of twelve. Similar brief references to ministers running schools are also found in Jamaica. It was not a time when new schools were founded in England. Certainly nobody had any idea of higher education in the West Indies, as the Puritan colonists in New England did with the foundation of Harvard as early as 1636. Intellectual life in the West Indies was sadly neglected.

It may be a libel to say that the main recreation of the West Indian colonists in the seventeenth century was eating and drinking, but there is little evidence of any sport. Colonel Drax, said Ligon, 'who was not so strict an observer of Sundayes, as to deny himself lawful recreations', would organize swimming contests for his Negroes, setting them to catch muscovy ducks on a pond. They had to swim underwater and seize them from below. Horses were raced for wagers between planters but there were no organized race meetings. Gambling with cards and dice was popular.

By the Revolution of 1688 the West Indian colonies were well established and no longer struggling. Fortunes had been made in Barbados, and in Jamaica there were planters with incomes of £4,000 a year and more. There were also paupers, substituting for the opulence, pompous dignity and worldly sagacity of the plantocrat the dejection, and guile of the underdog. Basically, the colonists were still very English in their ways, but differentiation was beginning to appear, notably the reliance on slave-labour and subservience to the sugar-cane. Whatever was said of the early West Indians – 'a stout and martial people', 'a people to be governed rather by persuasion than severity', or 'a people very capricious, jealous, and difficult to manage' – these early Jamaicans, Barbadians and Leeward Islanders were nothing less than a full-blooded race of pioneers, typical of the colonists who went to all the new lands on the western side of the Atlantic.

8
THE GREAT WARS,
1689-1815

In 1689 the English colonies in the West Indies consisted of Barbados, the Caribbee or Leeward Islands, Jamaica, and the proprietary colony of the Bahamas which numbered only a few hundred souls. There were also scattered unofficial settlements in the Bay of Campeche, the Bay Islands and the Moskito Coast. The total population amounted to about forty thousand white colonists, estate owners, indentured servants and seamen, and about eighty thousand Negro slaves.

Of the 126 years under review no less than sixty-four were occupied by war. Thus the problem of security was ever uppermost in the minds of the colonists. Every principal port was guarded by forts, and every able-bodied man continued to be required to serve in his island's militia. Garrisons of English regular soldiers and squadrons of the Royal Navy were always present, gradually relieving the colonial forces in the front line of defence and adding much to the social life of the island capitals. Wars meant interruptions in trade but they often brought a rise in the prices of island exports. In several cases they brought ruin when invasion and pillage occurred, and in the American War of Independence there was starvation and great distress. In spite of the wars, and partly because of them, the West Indies made remarkable economic progress. As a result of the Seven Years' War, Britain acquired Dominica, St Vincent, Grenada and Tobago. At the end of the American War she was lucky to lose only Tobago. In 1802 she kept Trinidad, captured in 1797, but restored other conquests including the future British Guiana – and Tobago. In 1815 Britain paid the Netherlands £3,000,000 and kept Guiana. St Lucia was ceded by France – so was Tobago. Why this small island was such a shuttlecock is a complete mystery.

In 1815, partly on account of new acquisitions, partly through expansion in Jamaica, the Virgin Islands and Bahamas, but mostly because of the slave trade the population of the British West Indies had risen to approximately seventy thousand whites, more than six hundred thousand Negro slaves and several thousand people of mixed blood, some of them free, some of them slaves. While the black element steadily expanded through slave importation rather than by natural increase, the white element expanded very little because it was continually shifting from island to island, or from the islands to the American mainland. It took a long time for Jamaica, by far the biggest island, to develop into the most important colony. Not till 1710 did it surpass Barbados in population.

Although the colonies were small and contained few people in comparison with the United Kingdom, where the population rose from six to more than ten million during this period, the eighteenth century was the most prosperous in West Indian history and they were recognized as the richest possessions of the British Crown. In the three years 1715, 1716, and 1717, the Leeward Islands, Barbados and Jamaica, in that order, each exported to the United Kingdom more than, or nearly as much as, *all the mainland colonies of America put together*. (Leewards £403,394, Barbados £364,577, Jamaica £332,266; North American colonies £382,576.) Towards the end of the century the younger Pitt estimated that four-fifths of British incomes derived from overseas came from the West Indies. The great Lord Mayor of London, William Beckford, father of the builder of Fonthill and the first Englishman to die a millionaire, drew most of his great wealth from property in Jamaica and profits in the lucrative West India trade. In the House of Commons of the eighteenth century some of the most influential voices were those of the West India lobby. To quote the younger Pitt again for an explanation of all this wealth and importance, on one occasion when he was acting in support of the West Indians, he started his speech, 'Sugar, sugar, sugar, sugar, Mr Speaker. . . . '

The acquisition of wealth was by no means a smooth and easy process. Attention has been drawn in an earlier chapter to how the natural drawbacks of the Caribbean come to interrupt the balmy days of the sunny climate. Among the most terrible of them was the earthquake that destroyed Port Royal in 1692 and set back the progress Jamaica was then making for a whole decade.

THE PORT ROYAL EARTHQUAKE

Popular legend is too fond of repeating how the great earthquake swallowed up the richest and wickedest city in the world. In 1692 Port Royal was prosperous but not as rich as London, or the trading cities of Holland. The Buccaneers had been gone for twenty years and the only pirates seen in the port were those brought in for trial and hanging in chains on the Palisadoes. Nevertheless, Dr Heath, the Rector, referred to his flock as 'a most ungodly and debauched people' and Captain Crocket described how some people that same night were 'at their Old Trade of Drinking, Swearing, and Whoreing, breaking up Ware-houses; pillaging and Stealing from their neighbours ... indeed this place has been one of the Ludest in the Christian World, a Sink of all Filthiness, and a meer Sodom'. To many the destruction of Port Royal appeared as a divine judgment.

All observers described how the fateful 7 June dawned clear and hot with scarce a cloud in the sky. In all there were three shocks, the first a mild one shortly after 11.30, then a second accompanied by a hollow rumbling sound – 'a warning to quit houses' – followed by the third violent shake which in the space of two minutes destroyed three-quarters of Port Royal. In some streets the sand rose and fell like the waves of the sea, graves were washed open and some unfortunates were swallowed and crushed by cracks in the streets' surface. There were some lucky escapes. Dr Heath was picked up by a boat, and Lewis Galdy was swallowed by the earth and then thrown up again, as his tombstone in the present Port Royal churchyard tells. All the northern side of the town, where the houses had been unwisely built on an accumulation of sand that had collected over the old coral reef that formed the Palisadoes, slid into the harbour, where in recent years their remains have been excavated by skin-divers to provide a unique archaeological collection.

Not only Port Royal was ruined by the earthquake. Houses and sugar-works all over the island were thrown down, mountains split and collapsed

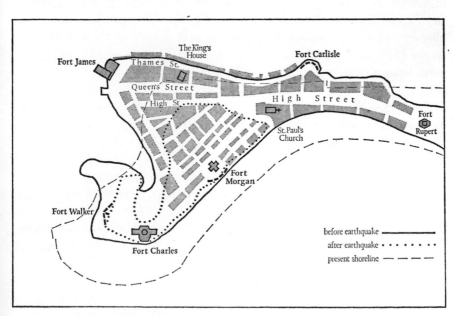

Port Royal and the earthquake of 1692

and rivers changed their courses. Then sickness struck. More people died of 'a malignant fever' than were killed by the earthquake. In all five thousand people lost their lives. At the time of the disaster Jamaica was without a governor, but John White, president of the council, and his fellow councillors dealt ably with the emergency. Less than three weeks after the earthquake orders were made for the survey of a new town on the far side of the harbour. Thus the present capital of Kingston was founded on a site which has allowed it to expand into the large metropolis of more than two hundred thousand people that it is today.

Port Royal never recovered. Silt accumulated to join the island left by the earthquake to the Palisadoes once more, but a fire in 1703 and two hurricanes in 1712 and 1722 discouraged any serious rebuilding. The navy used it as a base well into the nineteenth century, but it ceased to be notorious after 1692.

THE REPULSE OF MONSIEUR DU CASSE

It was fortunate for Jamaica that the Great Earthquake, terrible as it was, did not have more serious results than the deaths and damage it caused, for it occurred in the third year of the English Succession War when the coasts of Jamaica were under continual attacks from privateers, French, Dutch and Jacobite or mere renegade English, sailing under letters of marque issued by Monsieur du Casse, governor of the French settlements in western Hispaniola. Life on remote plantations was rendered insecure and frightening, for the privateers lived by no honourable code. Many planters had sent their families to Port Royal and Spanish Town for safety. At the time of the earthquake a French force had been plundering the north coast and were so frightened by it that they withdrew, but the real danger lay in what the French would do when they heard that the six forts at Port Royal had been shattered or were lying in six fathoms of water. If du Casse had acted promptly the French could have captured Jamaica. Instead he contented himself with privateering raids and it was two years before his main attempt materialized.

In the meantime Jamaica received a new lieutenant-governor when Sir William Beeston arrived in March 1693. Although new at the King's House, he was an old Jamaica hand of more than thirty years' standing. There could have been no better leader to cope with the dangerous situation, but he was fortunate to receive the necessary warning in a most extraordinary way. There could be nothing more graphic than Beeston's own account of what happened:

In the evening of Thursday, May 31st [1694] while I was sitting with some gentlemen, there entered my house Captain Elliott in a very mean habit with a meagre weather-beaten countenance, who told me that for the safety of the island he and two more had ventured their lives in a small canoe that would carry no more than three people, and had stolen away from the enemy on the Saturday night before, to warn me that the French had recruits of men and ships from France and Martinique, and that du Casse was coming against Jamaica with twenty ships and 3,000 men.

Captain Stephen Elliott's ship had been captured by the French in April and taken into Petit Goaves. It was from there that he had made his escape. Elliott and his two nameless companions had paddled nearly three hundred miles across the open sea, a magnificent heroic effort that brought timely warning of du Casse's approach and allowed Beeston to elaborate his plan of defence. Elliott's contemporaries recognized his services, the Lords of Trade recommending him to receive £500, a medal and chain, and his two companions £50 each. It was the most signal piece of individual service ever performed in the interests of Jamaica.

The position was grim. The last navy frigate had fallen into the hands of the French, leaving du Casse completely in command of the sea. His twenty ships could land their three thousand men wherever he chose. Beeston wasted no time. On the same night of Elliott's dramatic arrival he summoned the council, adjourned the assembly and proclaimed martial law. Colonel Peter Beckford was ordered to put Fort Charles at Port Royal into the best possible shape. With only 1,390 militiamen at his disposal, Beeston decided to concentrate his meagre force at Spanish Town. He ordered the evacuation of the eastern parishes and the concentration of the people, their slaves and cattle in the region of the capital. Any slave killing a Frenchman was to be granted his freedom and a reward. Sloops were dispatched to England and Barbados with the latest news.

When the French appeared on 17 June, Beeston took heart at their behaviour, for they settled down at Port Morant for a month, plundering, burning and torturing any prisoners who had disobeyed their governor's order to evacuate. If they had been intent on conquest, Beeston felt they would not have caused so much destruction. On 17 July seventeen French sail came in sight of Port Royal but passed on to leeward as dusk fell. Beeston recognized that their next point of descent could only be Carlisle Bay, thirty-five miles west of Spanish Town. Two troops of horse and a detachment of foot were ordered to march there at once. It was then that the Jamaica militia proved that it was no mere ceremonial soldiery. The long march continued through the night, the mounted men reaching their objective before dawn, the foot coming in soon after. The French landed on the nineteenth and scored an initial success over the local militia garrison, but the force that had marched so well, 'weary, lame and hungry', fell on the enemy and drove them back. Three days later the French advanced again, but a sound defence discouraged them. On 28 June they re-embarked and sailed back to Hispaniola. Later French plans to invade Jamaica never materialized because the Royal Navy thwarted them many miles away, under Rodney at Les Saintes in 1782, and in 1805 when Nelson chased Villeneuve back to Trafalgar. But in 1694 without any help from the navy, entirely from their own resources under the command of their planter-governor, the Jamaicans saved their island from the most serious invasion in its history.

On the departure of the French Beeston sat down to report the damage. Although only one hundred men had been killed in the fighting, the French had burnt over two hundred houses, destroyed fifty sugar-works and carried off 1,300 Negroes. Beeston asked for a grant of £4,000 to allow him to compensate the worst sufferers, otherwise people would leave the island. Not only was this request readily granted, but the English government sent out an expedition to attack the French in Hispaniola under Commodore Wilmot and Colonel Lillingston. It achieved little and its details do not concern this social history, but the danger to the English colony continued until the end of the war in 1697. At the Treaty of Ryswick France's colony of Saint Domingue on Hispaniola was recognized for the first time by Spain. As the nearest French colony to Jamaica it posed a threat whenever war broke out. In consequence English warships and English troops came to be permanently stationed in Jamaica and the island was not called to defend itself by itself again.

THE DARIEN SCHEME

Until the Act of Union with Scotland in 1707 the colonies in the West Indies were English and not British. This meant that Scotsmen were debarred from trading with them. In consequence the Scots made their tragic attempt to found a colony of their own. Perhaps if William Paterson, whose brainchild it was, had been less ambitious the venture might have succeeded, but fascinated as he became with the strategic importance of the Isthmus of Darien, he disregarded the equal importance attached to the place by Spain. He should have known better because he had been in Jamaica, whence he had returned to London with a fortune in 1684. He saw Darien as 'the door of the seas and the key of the universe', providing easier access to the Far East than the route round the Cape of Good Hope. He did not wish to oust Spain. He dreamt of the establishment of a free port on each side of the isthmus, joined at first by a waggon road and later by a canal. Completely ignorant of, or merely choosing to ignore, Spain's past exclusive policy in America he and the Company of Scotland Trading to Africa and the Indies went ahead with their plans, keeping the destination of their expedition secret. When he failed to secure any backing from London merchants, Paterson appealed to the people of Scotland and such was their enthusiasm that they not only found the £400,000 capital, but volunteered in their hundreds to participate in the venture. On 15 July 1698 all Edinburgh went down to Leith to bid godspeed to the five ships and the 1,200 colonists who had been selected to sail in them.

Although the secret of the destination had been well kept, English merchants had guessed at it, and King William III, whose personal consent had not been given, anxious above all things to avoid giving offence to Spain as a valuable ally against Louis XIV, issued secret orders to the governors of all colonies to have no dealings with the Scots colony. In April 1699, in compliance with these orders, Sir William Beeston at Jamaica issued a proclamation forbidding all subjects of William III to trade with the Scotsmen who had by then reached Darien.

Among the Scots events had been going from bad to worse. Although they had found a suitable harbour and had established friendly relations with the Indians, they had brought among their trade goods the most unsuitable items for a tropical climate, including bolts of Scottish serge, worsted stockings, 500 pairs of slippers, 1,440 Scots bonnets, 23,000 clay pipes and 4,000 periwigs, so that when ships from New York, Boston and the West Indies came by the colonists had nothing that any captain wanted in exchange for the provisions they badly needed. The most extraordinary orders for the government of the colony bedevilled any action and excluded Paterson from partaking in affairs – a short-sighted punishment for the theft of £17,000 of company funds with which a servant of Paterson's had disappeared. In April the rains set in and there were three hundred deaths from fever. In May news of Beeston's proclamation reached the colony. Realizing that King William had disowned them the colonists abandoned their settlement, leaving 750 graves.

In the meantime in Scotland, following the receipt of optimistic first news from the colony, reinforcements had been collected and a further four ships and 1,300 colonists sailed for the isthmus. But the mistakes of the first wave were repeated and by the time a leader of the right calibre arrived, in the person of Captain Alexander Campbell of Fonab, the rot had gone too far. Then a Spanish fleet appeared, as it was only inevitable, and the fate of the Scottish colony was sealed. On 12 April 1700 the last colonists were shipped away. No ship reached Scotland. Of the 1,300 members of the second expedition no less than 940 perished. The rest dispersed among the West Indian and American colonies in spite of the proclamations, and a number settled down in western Jamaica among the Surinam refugees. Down on the Isthmus of Panama today the only sign of the settlement of New Edinburgh is the overgrown moat that was cut across the little peninsula to protect the fort, and the local name for the place, Puerto Escoces.

William Paterson survived to return to Scotland to work for the obvious solution: the union of the governments of England and Scotland and the participation of the Scots in the henceforward *British* colonies, where his countrymen have since made such an enormous contribution.

THE GOVERNORS CODRINGTON IN THE LEEWARD ISLANDS

In small communities the personality of the governor exerts a disproportionate influence on events and the atmosphere in which they take place. In 1683 Christopher Codrington, son of one of the pioneer settlers in Barbados, moved to the Caribbees where he took up land in St Kitts and Antigua and, in partnership with his brother John, became the owner of the unoccupied island of Barbuda. He had already served in Barbados as deputy-governor – at the age of twenty-nine – and Speaker of the Assembly. In 1689 he became governor-general of the Leeward Islands.

It was a perilous time. At the news of the English Revolution few colonists showed much enthusiasm for Dutch William, and the Irish on Montserrat were expected to rebel in favour of the deposed James II. As France and England declared war, the French of St Kitts forgot the old treaty of neutrality that had been made by Thomas Warner and Pierre d'Esnambuc. Repeating their action of 1666 during the Second Dutch War, they invaded the English parts of the island and forced the outnumbered English forces to surrender. It was Codrington who organized the recapture of St Kitts in 1690 and urged the English government to attempt the seizure of Martinique and Guadeloupe. After the English attacks failed, there was no more fighting in the Leeward Islands. Codrington therefore turned to the resettlement of the English estates on St Kitts. For the future protection of the English colony he was anxious to encourage the settlement of small estates of twenty acres, whose owners would form the rank and file of the militia. More important, he persuaded the home government to keep two warships at the Leeward Islands. Meanwhile the handful of English regular soldiers at St Kitts, who had had no pay for months and whose uniforms were in tatters, were on the verge of mutiny. In such circumstances little planting could be done, a situation that was to recur too frequently in the century of the great wars.

Another unpleasant feature of West Indian life appeared during Codrington's regime. He became involved in a personal quarrel with Edward Walrond, a family name almost synonymous with trouble, as the early history of Barbados has shown. The details are immaterial, although the faults were not all on Walrond's side, for Codrington, as the colonels in

India were later to do, had developed under the tropical sun one of those choleric tempers that became as much a recognized attribute of West Indian planters as their fabulous wealth. There is no doubt that he indulged in illegal trade with interloping slavers and the Dutch on neighbouring St Eustatius, in contravention of the hated Navigation Acts, but he proved himself a brave and skilful leader in war. Like his fellow-planter, Sir Thomas Modyford, he proposed that the colonies should be represented at Westminster, and he wanted to see the establishment of schools and hospitals in the islands. His sudden death in 1698 prevented the execution of his schemes, but they obviously influenced those of his son, who succeeded his father not only to the estates of the wealthiest planter in the West Indies but also to the appointment of governor-general of the Leeward Islands.

The third Christopher Codrington was born in Barbados in 1668. His course of education has already been cited as typical of the schooling of the leading planters' sons. After completing his residence at Christ Church College, Oxford, and becoming a member of the Middle Temple, in 1690 he was elected a fellow of All Souls. Two years later, with leave from his college, young Christopher sailed with Sir Francis Wheler's expedition to the West Indies, where he joined his father in the vain attempt to capture Martinique. In 1693 the son was back at Oxford. Next year he went soldiering in Flanders where he gained the notice of King William during the siege of Namur. By the end of the English Succession War he was colonel commanding the Second Foot Guards and had become the lion of London society, so that the king, on hearing of the sudden demise of the governor-general, had no hesitation in appointing his son to succeed him. He was thirty – young, but superbly equipped for his task. The new governor-general, however, did not hurry to take up his appointment. He refused to move until the Treasury had paid the four years' arrears of salary owed to his father. When he arrived at Antigua in September 1700 Codrington was horrified at the confusion and corruption on every hand. He announced his intention of enforcing the Navigation Acts and made use of his legal training to reform court procedures which had developed on different lines in each island. This brought him face to face with the inter-island jealousy which thwarted his reforms and has continued to plague West Indian politics down to the present day. Some of the events which hit the headlines in 1969 were first put into rehearsal in 1700: the governor of St Kitts had been maltreating the governor of the little island of Anguilla. Codrington had the St Kitts man suspended. His attempts at reform naturally made him enemies, so that history repeated itself in a violent quarrel between governor-general and the leading planter of Nevis. Like the father's enemy, the son's went home to raise complaints with the home government against the governor-general. Fortunately Codrington's friends of his Oxford and London days sprang to his defence.

Exploitation of the slow communications between London and the colonies favoured a calumniator's dirty business, a danger of colonial service that governors like Clive and Warren Hastings in India as well as the Codringtons and others in the West Indies came to experience. Codrington III had the satisfaction of winning complete exoneration. When George Larkin, a travelling commissioner for the Council of Trade and Plantations, reported to the board in 1702, he wrote, 'What most surprises me is a complaint against the Governor of the Leeward Islands to the House of Commons, who truly . . . is the only governor that I have met withal since my coming into America that can be called a good governor.'

On the outbreak of the Spanish Succession War in 1702 Codrington acted swiftly, attacking the French at St Kitts with such promptitude that they surrendered in a week. Like his father before him he participated in an attack on another French colony, this time at Guadeloupe instead of Martinique, and like the earlier expedition this was no more successful. Poor intelligence was as much a cause of failure as anything else, but Codrington said there was also a social reason: the warm and liquid welcome of the English soldiers and sailors at Barbados, 'The Planters think ye best way to make their strangers Welcome is to murther them with Drinking. The tenth part of y^t strong liquor wch will scarce warme the blood of our West Indians, who have bodies like Egyptian mummys, must certainly dispatch a New-Comer to the other World.'

But the main cause of failure was one that had bedevilled English expeditions to the Caribbean since the last voyage of Drake and Hawkins: quarrelling leaders of a divided command, and it was not the last instance of this tragic occurrence.

Returning to St Kitts seriously ill, Codrington was able to do little more before he was relieved by Sir William Mathew, who died within four months. After a year's interregnum, in 1706 there arrived the new governor-general, Colonel Daniel Parke, who had been appointed by the petticoat government of Queen Anne as a reward for bringing her the news of Marlborough's great victory at Blenheim. His was the most nonsensical appointment in colonial history. An unscrupulous careerist, he earned the hatred of every planter in the Leeward Islands. On 7 December 1710, during the armed rising in which his unpopularity culminated, Governor Parke was brutally assaulted and left to die stripped naked in the blazing sun. It was a serious affray; eleven English soldiers and four islanders lost their lives in addition to the governor. Strange to relate nobody was ever brought to book. Colonel Walter Douglas, the new governor-general, was ordered to hold an inquiry and arrest the ringleaders, but he accepted large bribes. He was recalled in disgrace, fined and imprisoned, but Parke's murderers went free. Peaceful conditions were restored under the rule of Walter Hamilton, a leading planter, so that when he was succeeded in 1721 by Colonel John Hat, ex-governor of Maryland, Hat wrote a favourable first report, describing the Antiguans as 'a sociable and well-bred people', those of St Kitts 'a very brave people and very good seamen'. The colonists on Montserrat were 'two-thirds Papists, justly excluded by law from having any share in the government', but he found those on Nevis 'the most obstinate and particular tempered people I have ever conversed with'. The 1720s were the most prosperous period in the history of the Leeward Islands. Their exports were more valuable than those of any other colony and their white population reached its maximum of over twelve thousand. Antigua was the most productive island.

In 1707 Christopher Codrington had retired to Barbados broken in health and there he died in 1710, a bachelor of forty-four, leaving a will that became a milestone in West Indian history for the educational trust it established. First, he left £10,000 to All Souls College, Oxford, for the foundation of a library which is second only to the Bodleian at the university. In Barbados he left his two estates for the endowment of a college.

A Convenient number of Professors and Scholars [should be] Maintained there, all of them to be under vows of Poverty Chastity and obedience, who shall be oblidged to Studdy and Practice Physick and Chyrurgery as well as divinity, that by the apparent usefulness of the former to all mankind, they may Both indear themselves to the People and have the better oppertunitys of doeing good To mens Souls whilst they are Takeing Care of their Bodys.

He left the estates to the care of the Society for the Propagation of the Christian Religion in Foreign Parts, giving them discretion over the college's constitution. As a result vows of poverty, chastity and obedience were struck from the required conditions. A long time elapsed before any college materialized. First of all it took the form of a boys' grammar-school, started in 1745, and it was not until 1830 that a training college for young men, particularly those with a wish to enter holy orders, was started beside it. Although it was not specifically mentioned in the will, Codrington had a concern for the conversion of the slaves on the sugar-estates and he considered that a special college was necessary because he doubted that the secular clergy, 'who will be sure of their wine before they set about their talk', would lend themselves to such work. In fact there was considerable opposition to the idea of converting the slaves, especially among the planters, and the governor of Barbados at the time took measures to block the execution of the will.

A condition of the will was that the estates should be kept entire with three hundred negroes on them. This meant that the finances of the college were tied to the fluctuation of sugar prices, rendering their administration extremely difficult, for the profits varied from £4,000 in a good year down to less than £1,000 when conditions were bad. Later, too, the Society found itself embarrassed by the ownership of slaves.

Codrington's bequest, although not outstandingly munificent, was helpful. In the first hundred years of the college more than four hundred students passed through its halls to supply the West Indies with a line of bishops and clergy, chief justices, barristers, doctors, merchants and planters. In 1875 Codrington College became affiliated to the University of Durham, and has been since 1955 a priory adopted by the Community of the Resurrection, Mirfield. It appears like a corner of Oxford set down amidst the tropical beauty of Barbados.

Other educational bequests, like Codrington's, took a long time to produce any result. In Jamaica between 1667 and 1736 no less than 218 legacies were made to churches, poor relief and the foundation of schools, but only a few were executed. Manning's School, Savannah-la-Mar, was founded as a result of the will of Thomas Manning, a Westmorland planter who died in 1710, but the assembly did not pass the necessary act to start it until 1738. John Wolmer, a Kingston goldsmith who died in 1729, left his estate for the foundation of a free school which became the basis of the large schools for boys and girls that still bear his name, and Peter Beckford in 1730 left £1,000 for a free school in Spanish Town. Although these bequests showed the concern of leading colonists to correct the lack of schools, they were only a drop of water in the pail. The educational facilities of the British West Indies remained poor until long after Emancipation.

PIRATES AND THE BAHAMAS

On a map the Bahama Islands appear numerous and some of them are large. Because they are coral islands, however, with no depth of soil, it has never been possible to develop any notable agricultural industry. Their main attraction in the past lay in their strategic position, strung across the entrance to the Florida Strait leading to the Gulf of Mexico, and the Windward Passage, one of the gateways into the Caribbean. The only paying occupation for seventeenth-century colonists was piracy.

Adventurers from Bermuda formed the first small settlements, including that on the island of New Providence started in 1666, but the first official recognition came in 1670 when Charles II made a grant of them to the six Lords Proprietors of Carolina. Apart from appointing a succession of disreputable governors, the Proprietors did little for their colony. In 1676 the few hundred colonists were said to be living 'a lewd licentious sort of life'.

For adventurers who liked freedom from government restrictions and taxation these islands and the little Virgin Islands to the south of them were attractive. In 1684 the Spaniards had had enough of them. They destroyed the settlement on New Providence.

By 1690 the settlement was going again under Captain Cadwallader Jones, who, it was reported, 'highly caressed those Pirates that came to Providence', giving them commissions against the advice of his council, whose opinions he swayed by having the guns of his son's ship trained on the council chamber. The men with whom the Proprietors replaced him proved no better. Captain Nicholas Webb, who made a serious attempt to suppress piracy, found his position so uncomfortable that he fled. His successor was held up by the Speaker of the Assembly at pistol point, and, when the pistol was discharged in the ensuing scuffle, knocked on the head with its butt.

Disorders continued until the arrival of Captain Woodes Rogers, a great sailor who had circumnavigated the world and rescued Alexander Selkirk from Juan Fernandez. When he landed to take over at New Providence he was greeted by lines of friendly pirates who saluted him with continuous musket fire. Although Rogers persuaded them to give up piracy they were soon back at their old trade because a peaceful life was boring and there was nothing else for them to do. Strenuous efforts were then made to put them down. Edward Teach, or 'Blackbeard', was hanged at Jamaica in 1718. The women pirates, Anne Bonney and Mary Read, were sentenced there three years later but escaped the noose through convenient pregnancies. Rackham's Cay outside Port Royal marks the place of execution where their associate, 'Calico Jack' Rackham, met his end.

Like the Buccaneers before them, the pirates came from every nation and were notorious for their brutality and cruelty to prisoners, but where the former had directed their activities mainly against Spanish ships and towns, the pirates attacked ships of every country, including their own. Piracy continued to be a serious menace to trade and travel in the Caribbean off and on into the nineteenth century. As for privateering, letters of marque were only officially discountenanced by the Peace of Paris which ended the Crimean War in 1856. The Bahamas remained undeveloped for the rest of this period. In 1787 the Crown took over the last vestiges of the Proprietors' rights when for a few years American loyalist refugees introduced cotton planting, but the population rose to little over five thousand people, who, unlike all the other colonies, were almost equally divided into black and white. Gradually the islands' poor soil lost the competition against the greater fertility of the Southern States. The pirate tradition died hard. Whenever wars offered an opportunity, the islands came into their own as smuggling bases; they thrived in the days of American prohibition, and the present government of Cuba watches anxiously in their direction. No other ex-colony can claim to have had an ex-king as governor, for during the Second World War the late Duke of Windsor ruled at Nassau. In 1861 came the start of the industry that has been the most successful, when the first hotel was opened on New Providence. By the 1930s that island had become almost entirely a tourist resort. Hotels have since mushroomed in the out-islands as well, exploiting to the full the empty coral beaches and the limpid turquoise sea. Not since pirate days has so much money circulated in the islands.

THE NEW ACQUISITIONS

The most important point about the former British colonies in the West Indies is their great diversity, each ex-colony possessing characteristics that markedly distinguish it from its neighbours across the sea. Although Barbados and the Caribbees were founded in the same decade under the same Lord Proprietor, their governments were kept separate, and in the Caribbees each island was remarkable for some characteristic that distinguished it from the rest. Jamaica's main distinctive feature, apart from its government foundation, was its greater size and its separation from the oldest colonies by over nine hundred miles of sea. The poor natural environment of the Bahamas has just been described. The new acquisitions of the late eighteenth century were distinguished by their different origins. Before the British conquest Trinidad had been Spanish for two hundred years, Demerara and Berbice had been Dutch, and Grenada, Tobago, St Vincent, Dominica and St Lucia had been little or only lately developed by the French.

In the southern group, at first known as the South Caribbees and later as the Windward Islands, it took over forty years for British rule to become firmly established. In the American War and the French Revolutionary War there was bitter fighting up and down the whole chain of the Lesser Antilles, in which triangular contests between French and British planters and the Carib Indians took place. A successful tactic used by both sides to effect the surrender of local militiamen was to burn a few plantations and so induce the other watching owners in the hills to capitulate before their estates suffered the same fate.

Trinidad had been very little developed by the Spanish when it surrendered without any fighting in 1797. Only 36,000 acres were under the cultivation of sugar, coffee, cotton and cocoa. From 1783 the Spanish government had allowed the immigration of Catholics of any nation, so that there were a number of French royalist planters living there. The total population numbered less than eighteen thousand.

In the Dutch colonies of Berbice and Demerara-Essequibo, which had been founded about the same time as St Kitts and Barbados, about half the planters were British, who had moved there from their own colonies before and after the American War of Independence. The Dutch had founded no town, but this had been corrected by the French in their brief occupation between 1782 and 1784 when Stabroek (later Georgetown) was started. The plantations were devoted almost entirely to sugar, which thrived luxuriantly on the rich alluvial coastlands, protected by a typically Dutch sea-wall.

Differences of language, origin, law, religion and social custom existed to distinguish the new colonies from the old, and to these the British government added differences in constitution, for while in the acquisitions of 1763 elected assemblies were instituted, in St Lucia and Trinidad a form of Crown Colony government was set up, in which no assembly was to be allowed to cause the friction that had become traditional in the older colonies. To add spice to the variety Guiana kept its old Dutch constitution.

There was one common interest, however: all the colonies depended on the production of sugar by the labour of African slaves.

9

THE WEST INDIAN
SLAVE SOCIETY

The seventeenth-century living pattern described in Chapter Seven portrayed a society of pioneer colonists among whom slaves were becoming an important feature. A hundred years later the West Indian colonies had become completely dominated by the institution of slavery. In 1700 there were about 32,000 white inhabitants and 112,000 slaves in the English West Indies. By 1800 the figures were approximately 60,000 and 500,000 respectively, and about 15,000 free coloured persons of mixed race.

The cultivation of sugar-cane, which had created the demand for slave labour, had come to dominate the economy as much as the presence of slaves dominated the organization of society. The evil tide of slavery had reached its flood. Not only cane-fields were tilled by slave labour, but slaves had become a necessity in every walk of life: they waited at table, they combed their ladies' hair, nursed their children, and crept into their masters' beds; they ran shops and worked at trades, sailed boats and caught fish – all for their masters' profit. Ownership of slaves became a status symbol, while among the slaves themselves a man without a master was regarded as an object of derision. Slavery exerted an influence that West Indians could never recognize towards immorality, laziness, lack of initiative, callousness, egotism. Spoilt white children grew into little tyrants, speaking the Creole dialect with an accent indistinguishable from that of their slaves. Lady Nugent described in her journal a conversation with an unknown lady at a ball. To her remark that the air was much cooler than usual, the planter's wife replied, 'Yes, ma'am, him railly too fra-ish!'

It has been calculated that in the years between 1680 and 1786 more than two million Africans were shipped across the Atlantic and sold as slaves in the West Indian colonies. At Barbados the average annual immigration was 3,000, yet between the years 1700 and 1767, although more than 180,000 were brought in, the slave population only rose from 42,000 to 70,000. Planters reckoned that new slaves took three years to settle down and that losses of forty to fifty per cent would occur during that period. Over all, an owner could expect six deaths to occur for every live birth. Importation at a high rate was therefore necessary to maintain the labour supply or the whole sugar industry and its dependent trades would collapse. Prices of new slaves steadily rose. At Jamaica in 1689 the average price was £20; by 1745 it was £37 and in 1776, £50 sterling.

On arrival the slaves were sold by auction, stripped naked for purchasers to see the condition of the stock they were buying. Possibly on account of their relief that the dreadful voyage was over, slaves showed few signs of concern when they were sold. Then they were branded with their new owner's mark. Those of Codrington College carried the word SOCIETY (i.e. The Society for the Propagation of the Gospel) on their chests for the rest of their lives, a larger mark than the more usual initials that must have been painful to receive. (Later the Society ordered this brand to be discontinued.) Once branded the slaves were marched off to their estates and given names by the overseers, according to their tribal origin, personal characteristics, occupation or any whim that struck their new bosses: Mingo, Daphne, Fatima, Cato, Chocolate, Castoon, Coroo, Quobina, Mayfungo, Corrantee Quashey, Pawpaw Harry, Braveboy, Dumb, Sharper, Long Mary, Sloop Johnny, Cuffey (the) Potter, Quashey Hog (minder), Quashey (the) Boiler (man). According to each estate's custom the new slaves were allotted a hut or materials to build their own.

Coming from Africa, where clothing was more the exception than the rule, slaves in the West Indies were clad in the minimum. The most common material was 'osnaburg' canvas or linen (originally from Osnabruck in Hanover), brown, blue or white, of which the men were given a smock and the women a petticoat. In the cane-fields and about the estate they sometimes worked and walked naked, often laughing at the embarrassment of English visitors, who wore too many clothes anyway. In towns clothes had to be worn, sometimes just a blanket, or a jacket and trousers. Later in Barbados owners were required by law to provide at least a cap and drawers or a petticoat each year. Some gave more.

Plantation slaves were kept on minimum rations. The unpalatable 'loblolly' described by Ligon went out in favour of dry rations which the slaves prepared themselves. In the Leeward Islands slaves were issued with between four and nine pints of maize-flour and one pound of salt fish or half a dozen salted herrings a week. This meagre issue was supplemented by the ground provisions the slaves grew for themselves, but as cane cultivation spread, less and less land came to be spared for slave allotments, particularly in flat Barbados. In more mountainous St Kitts the allotments were pushed into the gullies and up the steep hill slopes. In Jamaica there was more land available and more was made of provision-grounds, so that

Saturday afternoons were reserved for their cultivation, whereas in the smaller islands Saturday was a full working day. Yet as the eighteenth century progressed reliance on imported food increased to such an extent that when supplies from the rebel colonies were cut off during the American War of Independence, three thousand slaves in the Leewards and fifteen thousand in Jamaica died of starvation. This disaster brought home to the planters the folly of relying on imported food. During that unhappy war the ackee and mango trees were transplanted from West Africa and India, to be followed in 1793 by the introduction of the breadfruit from Tahiti by Captain William Bligh. 'Pepper-pot', which was brought by the slaves from Africa and eventually found its way on to the planters' tables, the Jamaica dish of salt-fish and ackee, the Guyanese 'metagee', all favourites still today, owe their origin to the old slave diet.

As an illustration of the organization of slave labour, which followed a similar pattern in most of the islands, a description of what happened on the Codrington estates in Barbados may be taken as typical. In 1781 the Society for the Propagation of the Gospel owned 276 Negroes and hired twenty-nine more to work the two estates that supported the college. Two black drivers, Drummer and Johnny Sharry, were in charge of 'the great gang' of thirty-five men and forty-nine women who were employed in digging holes, planting, cutting and carrying the canes to the mills. Next a boy named Quawcoe Adjoe, and two women, Sue and Sarah Bob, led the second gang of ten boys and thirteen girls who performed the lighter work of planting maize, carrying cane trash to the boiling-house for fuel, turning manure and weeding. Old Dinah was driver to the 'meat-pickers', twenty-three boys and twenty-six girls of the third or 'hogsmeat' gang, employed in shovelling manure into the cane holes before planting, weeding, and gathering fodder for the livestock. The animals were stall-fed to save land for the canes so that slaves, in the Leeward Islands as well as in Barbados, were required to cut and carry grass growing on verges. The cattle, horses, mules and donkeys were used for working the cane-mills and carting produce. At Codrington ten men, five women, seven boys and one girl tended the animals or drove the carts.

Nineteen of the slaves waited on the white employees or cooked, nursed the sick and attended the piccaninnies too young to work. Seventeen men and one boy were employed at the sugar-works. Harry and Hog Dick put the canes into the mill; Billy Moore was the boiler, Tony General the clarifier. Cudjoe and Scipio were potters making the wooden curing pots. (The college and other estates in Barbados were exceptions in continuing to use pots for curing, for in other colonies the wet sugar was poured direct into the hogsheads, which had holes drilled in their bottoms to allow the molasses to drain away into cisterns underneath. The holes were then

Slavery and Abolition

A group of newly arrived slaves. After the horrifying voyage from West Africa they were glad to go ashore.

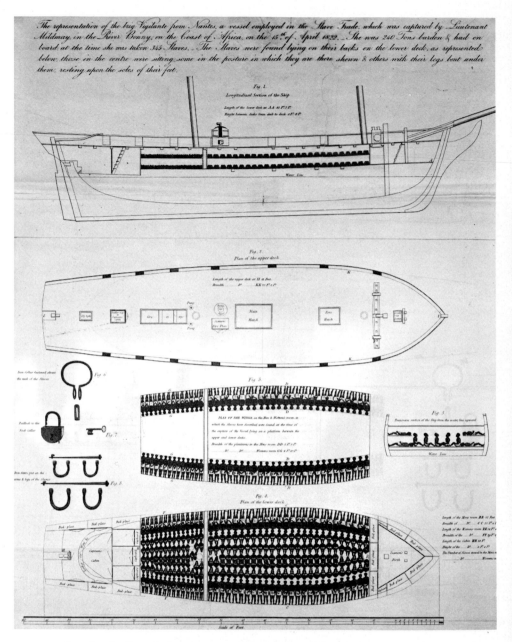

Details of a French slaver captured by the Royal Navy in West Africa in 1822 when slave trading had been declared illegal.

Top Captain Bligh's contribution to slave food was the breadfruit tree, introduced from Tahiti in 1793.

Bottom The ackee, another slave food brought to the West Indies from West Africa during the American War of Independence when thousands of slaves died from starvation as a result of the end of their imported food supplies from North America. Saltfish and ackee constitute the Jamaican national dish.

I would not have a Slave to till my ground

To carry me, to fan me while I sleep,

And tremble when I wake, for all the wealth

That sinews bought and sold, have ever earn'd.

We have no Slaves at home—why then abroad?

COWPER.

Anti-slavery propaganda. Slaves were not chained while working unless they had committed an offence.

O my great massa in heaven,
Pity me, and bless my Children!

The lot of the slave. It was a moot question whether they were much worse off than the English labourer at home.

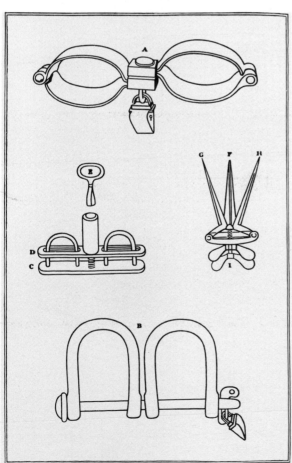

Top Newly purchased
slaves being branded.

Left Manacles used for
punishing slaves.

Above Examples of
branding irons.

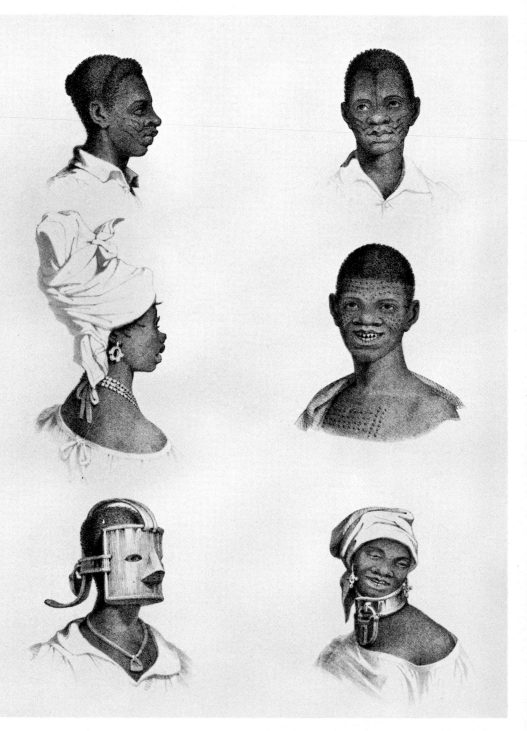

Negro heads sketched in Trinidad in 1851. The two lowest show how dirt eating and drunkenness were punished.

A peaceful scene on an Antigua mission station in mid-nineteenth century.

Top Slaves receiving news of their emancipation.

Bottom 'The New West India Dance' to the tune of £20,000,000, voted by Parliament for the compensation of the owners. The figure on the right is John Bull being presented with the bill. From the original lithograph by J. Doyle, 1838.

plugged before shipment.) Other employees were Sam the Basket-maker, Tackey and Quashey Madlew, smiths; John Bull, Caesar, Charles, Asia and the boy Rob were rangers and watchmen. At Codrington they were happy. As the abolition movement gathered momentum towards the end of the century, the Society were among the first owners to see to the improvement of conditions on their estates and their slaves took no part in the rebellion of 1816.

Of the 276 slaves owned by the Society, however, no less than fifty-four were exempt from labour. Forty-four were children and ten were too old or physically disabled. Thus one fifth of the slaves on these estates were unemployable, a testimony to the wastefulness of slave labour which men like Arthur Young attempted to point out and which the planters could not see. The human animal (for it was as an animal that they used the Negro slave) is the slowest animal to mature. While boys and girls were employed in light work – as African children still are used by their parents today – twelve years went by before they could be given a full day's work. In the 1780s the cost of maintenance of a field slave was calculated at approximately £5 sterling a year for food and clothing, but with all overheads, including purchase and maintenance in childhood and old age, the figure was nearer £10, and this was the annual wage paid by Parson Woodforde for a farm hand in Norfolk. The average wage of an English agricultural labourer at this time was £18 per annum. Slave labour was nowhere near as cheap as the planters supposed.

Slaves were hired by one owner from another. The Codrington trustees paid from sixpence to ninepence a day plus food, and a visitor to Antigua could hire a slave valet for eighteen shillings a month. Cooks, nursemaids, seamstresses and grooms were available for between £8 and £20 per annum – more than was paid for free servants in England. Slavery drove away the white tradesman and artisan. By the 1780s the white indentured servant had virtually disappeared.

In the first half of the eighteenth century the Codrington estates made a profit of £2,000 in a good year, but hurricanes, pests, floods and fluctuating sugar prices had to be contended with. Around 1780 the estates were only rescued from bankruptcy by the help of some of the leading Barbadian planters. In the nineties, with the introduction of the higher yielding Otaheite and Bourbon canes – also brought to the Caribbean by the obliging Captain Bligh – and the rising prices caused by the French Revolutionary Wars, prosperity returned: between 1814 and 1823 the average profits had risen to £4,000 a year. Bigger estates were much more profitable. In 1802 Lady Nugent stated that Hopewell Estate in St Mary, Jamaica, was worth £18,000 a year. In St Kitts in 1798 a 320-acre estate was offered for sale at £80,000 including buildings and slaves, and a ten-per-cent return could be expected. Many others, however, were in much less happy circumstances, heavily mortgaged until compensation paid at Emancipation enabled many mortgages to be cleared.

In the Leewards in the 1780s field slaves were worked from dawn until 9 am when they were given three-quarters of an hour for breakfast. At midday a break of one and a half to three hours was given, at the end of which each slave had to return with a bundle of grass for the estate's animals. Then they worked on until half an hour before sunset, when they were dismissed to gather another bundle. During crop time, however, they were often worked into the night. This was the routine for six days of the week. Sundays were free, and if this holiday was encroached upon slaves were paid. On this free day they usually went to market, selling the fruit and vegetables grown on their provision-grounds. Planters kept a wary eye open on these occasions, fearing that large market gatherings might turn into riots or even rebellion. Accordingly the militia provided patrols and let the slaves see that their masters were vigilant.

Because Sunday was the slaves' free day, when missionaries began work in the middle of the century they found the slaves reluctant to give up their free time for instruction and worship. Holidays were few. Christmas and Boxing Day were all that was given but individual owners occasionally declared an extra holiday. Thus when 'Monk' Lewis visited his Jamaica estates in 1815 he gave his slaves a holiday to mark his arrival and another before he sailed away.

In the course of time there developed a social distinction between mulatto and black slaves. The seventeenth-century practice of sending white indentured servants and black slaves into the fields together disappeared. As the white servants diminished, the increasing number of mulatto slaves took their place and gradually came to be excused from field labour altogether, being employed instead as artisans or domestic servants. Not that black slaves were never employed as personal servants: John Baker, Solicitor-General of the Leeward Islands in 1751 had a trusty personal attendant who gloried in the name of Jack Beef. Like many West Indians, when Baker visited England he took Jack Beef with him and used him like any white major-domo. Jack attended his master on horseback, was sent on shopping expeditions, and when the two Baker boys ran away from Winchester, it was Jack Beef who escorted them back to school. He was in great demand among John Baker's English friends for cooking turtles and bottling wines. He was on friendly terms with English servants, with whom he attended theatres. Eventually he was granted his freedom, but died before he was able to return to St Kitts.

Manumission was not uncommon in individual cases as a reward for faithful service. It was also possible for a slave to purchase his own freedom, but such cases were rare; it took a long time to save sufficient money from the meagre sales of produce in the Sunday markets.

Generally, domestic slaves were favourably treated. With a kind master they could live as happily as any white servants in England, so that Lady Nugent could say of the King's House slaves in Jamaica, 'I only wish the poor Irish were half as well off.' Those who transgressed, however, were severely disciplined. John Baker gave his slave Othello a severe whipping for sleeping out and another named Tycho 'a good smart one' for concealing it. A few pages on, his diary mentions, 'Uxor horse-whipped Patty [their ten-year-old daughter] for behaviour about minuit [midnight].' When the early abolitionists criticized the cruel use of the black drivers' short and long whips on the backs of lazy workers the planters pointed to the equally cruel flogging meted out to English soldiers and sailors.

The worst feature of the West India slave society was the poison worked into it by the planters' constant fear of the possibility of slave rebellions. As the slave population grew and the proportion of black to white inhabitants increased, the enhanced fear of rebellion led to mounting severity in the slave penal code. In Barbados a slave stealing anything of more than a shilling in value incurred the death penalty, but the sentence was usually compounded to save the destruction of valuable property. This consideration for property was responsible for a curious provision: an owner whose slave was executed for a criminal offence was paid compensation out of public funds.

Because of the planters' preoccupation with the danger of rebellion, slaves condemned for revolt received the most inhuman sentences. After the discovery of the great slave plot in Antigua in 1736, when the slaves had plans for blowing up all the white inhabitants attending a King's Birthday Ball, six were hanged, five were broken on the wheel and seventy-seven were burnt alive. The revolting punishment of castration introduced by the Leeward Islands legislature was quickly vetoed by the Lords of Trade and Plantations. Not without reason did Doctor Johnson refer to the West India planters as 'English barbarians', calling on his friends to drink a toast to the next insurrection in the West Indies. Yet the liberal-minded Lady Nugent, who was no lover of slavery, writing from her observations on the spot opined that the cruelties alleged by the abolitionists were exaggerated. On the way to church in Kingston she noted the heads of executed Negroes displayed on poles by the roadside but made no outraged comment. Nevertheless, the abolitionists exerted an ameliorating influence on the planters' treatment of their black property, for where at the beginning of the century no slave code existed, at the end of it most colonies had introduced laws regulating the treatment of slaves. Thus, whereas in Jamaica in 1725 all that happened to a white colonist killing a slave was three months' imprisonment and the payment of £50 compensation to the owner, by 1788 the mutilation of a slave was punishable by twelve months' imprisonment and a £100 fine, and slave-murder became a capital offence. Ten years later in the Leeward Islands the Assembly in the preamble to their Slave Amelioration Act could express their desire 'to extend every Blessing to a Race of People peculiarly under our Care and Protection'. In 1811, when news reached Governor Hugh Elliott (brother of Lord Minto, governor-general of India) that Arthur Hodge of Tortola had murdered sixty of his slaves by excessive punishment, he proceeded to Tortola in a warship, supervised Hodge's trial and witnessed his execution. Yet the year before in Nevis a planter named Edward Huggins, who had had thirty of his men and women slaves whipped in the public market place to the tune of 240 lashes each, was found not guilty of cruelty. The Nevis House of Assembly, however, passed a resolution describing Huggins's behaviour as 'an act of barbarity altogether unprecedented in this island . . . so disgraceful to humanity, so injurious to the fair character of the inhabitants, and so destructive of the best interests of the West India colonies'. The planters' consciences, after the abolition of the slave trade, were beginning to experience uncomfortable pricks.

Although unhinged individuals like Hodge and Huggins might behave in this way, the majority of owners had the sense not to damage or destroy their own property. It was on the estates of absentee proprietors that the worst treatment of slaves occurred, for the attorneys, managers and overseers were careless over their treatment of the absentees' slaves, who did not belong to them. Absenteeism was the greatest curse of the old West India society. It removed the men who should have been the leaders of the island communities and left second-rate individuals in charge. It had started with the Earl of Carlisle, Lord Proprietor of the Caribbee Islands, who never visited his estates, an example copied by the patent office holders who farmed out their posts to deputies. These men paid high prices for their appointments and then proceeded to mulct the colonists for as much as they could extort in fees. Consequently there was continual outcry against the patent offices. Bryan Edwards estimated that £30,000 in fees was remitted from Jamaica to England every year. Patent officers and absentee owners had their profits sent home and spent them in England instead of ploughing them back into their property in the colonies. As a result buildings and towns in the West Indies looked shabby and untidy. With the high proportion of wooden buildings fires were frequent and damaged buildings were left for long unrepaired. Although Monk Lewis found Montego Bay a neatly laid out and comparatively clean town, he could find no good word for Spanish Town the capital. 'The whole place wears an air of gloom and melancholy.' The King's House needed re-decorating and he did not like the fairly new Rodney Memorial. At the theatre he found an actor friend from Covent Garden and put the standard of performance on the same level with a good provincial theatre in England, but there was no orchestra – two fiddlers provided all the music. Kingston, he found, had a more cheerful atmosphere but the streets were dirty and unpaved. There was another theatre there.

Janet Schaw, the 'Lady of Quality' whose journal describes a visit to Antigua and St Kitts in 1774, liked the little town of St John's that rose from the harbour up a hill slope. Generally neat and pretty, it still bore the scars of the fire of 1769 and the hurricane of 1772. Public buildings were constructed of stone, and the church had an organ. Coming from Scotland Janet remarked on the low houses without chimneys. These were built on the street and friends passing by at meal-times would pop their heads in at the windows for a greeting and a chat. In contrast, Basseterre, St Kitts, had wooden houses set back from the street behind flower gardens. Janet landed at Basseterre from the back of a Negro slave who carried her through the surf. There was no large town in the West Indies at this time. Industrial development in the colonies was strongly discouraged by the English government as part of the mercantile system. Market towns and ports were all that could develop.

Although many of the considerable Jamaica planters kept a house in Spanish Town, they made the most of their great houses on the sugar estates, and a number of them have survived to the present day. Experience of hurricane and earthquake kept the buildings low and more than two storeys were rare. The main floor was raised from ground level by a terrace, often supported by rounded arches, access to which was provided by a double flight of stone steps leading to the verandas which surrounded the whole building and on which so much leisure-time was spent. One mile out of Basseterre and three hundred feet above the sea, Janet Schaw went to stay with her friend Lady Belle Hamilton at the Olivees. The house stood on a well-raised stone terrace paved with marble. Behind the spacious galleries and verandas was a great hall over fifty feet long with mahogany panelling and an ornamental ceiling. It was the scene of lavish hospitality. Behind it were the dining room and bedrooms, furnished in the English style. Few houses of the time had glass windows, because they stopped ventilation. Instead the jalousie was common, opened in fine weather like any window but capable of keeping out the rain without interfering with the ventilation. Many houses with exterior stone and brick walls had wooden partitions only nine or ten feet high dividing the rooms within. The tropics have always presented the choice between privacy or ventilation and not until the introduction of air-conditioning has it been possible to enjoy both. Monk Lewis was shaken at the first sight of his house on

Cornwall Estate near Savanna-la-Mar in Jamaica. It was entirely built of wood, raised on piles and completely lacking in privacy. Neighbouring houses were the same, 'absolutely transparent; the walls are nothing but windows and all the doors stand open. No servants are in waiting to announce arrivals: visitors, Negroes, dogs, cats, poultry, all walk in and out and up and down your living rooms without the slightest ceremony.' Even in the outside lavatory – 'The Temple of Cloacina' – latticed and pervious to the eye, old women passing would curtsy very gravely and say, 'Ah, massa! Bless you, massa! How day?' Most houses were roofed with wooden shingles, either imported from America or made locally. The days of corrugated iron, that abomination of the tropics today, had not yet begun. The approach to most houses was made impressive with avenues of coconut or royal palms and other trees.

The daily round started at dawn and most government business commenced at 7 am. The Nugents were very early risers, frequently 'up at gunfire', which was an hour before dawn when a gun was fired to notify ships outside that Kingston Harbour was open. On some days they were up at 4 am and off to Kingston or Stony Hill for a military review or down to Port Henderson opposite Port Royal for a row on the glassy water before breakfasting at the inn. Meal hours were elastic. If an early breakfast was eaten at 7 am, a second breakfast often followed it at 11 o'clock. Dinner was at any time between 3 pm and dusk, and there was usually a supper before bedtime. At every meal the men over-ate and drank too much. Although at breakfast there was tea, coffee and chocolate, most gentlemen insisted on drinking claret as well. Lady Nugent summed them up: 'The men of this country eat like cormorants and drink like porpoises.' In contrast most Creole women were extremely abstemious, eating little and rarely touching alcohol. This was probably the reason why on many occasions General Nugent and the men dined separately from Maria Nugent and the ladies. At midnight when the ladies took their leave the General slipped away, leaving the gentlemen 'to enjoy their bottle'.

In all the colonies there were frequent balls, at which, said Janet Schaw, 'all dance from fifteen to four-score', prolonging their enjoyment into the small hours. If there was no ball the men spent the time gambling. John Baker mentions winning sixty pistoles at Hazzard in Lindsey's Rooms in St John's, Antigua. There was cock-fighting, conducted on an inter-island basis, and even an occasional bear-baiting. Baker also enjoyed amateur dramatics and Janet Schaw went to a play given by professionals 'who had strolled right across the Atlantic'. By Lady Nugent's time racing had become well established in Jamaica. Prizes were provided by the Assembly to encourage the breeding of local thoroughbreds. She described a three-day meeting at Montego Bay. Two of the jockeys were white, the rest black, riding barefoot. It was a great occasion for the free blacks and mulattos who attended, 'dressed in the extreme caricature of English fashion, the females in muslins and ribbons of the gayest colours, with caps and turbans of the smartest silks and stuffs, silk stockings, and always red shoes, to which the shortness of their dresses gave ample display, and, above all, the gay parasols of green or pink, which the sable beauties displayed with infinite pride.' The 'gentlemen' wore blue coats with large brass buttons, waistcoats of silk or satin of the most gaudy pattern, set off by trousers of the whitest; but few wore shoes or stockings. Not only did they copy the white fashions: they affected their manners. 'How do, marm?' the black gallants greeted the ladies with deep bows hiding their broad smiles. 'Berry well, t'ank you, sah!' the black belles replied. There was little that escaped Maria Nugent's observant eye or her twinkling sense of humour.

On Sundays most townsfolk went to church, although there were times when no services were held because the parson was ill or the church was under repair. The clergy were a mixed bag, some good, others hardly qualified for their office. For Lady Nugent one service in Kingston was ruined by 'a Scots reader and a Welsh preacher'. At another in Spanish Town the preacher spoke 'of botany and astronomy as well as divinity ... more fit for the drawing room than the pulpit'. The Bishop of London, who was in charge of appointments to West Indian livings, had told General Nugent that it was difficult to persuade clergymen of character to accept livings 'when they are in dread of the climate'. It was the heyday of yellow fever.

Weddings and christenings were as often conducted in houses as in churches. When Captain Horatio Nelson was married in Nevis in 1787 the ceremony took place in the house of Montpelier, the home of his bride's uncle, John Herbert, president of the council of Nevis. It was an auspicious occasion, graced by the presence of Prince William Henry, the future William IV. Christenings often took place at night – the Nugents' first-born at 8.30 pm – and burials, always conducted with unceremonious haste in the tropics, were made round the plantation houses in the country, but in churchyards in the towns.

Inter-island travel in the Leeward Islands and the Windwards was made by schooner. In St Kitts a system of post-horses enabled John Baker, returning from St Croix, to land at Sandy Point in the north-west and reach Basseterre three hours later. In Jamaica the basis of the modern trunk road system existed but in a very indifferent state of repair. In 1802 the Nugents set out on a grand tour of the island that took them forty-eight days to complete. At only nine places did they spend more than one night and their average daily journey measured between twenty-five and thirty miles.

At each stopping place they were joined by the local planters in an immense cavalcade. Lady Nugent travelled in a carriage. At St Ann's Bay the governor left her to return to Spanish Town on government business. Two days later when he returned he had covered the forty miles in six hours in a gig over the two-thousand-foot Mount Diablo. Laconically, his wife noted, the poor horse died. George Nugent was a man of tremendous energy who left a trail not only of dead horses but prostrate staff behind him.

Sometimes road travel could be dangerous. A favourite resort of the Nugents was Mr Murphy's estate called The Decoy near the present Guy's Hill. On one occasion a kittereen went over a precipice on the hill known as the Devil's Racecourse and on another a sudden flood that came down the Rio Magno caught her ladyship in the middle of a ford. The local member of the Assembly gallantly rescued her and her baby. Admiral Duckworth, who was in attendance, got out on one of the carriage horses, but Lady Nugent's English maid was half-drowned before she reached the bank. Then behind an improvised screen the women stripped and rubbed themselves down with rum to prevent themselves from catching a cold. A more enjoyable experience was breakfasting at the Ferry Inn, halfway between Spanish Town and Kingston, and watching the travellers go by in kittereens and sulkies, on mules and donkeys. When Monk Lewis went from Savanna-la-Mar to Kingston he travelled in a kittereen and the journey took him three days of hard driving. Conch shells were blown on winding stretches of the road. Over the May Day Mountains he had to employ no less than seven horses and two mules, for the old roads in Jamaica went straight up and down the mountains and were not gently graded as the main roads are today. Inns and taverns of varying quality provided accommodation and changes of horses.

In none of the journals quoted is there any mention of absenteeism. Both Sir Nicholas Lawes, an earlier governor of Jamaica, and Edward Long, the historian, attributed it to the lack of schools. Long reckoned that three-quarters of the Jamaica planters sent their children to school in England and that barely half of them ever came back. Steps taken to discourage absenteeism met with no success. It varied from colony to colony. There were more resident proprietors in Barbados and Antigua than there were in St Kitts, but Jamaica was the hardest hit. In the French colonies there was a comparable situation: in Martinique and Guadeloupe most owners were resident but Saint Domingue suffered from absenteeism as much as Jamaica. There was one result that proved beneficial, not perhaps to the colonies but to Britain. When the American War of Independence broke out the large number of West Indian colonists living in England explained why the West Indies did not join the mainland colonies in their rebellion. They certainly objected to the English government measures that incensed the Americans, but the only action taken was the passing of resolutions of sympathy with the rebels.

Absentee owners appointed attorneys – either neighbouring estate owners or lawyers living in the towns – who left the running of the estates to managers or overseers, and 'book-keepers'. The attorney received a fee of six per cent of the sales of produce from the estate, but as managers were paid salaries of only £150 to £200 and book-keepers, £80 to £100, there was a strong temptation to enrich themselves at the absentee owner's expense until they had made enough money to become proprietors themselves. Monk Lewis, on his visit to his estates, commented on the unreliability of managers and the necessity of owners to make periodic inspections.

While managers might stand in trepidation of an owner's visit, the slaves welcomed it. Monk Lewis was greeted with cries of 'So long since none come see we, Massa; good Massa come at last!' So he gave them two heifers, rum and sugar for a feast and they kept him awake with their Johnny Canoe charades and dancing until the small hours. . . .

An exceptional planter was Samuel Martin, whom Janet Schaw met in Antigua in 1774. This charming old man spent no less than seventy of his eighty-six years on the island. His Negroes were healthy and well treated. He was 'a kind and beneficent master, not a harsh and unreasonable tyrant'. His slaves had increased so much that he had not had to buy a new slave for twenty years. His household slaves had been freed and waited on him with alacrity and devotion.

In addition to the influence of the abolitionists, the appearance of missionaries at the middle of the century contributed to the gradual amelioration of the slaves' living conditions. The spearhead had undoubtedly been the work of the SPG on the Codrington estates in Barbados. The founder of the college had wanted to see his slaves converted to Christianity without any consideration for their emancipation. Just as there had been slaves among the early Christians he saw no incompatability between Christianity and slavery in the eighteenth century. Towards the slaves' conversion the SPG went cautiously to work. Not until 1728 was the first baptism recorded, but five years later there were fifty-eight Christian slaves on the college estates. Among the colonial clergy there was no idea of working among the slaves, any more than their contemporaries in England felt any call to concern themselves with the workers in the new industrial towns.

The first missionary society to operate in the West Indies was the Church of the United Brethren or the Moravians, who within ten years of their foundation in Saxony had opened a mission in the Danish West Indies in 1732. From there by 1774 they had expanded their work into Jamaica,

Antigua and St Kitts. Like the beneficent Codrington they held no objections to slavery. In 1739 when Count Zinzendorff, the founder of the Moravian church, visited St Thomas he addressed the slaves as follows: 'God punished the first Negroes by making them slaves, and your conversion will make you free, not from the control of your masters, but simply from your wicked habits and thoughts and all that makes you dissatisfied with your lot.'

Moravian missionaries were always meticulous in their support of the civil power. So too were the Methodists who appeared in the West Indies at this time. Although John Wesley their founder declared himself against slavery Doctor Thomas Coke who arrived in 1786 to take charge of the Methodist missions modified the Wesleyan policy to accept the *status quo* and achieved successful expansion into the Windward Islands and Jamaica. By 1800 it was reckoned that one-quarter of all the slaves in the Leeward Islands were Christians.

Meanwhile on the Codrington estates in Barbados a number of other measures had been taken to improve the lot of the college slaves. The man mainly responsible was a far-sighted planter named John Blathwayt who leased the estates from the society from 1783 to 1793. Under his direction thatched stone quarters were provided, a better hospital was built and more land was turned over to slave allotments. Field labourers, no longer sent into the cane-fields in the rain, were issued with a daily tot of rum and a more generous scale of clothing. In consequence the number of slaves on the college estates showed a steady increase from 266 in 1793 to 355 thirty years later, without any new purchases being made. Whether the college set the pace it is difficult to determine, but similar policies were practised on other Barbadian estates with the result that between 1800 and 1833 the island slave population increased from 60,000 to 82,902. Humane treatment had been proved to be profitable.

Less spectacular increases occurred in other colonies so that the end of the supply when the slave trade was abolished in 1807 was not the disaster at first predicted by the planter interest. In this way the tactics of William Wilberforce proved successful: the end of the trade forced the planters to ameliorate the treatment of their slaves sufficiently to encourage them to breed. In this the missionary influence that demanded Christian marriage helped. Previously slave women had had no incentive to raise families; in fact, abortion and primitive methods of birth control had been practised.

On the promiscuous unions of white owners and overseers with attractive female slaves there was no restriction. Few writers of the time say much about it, but reading between the lines elucidates the position. By 1787 in Jamaica there were ten thousand free coloured people and over two hundred thousand slaves. As the child of a slave woman was born a slave, and the coloured people who were returned as free had either became so by manumission or were the issue of free coloured men and women, the presence of such a number of coloured people indicates the scale of miscegenation that had been going on. In Barbados about the same time there were about two thousand free coloureds. Illegitimate births were not confined to unions of mixed race: the respectable Christopher Codrington was careful to make provision in his will for his illegitimate son in Antigua, and John Baker mentioned illegitimacy in St Kitts. There was never any *marriage* between the races. Bryan Edwards explained: 'No white man of decent appearance, unless urged by the temptation of considerable fortune, will condescend to give his hand in marriage to a Mulatto: the very idea is shocking.' But most white men kept coloured mistresses – housekeepers, they were conveniently called – and in consequence of the shortage of brown women caused by this, free men of colour were forced to seek their wives and concubines among the black women slaves.

When Lady Nugent went on tour with her husband she met no white women between Kingston and Port Antonio; every night she was attended by mulatto ladies and recorded in her diary, 'The usual mulatto evening levee.' By the time the Nugents reached St Mary's Parish she became more explicit: 'they are all daughters of Members of the Assembly.' Army officers, too, added to the brown flood, and meetings with 'the half-black progeny of our staff' were faithfully recorded in her journal. A captain had died, leaving everything to his Jamaica black mistress and her children 'to the neglect of his children in England. . . . This is, I am afraid, too common a case in Jamaica.' Maria Nugent accepted the situation as the custom of the colony, but she did not condone it. Anxious to have her own King's House slaves baptized, she did not see how the Negroes could be expected to mend their morals as long as white overseers made free use of the female slaves. Thirty years earlier Janet Schaw, that 'Lady of Quality' had been shocked by the number of mulattos she saw in Antigua.

The free coloured people found themselves in an unenviable position. They were not socially acceptable, but they were expected to do their civic duty, like serving in the militia, without the enjoyment of any rights. In their turn the free coloureds came to despise the free blacks until there arose a caste system, in which the superiority of mulatto over black, of quadroon over mulatto, of octoroon over quadroon went on until a lucky combination of genes might produce a skin that could pass as the privileged white. Eventually the free coloured people of the Leeward Islands petitioned for political and legal equality with the white colonists, objecting to 'that policy which keeps the Coloured inhabitants at such an immeasurable distance from their Fathers, Brothers and Relations, the other inhabitants'. To their credit, the white colonists peacefully conceded. There was, of course, no move on the part of the coloured people to improve the lot of the slaves; they themselves were slave-owners, and few men, unless their minds are touched, give away their belongings.

From time to time the worst fears of the planters materialized in slave rebellions. They occurred in all colonies but with varying frequency. Thus there were twelve slave revolts in Jamaica during the century, but in Barbados none between 1702 and 1816. In the Leeward Islands there were few. Jamaica headed the list because of its greater size; its wild mountain interior provided an ideal refuge for runaways. Because of the rugged mountains there survived those fascinating communities known as the Maroons. Originating with the slaves set loose by the Spaniards in 1655 and augmented by runaways from the early English plantations, they had caused little nuisance until the gradual development of the colony had led to the settlement of the interior. In 1690 a serious slave revolt in the parish of Clarendon threw up a squat, strong and resourceful leader named Cudjoe, a Coromantee slave from what is now Ghana. For forty years Cudjoe and his runaway band conducted a series of raids from the mountains of upper Clarendon, having little to do with the original Spanish Maroons who were quartered on the northern slopes of the Blue Mountains at the legendary Nanny Town, built on the brink of a nine-hundred-foot drop above the confluence of two tributaries of the Rio Grande.

In 1730 the sporadic warfare against Cudjoe was intensified with the object of exterminating his guerrilla bands and with them the Maroons of Nanny Town. Two regular regiments were transported from Gibraltar, a bounty of £10 was offered for each Maroon's head brought in, and Indian trackers from the Moskito Coast were recruited. It was calculated that

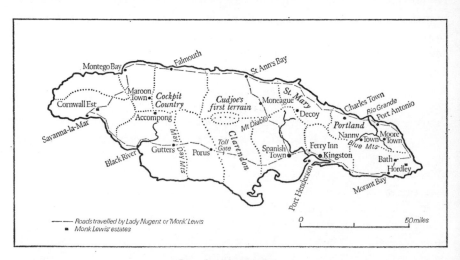

Jamaica about 1800

operations against Cudjoe over the previous forty years had cost the colony £240,000. Plantation life in the interior had been seriously disrupted and travel had become dangerous. By this time, however, Cudjoe's men had become experts in guerrilla warfare, trapping militia forces sent against them in ambush after ambush, and melting into the woods when pursuit became too hot. Cudjoe's main problem was the replenishment of his food and ammunition. The women cultivated concealed provision grounds, and raids on plantations, carefully planned with information from friendly slaves, produced the ammunition. A border life like that in the American colonies in conflict with the Red Indians became the order of the day, or, to take a twentieth-century example, similar to conditions in Kenya during the Mau-Mau rebellion.

In 1734 British troops succeeded in destroying Nanny Town by bombardment from swivel-guns lugged to the top of the Blue Mountain peak that still bears the name of the Captain Stoddart who was in charge of the battery. After the end of Nanny Town most of the survivors made the long trek over well-nigh impassable mountain country to join forces with Cudjoe. But the hunt was on. A ring of fortified posts was constructed round Cudjoe's country and tactics of destroying the Maroons' provision-grounds were adopted. A special corps of Rangers was created together with a company of trustworthy slaves known as the Confidential Black Shot. In desperation Cudjoe broke westwards into the terrible Cockpit Country, a plateau of two hundred square miles of honeycomb limestone, where deep sinks or dolines are separated from one another by precipitous ridges of saw-toothed rock. In spite of the absence of top-soil the ridges are covered in forest with trees growing straight from cracks in the rock. It was a guerrilla's paradise with only one drawback – an acute shortage of surface water. At two places where permanent springs existed the Maroons settled: in Petty River Bottom in the north-west and in the south at Accompong, named after one of Cudjoe's brothers. From these two fastnesses all military efforts failed to dislodge them.

Eventually in 1739 diplomacy succeeded where force had failed. A treaty was made with Cudjoe, by which the Maroons were granted 1,500 acres round Petty River Bottom and another thousand at Accompong. On these reserves Cudjoe enjoyed complete jurisdiction except for the death penalty. But there was a price to pay for their autonomy. The Maroons engaged to capture and return runaway slaves and to assist in the suppression of slave rebellions. More, their chiefs were required to wait upon the governor once a year, and a white superintendent was to be quartered in each settlement. The white planter government had successfully achieved a classic example of the maxim 'divide and rule'! It was a Maroon who captured Tacky, the leader of the great slave rebellion of 1760, and another who apprehended

Paul Bogle, leader of the Morant Bay insurrection of 1865. It is strange that the Maroons accepted these conditions, but they were exhausted and their women and children were starving. In the excitement of hunting runaway slaves they found an outlet for their spirits which had thrived so long on warfare. Cudjoe, who had led his people through fifty years of struggle, lived on in peace for a long time. In 1764 when well over eighty he waited on Governor Lyttleton at Montego Bay.

A few months after Cudjoe's peace, similar negotiations led to a treaty with the Windward Maroons – the remnant from Nanny Town – who had remained unsubdued in the Blue Mountains under their leader, Quao. They were accorded recognition for their settlements at Moore Town and Charles Town. The chiefs of the four settlements were called colonels, and on the model of the colonial militia they had a major and two captains under them. In 1802 General Nugent visited the Maroons of Moore Town and Charles Town in Portland Parish, who entertained him with feasts of jerked and barbecued hog, plantains and yams, their favourite delicacy. The annual visits of the Maroons to Spanish Town became picturesque occasions with the visitors dressed in finely laced coats, ruffled shirts and flowered waistcoats, gifts to them on previous calls on the governor.

In 1795 a second Maroon War broke out with the inhabitants of Trelawney Town, as Cudjoe's settlement had come to be called. Sensible treatment could have prevented fighting, but the Earl of Balcarres, the then governor, adopted an uncompromising attitude because the usual planters' fears had been augmented by rumours that agitators had landed from Haiti, then in turmoil as a result of the French Revolution. Once again after military operations had proved a failure, the officer in command, Major-General George Walpole, persuaded the Maroons to surrender on the understanding that there would be no question of deportation in the penalties imposed upon them. But Lord Balcarres and his advisers over-ruled Walpole's undertaking with the result that over five hundred men, women and children were deported. It is almost incomprehensible that they were sent to Halifax in Nova Scotia with its hard winters. Although there were scarcely any deaths from cold, the Maroons refused to work in the barren surroundings until four years later they won their petition to be transferred to Sierra Leone. A few of their descendants returned to Jamaica later. To his credit Walpole refused the gift of £500 for a sword voted by the Jamaica Assembly. Lord Balcarres took the £700 voted to him. Although he was popular with the planters, the discerning Lady Nugent was horrified by his filthy fingers at the table and the Augean stable that the King's House had become during his bachelor tenancy. Significantly, he kept a little black pig as a pet!

Similar conditions to those created by the Jamaica Maroons prevailed on a smaller scale from the presence of Caribs in St Lucia, 'Black Caribs' in St Vincent, and escaped slaves called Maroons in Dominica. Their presence disquieted the planters and in the French Revolutionary Wars provided fruitful ground for disturbances encouraged by *agents provocateurs* from Guadeloupe. Together with the Jamaica Maroons these isolated communities provide interesting examples of the influence of geography on history; they could never have survived without the forested mountain country that formed their refuge. In Jamaica Cudjoe and his marauding bands were partly responsible for the slow development of the colony in the first half of the eighteenth century. The service of his successors in hunting runaway slaves and suppressing rebellions built a social barrier between the Maroons and the majority of the Jamaican people that has led to the continuation of their proud, peaceful and dignified semi-isolation today.*

Distasteful as it is to present-day thinking, it must be admitted that the West India slave society worked, and produced the great wealth that helped to finance the revolution in industry which turned Britain into a modern state. The exports of sugar, coffee, cotton and other tropical products helped to finance the defeat of Napoleon, for by 1810 Britain controlled all the Dutch and French colonies except Saint Domingue, as well as her own. It was not entirely a coincidence that the slave trade was abolished two years after Trafalgar, because the command of the sea enabled Britain to enforce the abolition. Only after the peace was signed did competition arise with the countries that had not abolished the trade, but the cry of the planters that the sugar colonies were being ruined was drowned by the rising demand for emancipation. This social revolution destroyed the eighteenth-century West India society, which, profitable though it was, had always been rotten to the core. There was nothing noble about it. Although it worked, it was abominably wasteful: unwilling slave labour was only made productive because of compulsion and cruelty. Although the physical suffering of the African slaves was great, the effect on the white colonists was more subtle; it enervated and demoralized them. When a distasteful task had to be done hands were clapped for a slave to come and do it. As for the island militias, although they had fought with distinction in the wars at the turn of the century, by the end of it they were ridiculed by regular soldiers because the militiamen had slaves to carry their arms. Languid white women were waited on hand and foot by black girls. Extravagance

* When the author visited Accompong many years ago, he was welcomed by Major Hamilton, the deputy of Colonel Rowe, the then commandant. There was a well-attended school, in which the children, with their uniformly black, smiling faces, showed little of the racial mixture so evident in most parts of the island. (There was a unique cricket field sloping steeply on either side of the wicket which ran along a ridge. A breadfruit tree at square leg was worth two runs when hit.)

and peculation were rife and public duties were undertaken too often only because of the personal advantages to be extracted from them. When the abolitionists finally succeeded in emancipating the slaves, they freed the white colonists from the moral ruin into which slavery had been steadily dragging them.

10
EMANCIPATION

The details of the campaign for the abolition of slavery, fought in Britain under the leadership of William Wilberforce and Thomas Fowell Buxton, do not concern this social history of the British in the Caribbean. The effects of that campaign, however, causing as they did a major social revolution in the British West Indies, are very much to the point.

In 1823, the foundation year of the Anti-Slavery Society, the British government announced its resolve to work towards the abolition of slavery. Forthwith it started to exert pressure on the various colonial legislatures to pass ameliorating laws, such as a ban on carrying whips by gang drivers. In reply the colonists resisted, not so much because they were opposed to amelioration as because they considered that such demands constituted interference in their domestic affairs. As far as the treatment of the slaves was concerned, the colonial assemblies had all introduced *codes noirs* from before the abolition of the slave trade, but the effectiveness of such laws was doubtful as long as they were interpreted by planters sitting as honorary magistrates on the island benches. As for emancipation, the idea was greeted with full-throated cries of horror from every colony: it would mean the ruin of the British West Indies, the sugar trade and the merchant navy. Typical of the prophets of ruin was the father of young Elizabeth Barrett, whose family had owned land in Jamaica since the time of Penn and Venables. Born Edward Moulton, whose mother was a Barrett of Cinnamon Hill, Trelawny, the father of the poetess changed his name to Moulton-Barrett in 1798 on succeeding to his grandfather's Jamaica properties. In May 1833 Elizabeth wrote to a friend, 'The West Indians are irreparably ruined if the Bill passes. Papa says that in the case of its passing, nobody in his senses would think of even attempting the cultivation of sugar, and that they had better hang weights to the sides of the island of Jamaica and sink it at once. . . .' Another member of the family, the Honourable Richard Barrett, Custos of St James and Speaker of the

Jamaica Assembly, served on the Jamaica delegation to the English Parliament before the fatal Abolition Act was passed.

In the colonies the planters gave full voice to their fears, caring little what their servants overheard because they credited them with little intelligence or interest in the issues at stake. As early as 1816 there had been a slave rising in Barbados, caused largely by rumours among the slaves that freedom was coming but the planters were delaying it. Although only one white man was killed, considerable damage was done to buildings and works, so that harsh measures were taken. Several hundred slaves were killed in fighting or in executions afterwards and over one hundred were deported. Again in 1823 there was a considerable insurrection in Demerara and, in 1831, in north-west Jamaica, both caused by rumours similar to those that had disturbed Barbados. Although only two whites in Guiana and, three in Jamaica were murdered, the planters, taking the revolts as proof of their hallucinatory fears, indulged in orgies of retaliation.

In Demerara the prompt action of an east-coast estate manager in informing the governor that his personal slave had told him of plans for a Negro rebellion led to equally prompt action on the part of the governor, Brigadier-General Murray. Within a few hours a cavalry squadron of the militia was carrying a warning along the coast. Murray went out himself and met a large crowd of slaves a few miles from Georgetown. They refused to disperse. Murray returned to Georgetown, dispatched a detachment of the 21st Fusiliers and the 1st West India Regiment and declared martial law. Minor military operations followed in which over one hundred rebels were killed at the cost of a few soldiers wounded. In less than a week the revolt was over. Then the courts martial started, as a result of which forty-seven Negroes were hanged. But the principal figure of the trials was the Rev. John Smith of the London Missionary Society who was accused of instigating the revolt. He was given as fair a court martial as it was possible for anybody to be given. No planter was appointed as a member of the court and Smith was allowed legal advice. Nevertheless he was found guilty and sentenced to be hanged, subject to confirmation by the home government. In the long delay caused by the slow communications of the day Smith died in gaol of consumption. Although the abolitionists made the maximum capital out of the affair, the British government commended the local authorities for their firm handling of a dangerous situation. Though his sentence had been confirmed, Smith had been commended to mercy and deportation from the West Indies.

The local planters made their views explicit, voting generous presents to the various officers who had distinguished themselves, capping their gratitude with a vote of 1,200 guineas to Governor Murray. William Arindell and the Rev. W. S. Austin, who had respectively represented

Smith and protested a belief in his innocence, were socially ostracized to such an extent that Austin was compelled to resign his appointment in the established church. The planters campaigned for the deportation of all Nonconformist missionaries, but they reserved their special hostility for those of the London Missionary Society, in much the same way as their Boer cousins were doing in the Cape Colony.

In Jamaica it was the Baptists whom the planters hated in particular. No less than fourteen Baptist and six Wesleyan chapels were burnt down after the insurrection of 1831. This was a bigger and more serious affair than the Demerara revolt, involving fifty thousand slaves. Their leader, Samuel Sharpe, was an intelligent slave and a member of the Baptist church. The militia panicked and retreated into Montego Bay. Regular troops suppressed the rebellion in operations which cost the lives of ten soldiers and over four hundred slaves. About one thousand slaves were hanged and a further thousand severely flogged. The Assembly assessed the damage at more than one million pounds. They blamed the revolt on the missionaries and the measures under contemplation by the home government. There was open talk of independence and joining the United States.

In spite of these disagreeable upsets progress towards emancipation went on until on 29 August 1833 the Abolition of Slavery Act, after passing through Parliament without a division, received the royal assent. It was a remarkable piece of legislation, doing the maximum justice to the principal parties concerned. It set the date of implementation at 1 August 1834, and allowed for an apprenticeship system, varying from four years for artisans to six years for field labourers, during which the freed slaves were to work without pay for their former masters. In return for their labour, the planters were to house, clothe and feed the apprentices and pay them a supplementary wage if they worked for more than forty-five hours a week. To protect the apprentices from the planters' magistracy, a force of salaried magistrates paid by the British government was appointed. Last, but by no means least, a sum of £20,000,000 was voted to pay the slave-owners compensation for the loss of their human property, provided the colonial assemblies passed laws to implement the apprenticeship system.

Eventually £16,500,000 was paid to the West Indian slave-owners, the balance going to Cape Colony and Mauritius. The sum for each colony was worked out on an intricate system involving the ratio of exports to the number of slaves. Thus between British Guiana and Barbados, where the number of slaves was nearly the same, there was a difference of over £2,000,000 in favour of British Guiana, the average working out at about £20 a head in Barbados and £50 in British Guiana. Jamaica, with the largest number of slaves, received over £6,000,000, but this averaged less than £20 a head. The individual assessments varied from £19 for the lowest field labourer in Jamaica to £230 for a headman in British Guiana. Naturally the planters were far from satisfied. Edward Moulton-Barrett was expecting £140,000; he got £20,000. This financial blow over emancipation is thought to have contributed as much as the loss of his wife to his misanthropy.

The following amounts of compensation were paid in each colony:

colony	number of slaves	compensation £
Jamaica	311,070	6,149,955
British Guiana	82,824	4,295,989
Barbados	83,150	1,719,980
Trinidad	20,657	1,033,992
Grenada	23,638	616,255
St Vincent	22,266	550,777
St Kitts	19,780	329,393
Dominica	14,175	275,547
Tobago	11,589	233,875
Nevis	8,815	151,006
Bahamas	10,086	128,296
Montserrat	6,401	103,556
British Honduras	1,901	101,399
Virgin Islands	5,135	72,638
Bermuda	4,026	50,409

Nevertheless, the compensation was useful, allowing the redemption of many mortgages under which the majority of sugar estates had been operating. Where it was inadequate was in the lack of provision of capital to allow the owners to adjust to paid labour and the anticipated reduction of the labour force at the end of the apprenticeship period.

When it came on 1 August 1834, Emancipation Day passed without violence in any of the colonies. For this considerable achievement the missionaries' influence was largely responsible, as the day was marked by thanksgiving services in all the churches. In Georgetown the governor, Sir James Carmichael Smyth, attended St George's Anglican church in the morning and St Andrew's Kirk in the afternoon. The freed slaves went to church too. Only in Trinidad was there rowdyism, but Sir George Hill, the governor, refused to declare martial law and no violence occurred.

The apprenticeship system proved a failure. Designed to guarantee labour to the planters and time for the slaves to prepare themselves for the responsibilities of complete freedom, it satisfied nobody. In Bermuda and Antigua, where the slave-owners had decided to dispense with apprenticeship, the slaves were given complete freedom in 1834. In British Guiana

Governor Smyth managed to keep the ex-slaves near Georgetown informed about the system, but in remote Essequibo they refused to continue working for their former masters until stern measures were taken. In Jamaica the planters sulked. In that large island and in British Guiana with its vast hinterland many apprentices decamped into the interior. The planters had been convinced that emancipation would spell ruin, so they made little effort to make a success of apprenticeship, taking no steps to build up good relations with their labour for the complete freedom scheduled for 1840. But there were exceptions, and where individual planters looked after their people they suffered no shortage of labour when complete freedom came. In the smaller islands there was less of a problem because there was no vacant land to which the Negroes could run away. Barbados, Antigua, St Kitts, St Lucia, Dominica and Grenada passed into freedom without labour problems and made no clamorous demands for immigration, as Trinidad, Guiana and Jamaica were to do. In the French colonies of Martinique and Guadeloupe, however, where slavery continued, guards had to be posted to prevent their slaves trying to escape by boat to the British islands. Martinique lost three thousand slaves in this way.

The abolitionists had always maintained that a slave economy was wasteful, so that when one of their leaders, Joseph Sturge, and his fellow Quakers, Thomas Harvey, John Scoble and William Lloyd, arrived in the West Indies towards the end of 1836 to see how apprenticeship was working, Sturge was delighted to find in Antigua planters who told him that they were making better profits with paid labour than they had done with slaves. He thought the Negroes' houses were poor, but Sunday observance impressed him. On Sundays it was not uncommon 'to see *ladies*, who had toiled under a burning sun during six days of the week, attired on the seventh in silk stockings and straw bonnets, with parasol and gloves, and the *gentlemen* in black coats and fancy waistcoats.' Once wages were paid the import trade increased, for the Negroes liked spending their money. One of the planters in favour of emancipation was Colonel Samuel Warner, president of the council of Antigua and a descendant of the founder of St Kitts.

The more sensible planters turned their attention to improved methods of cultivation. Sturge saw newly introduced ploughs in Antigua. In St Lucia on one estate he saw rows of cane planted five feet apart to allow the use of a horse hoe for weeding. Scots peasants were being recruited to demonstrate the plough and train Negroes in the use of it. On Christmas Day a military band played outside the officials' homes, including a tune called 'President Jeremie' composed by the Negroes.

One of the main principles written into the apprenticeship system by the abolitionists was that the planters should no longer have the right to punish their former slaves. Hence the appointment of the stipendiary magistrates. These were a mixed bag, their effectiveness varying from island to island. But if the planters were no longer able to give punishments, the apprentices, although protected in many ways, were severely punished if they misbehaved. Most gaols were equipped with dark cells, and treadmills upon which the progress of the prisoners was encouraged by touches from the cat-o'-nine-tails. For outside work there was the chaingang. This heinous code was not peculiar to the West Indies: it was copied from the current system in the United Kingdom; among the prisoners in two of the Jamaica gaols the Quakers noted English soldiers and sailors. Sturge and Harvey remonstrated with the authorities whenever they came upon excessive cruelty. It helped to add to their conviction that the apprenticeship system was merely a name disguising the legalized extension of slavery. Largely due to their representations on their return home, apprenticeship was terminated for field as well as domestic workers and artisans on 1 August 1838, the day ever since celebrated in the West Indies as the real Emancipation Day. The planters welcomed the end of apprenticeship as much as their erstwhile slaves.

The tour made by Joseph Sturge and Thomas Harvey – entirely at their own expense – was extensive. In Jamaica they travelled between one end of the island and the other and penetrated the fastnesses of the Blue Mountains, where they were duly impressed with the gorgeous scenery and the bird's-eye views over Kingston and the Liguanea Plain. In the Botanic Gardens in St Andrew they saw the trees brought to the island by Captain Bligh and in the mountains met Wiles, Bligh's former botanist. By then an old man, he told them how Rodney not only saved Jamaica from the French, but from a French prize presented the colony with mango seedlings – a service almost as valuable as his defence. With their firm belief in the Negro's capabilities they recorded with delight their meeting with the septuagenarian, Whitehall Ellis, the headman at Farm, Lord Carrington's well-run estate. He invited the Quakers into his house and offered them glasses of madeira. While still a slave, Ellis had himself owned nine slaves, twenty cattle and seventy sheep, officially registered as a free friend's property. He told a story against himself, relating how one of his slaves had stolen one of his cows, sold it in the Kingston market, and then half killed Ellis walking in the Ferry swamps where the missing animal was allegedly lost. It was a case of 'dog eating dog', as they might say in Jamaica. Sturge noticed with approval a black overseer on one of the Barrett estates and a coloured overseer, William Hamilton, at Lenox, near the St Elizabeth-Westmorland border. He had purchased his freedom for £209 and was the proud owner of seventy acres of his own land. Near Bath Thomas Harvey approved the sample of mountain-crab he tasted, described by Bryan Edwards as 'the most savoury and delicious morsel in nature'. The estate crab-catcher was expected to produce between fifty and sixty crabs a week.

At Bath there were more breadfruit trees, and over the Cuna Cuna Pass in the Rio Grande valley Harvey visited Altamont, where a recently established colony of Scottish immigrants were struggling to make a living. They reminded him of the 'red-shanks' he had seen in Barbados. He was suspicious of 'poor whites' having a demoralizing effect on the innocent Negroes; in Barbados there had been far too many rum shops. ... At Moore Town he noticed an interesting custom of the Maroons. For cultivating their plots they disdained to use the hoe as an emblem of slavery. Instead they used a cutlass. This custom has now spread all over the island, for the cutlass makes a versatile hand-tool: spade, trowel, hand-hoe and axe, all in one. Sometimes used as a cruel weapon of offence, it is a source of comfort when held in one's hand on a dark night, against enemies both of this and the spirit world.

When the slaves were freed they needed a surname as well as the single name or character names recorded in the estate slave book. Many took the names of their former owners, their estates or the towns near which they had lived. Some borrowed the name of the then governor. Hence the striking combination of black faces and British surnames. Where faces are brown there may be more intimate reasons. Christian names, under missionary influence, have been chosen from the Old Testament with the same relish that marked the enthusiasm of Puritan England in the seventeenth century.

Soon after 1838 the important social changes resulting from emancipation began to appear. The detailed picture is fogged. Where a living wage was paid the field worker stayed on his old estate, for his house and effects were there, but in many cases where the slave-owners vented their resentment at emancipation on their former slaves by paying them low wages – often months in arrears – or charging exorbitant house rents, the new freemen quietly packed up and left. In Jamaica all land had been taken up by 1815, but before 1833 sugar production had begun to fall away in the face of competition from new estates in Java and Cuba. After 1838 the competition became harsher as the British West Indies turned over to paid labour and the higher cost of production it entailed. Between 1836 and 1846 157 Jamaica sugar estates were abandoned. Thus land became available, but the government had no plans worked out for peasant proprietorship and many planters were reluctant to sell land to Negroes. It was here that the missionaries stepped in to help their converts, spearheaded by the Baptists under the leadership of William Knibb. By 1842 between 150 and 200 Free Villages had been founded on 100,000 acres of land. By 1845 when

Knibb died there were 19,397 small holdings of less than ten acres each. As an example, John Clark the Baptist minister at Brown's Town bought 120 acres for £700. This land was divided between eighty or ninety people who paid £400 down between them – an interesting sidelight on the comparative prosperity of the slaves – and settled the balance by instalments. When the land had been paid for, church, school and mission house were built. As for a name, on Clark's suggestion, the new settlement was called Sturge's Town, in honour of the Quaker abolitionist. Other villages were named for Wilberforce, Clarkson and Buxton. Still more were christened with the happy optimism in which they were founded: Liberty Valley, Content, Fellowship, Harmony, Friendship Castle, Amity and Unity. Others were given a religious flavour: Wesleymount, Bethlehem and Mount Zion. And there were those of a more cryptic character including Hard Bargain, Bold Attempt, Come See, Needs Must, Wait-a-bit and Shambles. Emancipation has left its stamp on the modern map of Jamaica.

In British Guiana similar settlements were made on abandoned sugar estates where the land was communally purchased and divided among the new peasant proprietors. Once again they received no government assistance and the missionaries did far less than those in Jamaica. In consequence the new villages, although not named so, often became shambles, with drainage canals blocked by mud and debris, and dams and sea-walls crumbling in decay; and yet life was easy. Mangoes and guavas dropped from the trees and fish were not difficult to catch in the rivers and canals. Planters complained that the Negroes would not work and cut down the fruit trees to force them into it. The cry went up that echoed down the years into the twentieth century that the black man was lazy and stopped work as soon as he had earned enough to fill his belly. Nobody understood how to attract labour; nobody realized that malaria sapped energy; nobody knew that mosquito bites caused malarial infection. And yet it was true that in Guiana life was easier than in the islands, for that flat country is seldom visited by hurricane or earthquake.

With the exception of Trinidad, where new villages were formed, in the Lesser Antilles there was no spare land in the small mountainous islands for peasant settlement. Their proprietorship developed slowly as estates came on to the market. In Barbados Sturge noted as an exception a coloured owner of seven and a half acres who had a small sugar-mill and boiling-house, at which he ground other people's cane as well as his own. Ex-slaves in crowded Barbados were lucky if they could boast of owning half an acre. Those who grew sugar-cane usually took it to the nearest planter's mill, where a custom originating in the French islands came to be adopted: in return for the use of the mill the owner took one-third of the peasant's canes. Known as the metayer system, this arrangement spread through most of the small islands and lasted into the twentieth century. If the canes were cultivated on estate land the grower received half instead of two-thirds of the sugar and a bottle of rum for every sugar barrel filled.

Almost as great as the demand for land was the need for education. The foundation of the handful of trust schools has been mentioned in Chapter Eight but these were for secondary education. What was needed was the most rudimentary grounding in the 'three Rs'. To their credit the abolitionists had made provision for this, abstracting from the British Parliament, in addition to the £20,000,000 compensation and the salaries of stipendiary magistrates, a Negro Education Grant. An annual sum of £30,000 for five years was voted, followed by a diminishing grant which was to terminate in 1845. The object was to provide buildings for which the various missionary societies would find the teachers, as well as one-third of the building costs. In addition Zachary Macaulay, secretary of the London Anti-Slavery Committee, secured from the Charity Commissioners the application of the trust founded by Lady Mico in 1670 for the redemption of English slaves in the hands of the Barbary pirates, a cause for several years extinct. In 1835 there was £115,000 in the fund. The Mico commissioners went to work with lightning speed. Within a fortnight of his arrival in Kingston in December 1835, the Rev. J. M. Trew announced the opening of the first Mico 'normal' school. He had brought from England a nucleus staff of three married couples and two bachelors. After six months' training the teachers were sent out to start new primary schools and two more normal schools were opened. This resulted in a mushroom growth, not only in Jamaica but in every colony. Trew, proving himself a great organizer, left a young deputy, Edwin Wallbridge, in charge at Kingston and went to visit the schools in the south Caribbean. In 1841 he called a conference of Mico superintendents at Antigua, where it was decided that with the end of the parliamentary grant the Mico Charity should hand over to the missionary societies all the primary schools except those in St Lucia and concentrate only on teacher-training at Antigua and Jamaica. In 1845 the Kingston Mico College, which incidentally can claim to be one of the earliest training institutions in the New World, reduced the number of male students in training to fifteen and increased the length of the course to three years. The aim was to produce quality, not quantity.

Among the 158 Mico trainees from the crash courses of its first decade there were nineteen European men (including eight discharged soldiers), two European women, ninety 'Native Males', and forty-seven 'Native Females'. Trew had relied on the recruitment of coloured teachers, but had been disappointed in their tendency to drift away into other occupations. A main cause of this was the low salaries paid – an unfortunate tradition that has persisted in Jamaica. The lay teachers, as distinct from the missionaries, were also accorded a low status. Joseph Sturge, referring to coloured orphan girls at school who were destined for the teaching profession, added 'but when that class is sufficiently numerous, they will be placed out as domestic servants'.

Conditions at Mico were strenuous. The students' day started in the dark at 5 am with three hours' work before breakfast. After an hour's break another three hours were put in until noon, when only fifteen minutes were allowed for second breakfast or lunch. All through the hot tropical afternoon classes continued until dinner at 5 pm. At 5.30 pm, without thought of indigestion, there was an hour's physical exercise, followed by family reading and prayers. At 7 pm the students started 1½ hours' private study to complete a 15½-hour day. Lights went out at 9 pm. This regimen was nothing less than the application of estate slave hours to teacher-training and it lasted well past the middle of the century. In 1882 the Mico day stretched from 7 am till 9.30 pm with a half-holiday on Saturday. In 1896 Wednesday afternoons became free after 2.45 pm. There was no lying in on Sundays: the day started at 7 am with an hour and a half of scripture and vocal music, and there was to be no bathing during the day.*

In 1870 the number of students was increased to thirty, in 1891 to eighty, including men from other colonies. For women students, who had been excluded from Mico in 1839, there were no training facilities until Shortwood College opened in 1883. In Trinidad the government college, opened in 1852, kept more reasonable hours, with sessions from 7 to 9 am, 10 am till noon, 1 to 3 and 6 to 8 pm. It is sensible to start the day early in a tropical climate.

Long before Mico College was founded, the missionary societies, led by the Moravians, had attempted to provide education for the slaves, but the long estate hours for six days a week left no time for schooling except at night and on Sundays, where the only subjects allowed on religious principle were Bible study and catechism. At least this taught some to read.

In 1824 when the dioceses of Jamaica and Barbados were formed, the Anglican church turned from its former pro-planter attitude to consider the needs of the black people of the islands. When Sturge visited Barbados in 1837 the bishop told him there were eight thousand children in his church schools under black and coloured teachers. During the four years of the apprenticeship scheme, when children under the age of six were

---

* Long hours became another Jamaica tradition. When the author took up a teaching appointment in the island in 1934 his time-table consisted of teaching forty out of forty-four periods and an hour and a half of scripture on Sundays – without the vocal music.

immediately emancipated, a start was made with infant education which built up into a useful primary system by the time total freedom came in 1838. In Barbados and Tobago the free coloured people, mostly artisans living in the towns, took the initiative in providing schools for their children, receiving sympathy but too little financial help from church and government. So great was the demand for education that in the evenings parents made their children pass on what they had learnt in school that day, and the children sometimes walked as much as five miles to school. Sturge described coming across a Mico day-school in Jamaica where the children were eating from a cloth spread on the floor a second breakfast of cold yams and cocos.

Although teachers trained at the Mico colleges were of a satisfactory standard, the great majority of teachers in the West Indies received no training at all. Shortly after the free school opened in Tobago two members of the management committee commented on the rowdy behaviour of the children and so a letter was written to the master, ending: 'In our opinion the attributes of a good and efficient schoolmaster are the eyes of Argus, the hundred hands of Briareus and the wings of Mercury.' Forty years later a Tobago inspector of schools was wagging his head: 'It is hopeless to expect this rising generation to arrive at . . . a fair knowledge of the tongue they speak, when they hear from their teachers such phrases as "Where did Moses born?" . . . "I eats yam" . . . "I did come yesterday", and so on.' Perhaps the worst case came from British Guiana where a mid-century inspector found a man teaching who had previously been a cart-driver, 'whose capabilities consisted of his wearing glasses, looking wise, being of a very plausible address, able to scratch his name and repeat – we cannot say read – the Lord's Prayer and most of the ordinary portions of the Church of England service. . . .' From such uneducated teachers has the ungrammatical idiom of the West Indies spread across the Caribbean. During the twentieth century, however, much leeway has been made up.

Emancipation led to one completely unanticipated benefit throughout the West Indies: the reform of the extraordinary currency arrangements under which the colonists had conducted business for so long. From the foundation years of the seventeenth century the lack of any local currency had imposed the necessity for the payment of salaries, debts and land purchases in kind, at first in tobacco, then in sugar. Only in 1751 was sugar no longer accepted as currency in Jamaica. In Guiana, however, taxes could still be paid in sugar thirty years later. Planters lived on credit until merchants in England had sold their crop. Even then they saw no cash. The inconvenience had long been recognized. In 1707 Governor Crowe of Barbados had written, 'This island is so drained of cash that there is little to be procured for the minutest occasions, which is one great reason for the poorer sorts leaving us'. Complaints about the shortage of coin echoed down the century. From Jamaica in 1733, a letter read, 'If any Body has any, they keep it by them for Fear they should never see it again.'

The French colonies issued small coin for local trade, but in the absence of such official coinage in the British islands, coins of all countries were accepted: Spanish doubloons and pieces of eight had been common in the seventeenth century; when John Baker went gambling in the Leeward Islands in the 1750s he collected his winnings in French pistoles (worth 20s) and he paid for his daughter's music lessons in the same coin, but he bought a horse for twenty-three and a half guineas and accounted for slaves purchased in pounds. Copper coins called 'Leeward Island Dogs' were issued; there were also 'Black Dogs' cut from Spanish silver dollars, sometimes known as 'stampees' on account of the initial letter of each island impressed on them. In Trinidad at the opening of the nineteenth century there was a variety of coin, which might have delighted a modern coin-collector, but hardly facilitated local business: 'douro fuerte', quarter dollar, 'two-bit piece', the 'cinq sous clou' or 'cinq sous croix' – of irregular shape stamped with a cross – and often cut into quarters known as 'cinq sous coupés' or 'Moco pa Jim'. In St Lucia they dealt in sols, deniers, livres, Louis d'ors, 'three-man pieces', British pennies and 'Leeward Island Dogs'; in Grenada it was stamped colonial monetas and moidres; in Guiana, Dutch guilders and stivers. In all colonies the Portuguese gold Johannes were acceptable, known throughout the eastern Caribbean as 'Joes'.

In 1811 Governor Munro of Trinidad issued twenty-five thousand silver dollars, cut in Port of Spain, valued at nine shillings each. A further issue was made by his successor. When short of small coin shopkeepers issued their own token 'marks'. This continual shortage of coin got a colonial treasurer into serious trouble. To help his merchant friends he lent them government money until he was caught by a surprise inspection with the treasury vault nearly empty. Setting the inspecting committee counting £1,500-worth of silver threepenny and penny-halfpenny pieces he sent an SOS to his friends and was soon hauling baskets of doubloons through a back window. He was caught out on a second visit, sacked and imprisoned.

Occasionally coins were struck in Britain specially for a colony. Thus Barbados had a 'pineapple penny' in 1788 and 'silver anchor money' in 1822. In Jamaica, apart from 'macaronies' of five, ten and twenty pence, there were the 'quattie' and 'bit' worth a penny-halfpenny and fourpence respectively. Although coins of these denominations have long since disappeared out of circulation, the terms 'quattie' and 'bit' are still used by country people.

With all this complicated variety of currency it must have been extremely difficult undertaking a simple transaction like buying a drink, and the temptation to swindlers was great. As long as slave labour continued there were no wages, but with the start of apprenticeship cash became urgently required; after complete emancipation it became a vital necessity. To meet these needs, both new and long standing, the Colonial Bank (later Barclays, Dominion, Colonial & Overseas Ltd)* was incorporated in 1836 and branches were opened in Jamaica, Trinidad, Barbados and British Guiana. In 1838 British coins were placed in circulation and continued until 1951 when they were replaced by special West Indian coinage. Until then in the south Caribbean a system in the eighteenth-century monetary tradition survived: although accounts were kept in dollars and cents, United Kingdom coins were used, with the West Indian dollar tied to sterling at 4s 2d, or $4.80 to the pound. An English visitor found it strange calling a half-penny a cent, a shilling twenty-four cents, and a half-crown sixty cents, but the system worked with commendable economy. Paper dollars were issued for higher denominations.

While the new free citizens were stretching their unshackled limbs, the planters were reacting in different ways from colony to colony. In Jamaica, with a few notable exceptions, the tendency was to throw up hands in surrender to ruin. By 1852 over 240 estates had been abandoned. Sugar production, which had averaged more than 68,000 tons per annum in the decade preceding 1833, sank to an average of 27,474 tons per annum in the mid-fifties and continued this downward trend until the end of the nineteenth century. In British Guiana production declined and then rose again. In Trinidad, where the sugar output was less than one-fifth of Jamaica's at emancipation, it steadily increased until by 1870 it was nearly four times its pre-emancipation figure and nearly double that of 1870 Jamaica. Barbados also suffered no setback and nearly doubled production between 1833 and 1860. In that small island, as well as in the Leewards and Windwards, a serious labour shortage was never experienced because the new freemen were forced to remain on the estates through the lack of empty land to which they could remove.

A generalization that emancipation ruined the West Indian sugar industry would not be true. Sugar prices in London had been falling steadily from approximately £70 a ton in 1815 to £25 a ton in 1830. Good businessmen saw the writing on the wall and cut their losses, among them Sir John Gladstone, the father of the future premier. In 1838 he sold his three estates in British Guiana for half of their 1819 value; all the same he received £60,000. Good estate management kept wise heads above water, but competition with new sugar estates in Cuba and Java as well as those

* Now Barclays International.

in Brazil, where slave labour still existed, increased the British planters' difficulties. The greatest blow was the repeal of the Navigation Acts in 1849 and the gradual removal of protective sugar duties on foreign sugar by 1854.

Gallantly the planters in the south Caribbean area resorted to improved agricultural and manufacturing techniques to reduce their cost of production. In Barbados, where the proportion of resident proprietors was higher than absentees, agricultural societies were formed among whose members news of new methods was circulated. At breakfast meetings reports on visits of inspection by planters' committees were read out and discussed. By 1850 the plough, grubber and horse-hoe were all in use in the fields and vacuum pans, centrifugals and roller-mills were being introduced into the sugar-works. It is important to remember that sugar production consists not only of farming but also of a manufacturing process. As the new machinery came into use the sugar-works, where the simple processes of boiling, skimming and cooling had gone on for two hundred years, were converted into complicated factories, deriving their power from the steam-engine in place of draught animals or windmills. It became necessary for an owner or manager to be an engineer or to employ one to supervise the machinery, for a breakdown in busy crop-time would entail the loss of the year's growth of cane. Similar technical advances were made in Trinidad and Guiana but there the planters suffered from a labour shortage which their Barbados friends escaped. Their remedies for this led to vital social consequences.

In their search for immigrant labourers the planters scoured half the world. Within a year of emancipation the first Portuguese from Madeira arrived in British Guiana. News from distant Mauritius told of the success there of the importation of Indian coolies, so agents visited India to make arrangements for coolies to be sent to the West Indies where, to distinguish them from the black, brown and white Creoles, they have been known ever since as East Indians. Over seven thousand had arrived by 1841 when the abolitionists persuaded the British government to stop the traffic as it bore too close a resemblance to the slave trade. By 1845 the West Indians had succeeded in reversing the decision. In consequence, up to 1917, 239,000 Indian immigrants had arrived in Guiana, 134,000 in Trinidad, a few thousand in St Lucia, Grenada and St Vincent, and after a later start, 33,000 in Jamaica. All immigrants were given the option of repatriation after completing their five years of indenture, but the majority elected to remain and turn the West Indies into a racial hot-pot. To add flavour, after 1850 Chinese were brought in, the majority going to Guiana, a considerable number to Jamaica and others to Trinidad. Negroes from Sierra Leone and the USA, and others rescued from slave-runners by the Royal Navy provided another strain. Even European labourers were tried. Over two thousand British and one thousand Germans went to Jamaica, where Thomas Harvey had visited one of their settlements at Altamont, and others to Trinidad. Many of them died.

Naturally as in most experiments there were failures. The Chinese and Portuguese soon left the cane-fields in search of more lucrative employment. The Portuguese became the principal shopkeepers in Guiana, and as such presented a target for Negro enmity. The first anti-Portuguese riots occurred in 1847, to be followed by the serious 'Angel Gabriel' riots in 1856. The Chinese turned grocers and laundrymen. Gradually as the second and third generations became educated, and family ties and cultural links with their countries of origin weakened, immigrants grew to regard themselves as West Indians and began to rise to the highest positions in their new homes. Yet much of their native culture has remained. In Trinidad and Guiana mosques and Hindu temples are a feature of the roadside scene. The year 1863 saw the start of the Islamic festival of Husein in Trinidad – three days of parades, dances and feasting. Already the Catholic carnival of Mardi Gras had become well established, absorbing the still earlier torchlight processions of Canboulay, a name debased from the French *cannes brulées* ('burnt canes') when slaves were called out at night to fight cane-fires. It is not easy for different races to live together peacefully on a basis of equality, as Britain and the United States have been recently discovering from bitter experience. In the nineteenth-century West Indies, society became dangerously segregated into three tiers distinguished by race as well as by wealth and occupation: the white plutocracy, the coloured middle class and the black working class. In Trinidad and British Guiana the working class became ominously subdivided into Negro and East Indian elements. As with a sleeping volcano, long years have passed without disturbance, but when disturbances occur they erupt violently along racial fissures. All these present-day features of Caribbean life stem from the immigration policy of the post-abolition period.

To begin with, immigration did little to improve economic conditions. It was expensive to arrange and uncertain in its working. By mid-century the West Indies reached their nadir. As banks and trading firms failed, wages were cut to two-thirds or a half of their previously low rates. Into the area at this time came a visitor of literary talent – Anthony Trollope. Between 1858 and 1860 he made an extensive tour of the Caribbean on post office business, as a result of which the post offices in the West Indies were made the responsibility of their colony governments, instead of being controlled from London. His book, *The West Indies and Spanish Main*, provides an interesting picture of life in the colonies in their worst period.

Trollope found all the towns depressing. The whole of Kingston was a dilapidated slum of unpainted brick and wooden houses, uneven pavements and rutted, undrained roads, which became death traps at night. In contrast to the oil lamps of Havana and the recently installed gas-lighting at Cienfuegos in Cuba, there was no street lighting at all. Grass was growing in the streets of Roseau, Dominica. In Spanish Town, a drab town, half dead, 'with buildings as yellow as the fever', scrawny pigs roamed the dirty streets. When he asked the way to the inn, he received an uncomprehending stare for the term is not used in Jamaica: instead there are *taverns* in the towns. In Georgetown, Guiana, he lodged in 'a rickety, ruined, tumble-down wooden house', where a faulty lock compelled him to bolt the door to secure privacy and rise from his bed in the morning to let in the big black chambermaid with a huge tub of bathwater on her head. The majority of the hotels or lodging houses Trollope stayed in seemed to be kept by coloured ladies, always known by two names such as Betsey Austen or Caroline Lee. He deprecated the tendency always to serve English dishes and treat local dishes with disdain, complaining of a surfeit of roast beef, steak and oxtail served with bad English potatoes, to the exclusion of turtle soup, yams, avocado pears, mountain cabbage and plantains after which he was hankering.

Travel was an unpleasant ordeal. Owing to the disrepair of the roads – seriously deteriorated since Lady Nugent's day – Anthony Trollope travelled in Jamaica on horseback, hiring four horses, two for his servant and their baggage and two for himself as he was a heavy man. In spite of the rough conditions he travelled extensively, even climbing Blue Mountain peak to see the sunrise. Like many subsequent travellers he was disappointed, arriving at the summit in a cloud, shivering all night in spite of a liberal supply of wine, brandy and rum, and leaving in a cloud. . . . In the west of the island he stayed several days with a Westmorland planter. In spite of depressed trading conditions, estate life was still pleasant, with fishing and shooting to take the mind off the miserable prospects of sugar. Coffee was brought to his bed at 6 am. After a leisurely toilet he was taken out riding, returning between 10 and 10.30 am for a heavy breakfast of fish, steak and tinned meats, potatoes, yams, plantains, eggs and a choice of tea, chocolate, beer, wine, rum and brandy. He admired the good stock on the 'pens' into which many sugar estates were being converted at that time. Dinner was usually eaten at 6 pm after a leisurely hour dressing in a black suit (*de rigueur* in Jamaica) and the evening ended at 9 pm after coffee on the veranda. Sherry and bitters was the fashionable drink, and dancing, 'the elixir of life', was as popular with young and old as it had been in the days of John Baker, Lady Nugent and Monk Lewis. Everyone dispensed the traditional hospitality even though, Trollope suspected, there was little reserve stock in the larder and a large overdraft at the bank.

Both in Jamaica and British Guiana Anthony Trollope travelled on the

The Planters' Society

Planter, attended by his negro driver.

Right John Gregg, a Jamaican planter. Eighteenth century.

Centre The laziness bred by slavery.

Bottom A funeral in Dutch Surinam, *c.* 1839.

Above A man of quality and his wife attended by six slaves – a status symbol.

Below A drawing by James Hakewill (1820) of the gates of Rose Hall, near Montego Bay, Jamaica, the home of the notorious Annie Palmer. The house has now been reconditioned as a tourist attraction. It dates from about 1780.

Above Holland Estate, St Thomas-in-the-East, Jamaica, the neighbouring estate to 'Monk' Lewis's Hordley, painted by Hakewill in 1820.

Below Cardiff Hall, St Ann's, an example of a Jamaica Great House, also by Hakewill. The house was built about 1770.

Above Gracehill, Antigua.

Below Hakewill's picture of Spring Garden Estate, near Buff Bay, Jamaica, then the property of L. R. Grasett, M.P., an absentee owner. Planters sited their houses on hills for the cool air and supervision.

The Jamaican earthquake of 1692, as depicted in a contemporary broadsheet.
2,000 people perished in two minutes. According to the key on the original:
A Houses falling. B Churches. C Sugar works. D The mills. E The Bridges in the
whole country. F The Rocks and Mountains. G Capt. Ruden's House Sunk first
into the Earth with his Wife and Family. H The Ground Rolling under the
Minister's feet. I The Great Church and Tower falling. K The Earth Opening and
Swallowing Multitudes of People in Morgan's Fort. L The Minister kneeling down
in a Ring with the People in the Street at Prayers. M The Wharf covered with the
Sea. N Dr Heath going from ship to ship to visit the bruised people. O Thieves
Robbing and Breaking open both Houses and Warehouses. P Dr Tapham hanging
by the Hands on a Rack of the Chimney and one of his children hanging about his
neck seeing his Wife and the rest of his children a'sinking. Q A boat coming to save
them. R The Minister preaching in a Tent. S Dead bodies floating. T The sea
washing the dead Carcases out of the Graves and Tombs. V People swallowed up
in the Earth, several as high as their Necks, with their Heads above ground. W The
dogs eating of Dead Men's Heads. X Several Ships Cast away and driven into the
Very Town. Y A Woman and her two Daughters beat to pieces one against the
other. Z Mr Beckford his Digging out of the Ground.'

Lewis Galdy's tombstone in St Peter's Churchyard, Port Royal. The inscription reads: 'Here lies the body of Lewis Galdy who departed this life at Port Royal the 22 December 1719 aged 50. He was born at Montpellier in France but left that country for his Religion and came to settle in this island where he was swallowed up in the Great Earthquake in the year 1692 and by the Providence of God was by another shock thrown into the sea and Miraculously lived by swimming until a boat took him up. He lived many years after in great Reputation beloved by all that knew him and much lamented at his Death.'

Above Guns recovered by a recent marine archaeological project from HMS *Swan*, which sank in the Great Earthquake.

Left Pewter implements recovered from the sea off Port Royal.

nascent railways, stretching in each colony about fifteen miles from rail-head. In Jamaica there was a train every four hours, taking just under the hour for the thirteen-mile journey between Kingston and Spanish Town. In Guiana he completed the sixty-mile journey between Georgetown and New Amsterdam by dilapidated mail phaeton which ran three times a week. A broken axle delayed him on the road for five hours, so that he reached the end of his journey long after nightfall, eaten by mosquitoes and crossing the Berbice river by flimsy ferry-boat. The hotel, kept by a former slave, was the best he found in the West Indies. After the sorry villages of the free Negroes along the coast, Trollope thought New Amsterdam a clean and orderly little place, where 'three persons in the street constitute a crowd, and five collected for any purpose would form a goodly club'. The wooden houses standing in their own grounds were neatly kept. He found a coastal steamer to take him back to Georgetown.

In Barbados, where the white roads were painful to the traveller's eye, Trollope was impressed by the statue of Nelson standing in Bridgetown's Trafalgar Square. He was gently amused by the 'Bims', the white Barbadians, who possessed a high opinion of themselves and their sugar. He saw few coloured people except in the shops. They were socially ignored by the whites, and in contrast to Jamaica, where there were two black and a number of coloured assemblymen, all the Barbados Assembly was white. All the same the Bims were admirable people. Barbados, con-cluded Trollope, 'owes no man anything, pays its own way and never makes a poor mouth.'

Consorting with planters as he did, it was not surprising that he came to share their opinion of the free Negroes. The main complaint against them was that they were too lazy to do a proper day's work. From 6 to 10 am was long enough. 'The negro's idea of emancipation was, and is, emancipa-tion not from slavery but from work.' At the most they only worked five days a week and lived in better circumstances than the English labourers of his day, who were working a six-day week. Contrast with Trollope's the remarks of John Candler, a Quaker visitor to Jamaica in 1850:

I could scarcely believe that slavery ever existed here. . . . Some of the planters still insist that they are an idle people because they do not, on the whole, perform as much work as in slavery; but who that has seen them at work in the cane-fields or hoeing coffee on the steep hills, or has travelled among their provision grounds in the mountains, can call them an idle people? I have seen them, men, women and children, loaded with provisions and fruits which they carry on their heads . . . weights which no European would ever encounter, and sweating under the heavy toil, yet all labouring cheerfully because they are free.

Governor Sir Henry Barkly hit the nail on the head in 1854: ' . . . they gladly labour for their former masters, *provided a remunerative rate of wages is offered.*' Lastly Captain George Price, a planter himself, resident owner of Worthy Park, Jamaica, between 1842 and 1865, said of the Negro,

I know his many grave faults, but I know faults as numerous and grave in English and Irish men of the lowest class . . . the negro compared with the white man is sober. On the roads in the environs of Kingston and in its streets to one drunken negro 20 drunken white soldiers and sailors may be any day seen, yet the low class negro of Kingston is probably the worst to be found in the Island.

Conflicting opinions about the Negro were as responsible as any cause for the series of events known in Jamaica as the Morant Bay Rebellion of 1865. In that large island the nadir of mid-century referred to above lasted for over a decade. By 1865 the general economic depression had permeated society to the humblest labourer. Because of the decay of the sugar industry wages had been reduced from an average of 2s 6d a day in 1838 to less than a shilling for a twelve-hour day in the 1860s. Droughts over the previous two years had hit the provision-grounds of the peasant cultivators, there was no work for them on the estates, and prices had risen as a result of the American Civil War.

Economic and social distress, emphasized by a marked increase in crime, particularly of predial larceny (the theft of estate produce), engendered political action for redress. In the Assembly the impassioned speeches of George William Gordon received publicity not only for their content but for their oratory. Like the English radicals of the previous generation, Gordon saw the solution for social distress in the reform of the constitution, especially the widening of the franchise. His was an interesting career. Born a slave about 1820, the son of a Scottish estate attorney and a black concubine, and freed not by his father's manumission as was customary but by the general emancipation of 1838, George made a small fortune for himself from speculating in property and succeeded in being elected to the Assembly. This two hundred-year-old legislature then consisted of forty-seven members returned by only 1,903 registered electors in the island's twenty-three constituencies.

It was Gordon's fatal misfortune that the governor since 1862, Edward John Eyre, was a man with no sympathy for anybody. Twenty years before Eyre had made his name by his explorations in Australia and had subsequently held the appointments of lieutenant-governor of New Zealand and St Vincent and acting-governor of the Leeward Islands. Since his arrival in Jamaica he had made himself unpopular with everybody, particularly the planters. To Eyre Gordon was a seditious agitator. His dislike was increased by his detestation of the Baptist church in which Gordon was an active member.

To the local political activity of Gordon there was added the support of

Dr E. B. Underhill, the Secretary of the Baptist Missionary Society in England. Dr Underhill, who had paid a visit to Jamaica at the same time as Anthony Trollope, had been kept in touch with conditions in the island by letters from Baptist missionaries. So concerned did he become that in February 1865 he addressed a letter to Edward Cardwell, the Liberal Secretary of State for the Colonies, drawing his attention to the serious situation in Jamaica. Cardwell referred the letter to Eyre for his comments and Eyre told him Underhill had exaggerated. Although he admitted that there was distress, due partly to low wages, high prices, unemployment and drought, the main cause in his opinion was nothing less than 'the idleness, improvidence and vice of the people'. No action was therefore taken on the reasonable and practicable suggestions made by Dr Underhill.

In similar vein no sympathetic consideration was accorded to a petition to the queen by peasants in St Ann's Parish, asking to be allowed to cultivate unoccupied Crown lands in return for rent. The official reply to this reasonable request, although composed by officials in the Colonial Office, is known in Jamaica annals as the Queen's Letter. It contained the following almost incredible dictum:

The prosperity of the labouring classes depends, in Jamaica, and in other countries, upon their working for wages, not uncertainly, or capriciously, but steadily and continuously, at the times when their labour is wanted: and that if they would use this industry, and thereby render the plantations productive, they would enable the planters to pay them higher wages for the same hours of work than are received by the best field labourers in this country . . .

Governor Eyre was so delighted with this letter that he had printed copies of it placed on display all over the island, and became highly incensed when certain free church clergy refused to publicize it among their congregations. They and many other people were flabbergasted. George Gordon arose in the Assembly to say that the queen's ministers had been deceived and misled, 'constituting a serious grievance to our people, but we advise them to be prudent yet firm in their remonstrances and we have no doubt that truth will prevail.' Eyre considered these words seditious.

Meanwhile in the parish of St Thomas discontent was mounting to a dangerous level. In that south-eastern corner of the island, cut off from the rest by mountain walls and unbridged rivers, apart from the common grievances there was strong local resentment against the biased and completely unsympathetic attitude of the local justices of the peace, headed by the Custos, Baron Maximilan von Ketelholdt and the Rector, the Rev. S.H. Cooke, whose son was clerk of the courts. Appeals and deputations were totally disregarded, while warrants of arrest were issued in cases where only a summons was legally justified. George Gordon had become involved here for he was a member of the parish Vestry until Eyre ordered his removal from the bench on the representations of the Custos. A stipendiary magistrate who had criticized the questionable use of warrants of arrest had been transferred. At the time of publication of the Queen's Letter Gordon was in Kingston, but Paul Bogle, a deacon of Gordon's church near Morant Bay was so incensed after reading the letter that he walked the forty-five miles to Spanish Town to warn the governor there would be trouble if unemployment went unrelieved. Eyre refused to receive him. On his return home Bogle was seething. He decided to take the law into his own hands and his first action was to resist the illegal warrants of arrest which the local magistrates were continuing to issue.

On 7 October a prisoner arrested by a constable on a warrant was freed by Bogle's followers. Then seven constables arriving to arrest Bogle were overpowered and sent packing. Hearing about this, Custos von Ketelholdt summoned the parish Vestry to meet on 11 October and called up the local Volunteers for security. Shortly after the Vestry meeting started a mob of between three and four hundred people, led by Paul Bogle's brother, Moses, appeared before the court house. They refused to listen to the Custos. After he had read the Riot Act and missiles had started to fly, the Volunteers opened fire. This caused a temporary retreat on the part of the rioters until the arrival of Paul Bogle. When he heard that seven men had been killed he ordered the killing of the members of the Vestry in retaliation. They died bravely and horribly. The rioters smoked them out of the court house and adjoining small fort and hacked them down with cutlasses as they ran out, Bogle himself dispatching the Custos. Meanwhile the wily Rector escaped through a back door. In all fourteen Vestrymen including the one black member died. When all was quiet Bogle returned home and held a prayer meeting of thanksgiving. There had been no looting. No women or children were molested, but three white estate managers were murdered over the next few days.

It is plain from the facts that this was no organized rebellion but a demonstration in force that developed into a riot. Once the fat was in the fire Bogle tried to rouse the parish without any success.

Retribution descended swiftly. Governor Eyre heard of the riot twenty-four hours after it had occurred while he was at Flamstead in the Port Royal mountains. He acted with lightning speed. A company of the Royal Regiment stationed at Newcastle set off that same night, marching overland into the Morant river valley. By midnight Eyre was down in Kingston conferring with his council. Martial law was declared in the county of Surrey and Eyre sailed in the early hours on HMS *Wolverine* for Morant Bay with a strong force of soldiers. After landing troops of the West India Regiment there, Eyre sailed on to Port Antonio, where he dropped more troops to march down the east coast and prevent the trouble from spreading into Portland. His prompt measures undoubtedly prevented the disturbance becoming general but he then overreached himself: his punitive measures became a massacre. Worst of them all, in the search for a scapegoat, George Gordon was seized in Kingston, taken out of his sick-bed, from which he had obviously had no contact with the rioters, and transferred to Morant Bay. There he was tried by court martial without legal aid or permission to call witnesses. On 23 October he was hanged, protesting his innocence. On the previous day Paul Bogle was captured by Maroons from Hayfield, who had come to the government's aid in fulfilment of their ancient treaty. After a quick court martial, Bogle was hanged like a pirate at the yard-arm of the *Wolverine*. It was not without significance that the naval vessel involved in quelling the 'rebellion' was named for one of nature's most savage animals. In all 439 people were killed in the suppression of the rising, six hundred men and women were severely flogged and over a thousand houses were burnt down.

Such a savage story could have no sudden ending. Before his turn came, Eyre succeeded in persuading the Jamaica Assembly to agree to its own abolition and it voted itself out of existence. A royal commission of inquiry concluded that Gordon was culpable of agitation; it commended Eyre for his prompt action that had prevented a general insurrection, but strongly criticized the extremely repressive measures taken after the fighting was over. Eyre was recalled, to become the centre of a bitter controversy in England. He maintained a dignified silence until his death in 1901.

The full implications of the Morant Bay affair were sufficiently resounding to alter the course of Jamaica's history, as will be seen later on in this book, but a postscript will not be out of place here. In 1965, to commemorate the centenary of the Morant Bay Rebellion the then independent government of Jamaica dedicated a monument to the national heroes, George William Gordon and Paul Bogle. It stands, an impressive modern sculpture by Jamaican artists, at the long since tranquil port of Morant Bay.

11

THE MAIN, THE BAY
AND THE SHORE

With the foundation of St Kitts, Barbados and Providence, the English had directed their main attention in the Caribbean to the islands, leaving the Spaniards in possession of three thousand miles of mainland coast. Spain excluded all foreigners from any trading activity with the vast area lying behind and so, with one remarkable exception, English concern with the Spanish dominions was confined to warlike attack.

The exception was Thomas Gage who in 1625 arrived to spend twelve years in Central America, working as a Dominican priest, mostly in Guatemala. His experience showed that the main Spanish objection to Englishmen lay in their heresy. Foreign individuals who were good Catholics were not unwelcome, and the Gages were among the staunchest of English Catholics, bent on the recovery of their country by the true church. Obedient to their father's wish four of the five sons of John Gage of Haling Park, Surrey, entered the service of the Roman church. It was intended that the second son Thomas, born in 1600, after education under the English Jesuits in St Omer and Valladolid, should devote his life to missionary work in England, but he incurred his father's wrath by forsaking the Jesuits for the Dominicans and disappearing on a Dominican mission to the Philippines. A half-hearted attempt was made to prevent him from sailing to Mexico (on the regular route to Manila) not because an English priest would be unwelcome there, but for the reason that, 'having a country of their own to convert', English priests were expected to devote their proselytizing energies to England. Remaining hidden in a biscuit-barrel until the ships were at sea, Thomas Gage was treated when he emerged as one of the mission party. During a five months' rest in Mexico, Thomas decided that work in America would be preferable to the Far East. Eluding the friar in charge, he escaped with an Irishman and two others – in a later age Gage could have stood in for Houdini. They made their way to Chiapa, where the Englishman spent five months teaching Latin grammar, and eventually reached the Antigua Guatemala of today. Three and a half years lecturing in logic at the university were followed by six as a parish priest among the Indians. In all this time Gage made no secret of his nationality, being treated always with courtesy, often with curiosity, never with hostility. His parish work was remunerative, for Indians were encouraged to look after their spiritual fathers. When the time came for him to go, Thomas Gage found himself the possessor of more than £2,000.

In spite of permission all the way from distant Rome to return to his own country, the Provincial of Chiapa refused to release him, so Gage turned Houdini again. Laying a false trail to the north, he left at midnight southwards and after many adventures reached Costa Rica. No sooner had he embarked on the short voyage to Porto Bello, however, than his ship was captured by a Dutch mulatto privateer. It was ironic that the sole Englishman in Spanish Central America should suffer thus from privateering, the favourite pursuit of his nation. Only the pearls stitched into his travelling quilt were kept from his twelve years' savings. Eventually he reached Cartagena, whence he sailed for Havana and Spain in company with William Rous and other prisoners from Providence (see Chapter Four).

By the time Gage reached England at Christmas 1637, after nearly a year's travelling, he found he had forgotten most of his English. He had been away for twenty-four years. As time went by, Thomas Gage turned

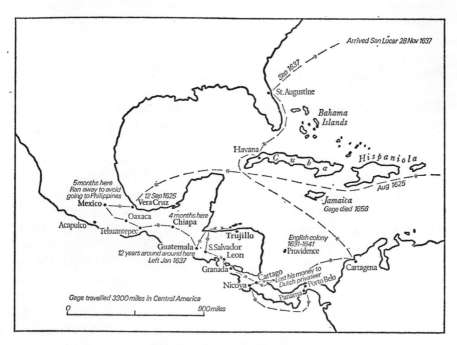

The travels of Thomas Gage

apostate, betrayed several of his former friends, married, and was granted a living near Deal. In 1648 he published the account of his travels, carefully slanted to convince the new rulers of England of the ease with which the Spanish empire could be conquered. Seven years later he sailed as chaplain to General Venables on the mismanaged Western Design. A second edition of his book came out under Cromwell's patronage soon after the expedition sailed, but Gage reaped no benefit: he died in Jamaica in 1656.

His book, *The English American, or a New Survey of the West India's* [*sic*] gives an interesting description of life in the Spanish colonies, which concerns us here only for the contrast it provides between them and those founded by Englishmen. Spanish authoritarian government was established on a uniform pattern in every colony; the church was the equal of the civil power and had worked hard from the earliest days to convert the native peoples, as never happened in English lands until the eighteenth century. But the Indians, even if converted, were completely subjugated. Generally they lived in their own towns and settlements, whence they were summoned when labour was required. They were expected to provide Spanish travellers with mules and guides, and they paid heavy tribute. In consequence, Spanish colonists lived splendidly, in fine town houses built round patioed gardens. Particularly in their towns did the Spaniards surpass the English. They built great churches and governors' palaces, bull-rings and theatres, seminaries and universities. The mineral wealth was fantastic. Gage described a silver lamp in the Dominican church at Guatemala, so heavy that three men were required to lift it, and there was a life-size silver statue of the Virgin valued at a hundred thousand ducats. How English mouths must have watered at the prospect of such plunder!

After Thomas Gage, the main activities of the English were planting in their small colonies, buccaneering and logwood-cutting. Then in 1711 came the first attempt at open trade, with the foundation of the South Sea Company and its subsequent operation of the *asiento*. By 1700 Spain's exclusion of foreign traders had backfired badly by depriving her colonies of African slaves, and exceptions had had to be made to correct this. At first Genoese merchants were given a contract or *asiento* to supply the slaves for a limited number of years. During the 1680s a naturalized Spaniard living in Jamaica, James del Castillo, obtained a contract by which Spanish ships came to Jamaica to buy the slaves he procured from the Royal African Company. During the War of the Spanish Succession the French operated the contract, so that it was considered a diplomatic triumph when the Treaty of Utrecht of 1713 awarded the *asiento* to the United Kingdom. By the terms of the separate treaty signed in March 1714, Britain engaged to supply a thousand gross of Negroes to the Spanish colonies over the next thirty years. The South Sea Company, to whom the government awarded the monopoly, agreed to pay an import duty of thirty-three and a third pieces of eight on each slave (i.e. a little more than £8). In addition to the slave ships the company gained a special concession: the privilege of sending one ship of five hundred tons filled with general merchandise to the annual fair at Porto Bello, provided that one-quarter of the profits went to the king of Spain plus five per cent of the remainder. It was a complicated arrangement but to the company it allowed a foot in the tightly closed door. To smooth the operation of the more important slave supply the company was granted licences for six factors to reside at each of the towns of Vera Cruz, Cartagena, Panama and Buenos Aires, and four representatives at Havana, Porto Bello and Caracas. In 1731 the magnificent style and consequent popularity of the company's factors in Porto Bello was the subject of admiring comment.

Yet the magnitude of the trade must not be exaggerated. The Spanish government had granted the concession in the hope that it would reduce smuggling. In 1717 the first 'annual ship' carried to Porto Bello merchandise valued at a quarter of a million pounds. Then a short war in 1718 interrupted the voyages until 1721. Only seven ships actually sailed in the twelve years to 1733, but by then breaches of the law, typical of the Caribbean, were being winked at, for a small convoy accompanied the annual ship and waited below the horizon to replenish by night the stocks of the single official concessionaire. Naturally such practices were not publicized, so details are lacking.

Concurrently with the official *asiento* trade, logwood-cutting went on along the coasts of Central America. Like the South Sea Company traders, the cutters sought no publicity for in Spanish eyes they were trespassing. Of course the Spaniards were doing nothing with the land. There were small British settlements along the Moskito Shore where a tradition of friendship with the Indian inhabitants had survived from the time of the Providence colony and the heyday of the Buccaneers, among whom a Dutchman named Blauvelt was remembered at Bluefields Bay. It was the Indians, calling themselves *Miskito*, with the accent on the first syllable, who gave their name to the shore. By coincidence there has always been a superabundance of the insects, so the spelling confusion is explicable. Round the corner of Cape Gracias a Dios (a reminder that the pious Columbus once passed that point) is the wide Gulf or Bay of Honduras, known to seventeenth- and eighteenth-century Englishmen who went there simply as 'the Bay'. Hence the names 'the Baymen' for those who traded there, and the 'Bay Islands' for the islands of Utila, Ruatan and Bonacca, where they stopped on their way to the river of 'Bullys', 'Vallis' or Belize, where the best logwood grew. During the time of the South Sea

Company logwood worth £100,000 annually was being cut. This was sour grapes to the Spaniards: in 1730 they destroyed the English cutters' camps on the Belize river.

By this time Spain had taken a page out of the Jamaica history book. Instead of sending expensive fleets to defend her outposts and enforce her laws, a policy was adopted of employing privateers on the old terms of 'no prizes, no pay'. Consequently these *guarda costas* were not overscrupulous in their actions against foreign ships. In 1726 British merchants complained that they had lost £300,000 in unwarrantable *guarda costa* attacks, so a British squadron under Admiral Hosier went to blockade Porto Bello. In 1731 a certain Captain Jenkins in a brush with a *guarda costa* lost one of his ears. Seven years later he displayed what was left of it to a committee of the House of Commons. This is too often quoted as the main cause of the War of Jenkins's Ear. What it really marked was the culmination of a series of provocative attacks on British traders both lawful and unlawful. The logwood-cutters had been attacked on two other occasions and it was the attack of 1739 which led to the war as much as the pickled ear. Also contributing to it were the unsatisfied claims of the South Sea Company for trading losses.

The war of 1739–48 achieved little. The Peace of Aix-la-Chapelle renewed the *asiento* until 1752, after which it was discontinued by mutual consent, but the South Sea Company survived until 1854 when its business was wound up. It proved better to let the Spaniards come to Jamaica and buy their slaves there as they had done in the days of Castillo.

In the Bay of Honduras the logwood-cutters continued their activities under the most insecure conditions. They never knew when a Spanish attack might materialize. Attempts to obtain recognition as a colony received no response from Britain, so they organized their own few government requirements in a delightfully informal but practically efficient way. At a public meeting on the first Monday in May all the cutters present elected two magistrates and five assistants. These officers were authorized to impose taxes and settle disputes according to 'the Custom of the Bay'. Along the Moskito Shore the few functions of government were attended to by a Superintendent appointed by the governor of Jamaica.

At last by the Treaty of Paris in 1763 official recognition of logwood-cutting rights was acknowledged by Spain, but all fortifications had to be demolished and no plantations or industries were to be started. Next year Admiral Sir William Burnaby came from Jamaica to straighten out the cutters' affairs. He had the 'Customs of the Bay' written down in what came to be known as Burnaby's Laws. They included a decree, with Puritan reminiscences, against 'profane cursing and swearing in disobedience to God's command and the derogation of His honour'. A fine of half a crown was to be imposed for each offence. The principle of no taxation without representation was included and provision was made for future legislation by a majority vote of the inhabitants at the annual public meeting. Among the four ships that accompanied Burnaby was that of Lieutenant James Cook, the future explorer of the Pacific. He wrote an account of an official mission he conducted to the Spanish capital of Yucatan.

But recognition as a colony was not granted. In spite of the Treaty of Paris Spanish attacks continued, culminating in the expulsion of most of the settlers in 1779. Further negotiations were included in the Treaty of Versailles four years later. In return for British evacuation of the Moskito Shore Spain authorized the settlements between the Belize and Sibun rivers and on St George's Cay; but once again restrictions were placed on planting and industry. These arrangements were supplemented by the Convention of London in 1786. To stress that Spain still exercised sovereignty over the land, Spanish commissioners were to make two visits a year to satisfy their government that the restrictions were being observed. At the request of the cutters a Superintendent was appointed from Jamaica. In 1787, to the 537 whites and free coloureds and their 1,677 slaves were added two thousand settlers and slaves from the Moskito Shore, doubling the population of the settlement. The Moskito Indians, however, refused to give up the vague protectorate Britain had exercised over them and declined to submit to Spanish government. As the Spaniards were not interested in their affairs this meant no change in the *status quo*. When a new Moskito king was to be crowned he continued to go to Jamaica for his coronation. As missionaries of the SPG had been working among the Indians since 1741, this ceremony was performed in church.

During the 1780s, as the demand for mahogany furniture appeared in Europe, mahogany-cutting surpassed logwood in importance and large shipments were made. But insecurity remained to cramp development. In 1798 a force of 2,500 Spaniards in thirty-two vessels appeared from the direction of Yucatan. The settlers had been expecting them. HMS *Merlin* and two hundred soldiers of the 68th and 6th West India Regiments made up the sum total of the official garrison, but they were supported by every able-bodied man to the number of 350, disposed among a small flotilla of little local ships each armed with a single gun and manned by Negro crewmen. After a week of minor skirmishing the Spaniards assaulted the main defences on St George's Cay. In a two-hour engagement they were soundly beaten off, never to appear in force again. From then on the settlers considered that in addition to their ancient right of occupation they had added the right of conquest. 10 September, the anniversary of the battle of St George's Cay, is celebrated still as the indisputable birthday of British Honduras.

This complicated story of the early years of British Honduras has been included in some detail because it is necessary for an understanding of the social conditions under which this small unique dependency came into existence. The rest of its political history can be dismissed in five sentences. In 1862 the settlement was at last constituted a colony with the Superintendent becoming a lieutenant-governor under the tutelage of the governor of Jamaica. In 1884 the two colonies were separated. In 1854 a legislative council had replaced the traditional public meeting. With minor changes British Honduras has continued as a colony into the second half of the twentieth century, attaining internal self-government in 1964. Independence has had to wait because of a historical skeleton in the cupboard: the neighbouring republic of Guatemala has revived the old Spanish claims to sovereignty and has insisted that the colony should be incorporated, even to the extent of an invasion threat in 1948; as long as this threat to the colony's security exists, it remains under British protection.

Because uncertainty has bedevilled the development of this oddity of the British Commonwealth, the population has remained small, with approximately 105,000 people at the last census on an area (after various extensions) of 8,867 square miles, one-tenth that of the former British Guiana, which it most closely resembles. In spite of attempts to find alternative or additional occupations, the forests, covering sixty-five per cent of the area, have continued to provide the main exports of the colony. Chicle, the rubbery basis of chewing-gum, joined logwood and mahogany as a product at the end of the nineteenth century.

In 1882 the colony was visited by Daniel Morris, then Director of Public Gardens and Plantations in Jamaica, to make recommendations for possible new enterprises. Later as Sir Daniel Morris he became Imperial Commissioner for Agriculture in the West Indies. He left an interesting description of the logging industry. Trees were being dragged as far as ten miles to the rivers, either on primitive wagons with broad wooden wheels or on 'slides', a kind of sledge, passing over skids of long hard posts placed across the track at yard intervals. Trucking was done at night to save the oxen from heat exhaustion by day. 'The lowing of the oxen, the creaking of the wheels, the shrill cries of the men, the resounding cracks of their whips and the red glow of pine torches in the midst of the dense dark forest, produce an effect approaching to sublimity.' After squaring on the river bank the logs were floated downstream to the boom, a chain across the river ten miles from the mouth. Here the logs were sorted by their owners, made up into rafts and floated down to the sea for export. The loggers worked the same circuit every thirty years until over-cutting led to exhaustion of supply. Already, however, demand had fallen off in the 1860s when iron began to replace wood in shipbuilding, and by 1900 the bottom had fallen out of the mahogany market.

Logwood cutting was much simpler and less strenuous, as Dampier's description has been already quoted to show, because the trees were rarely more than one foot in diameter. After the tree had been cut down and the outer sapwood had been removed, the dark heart-wood, from which the dye was extracted, was carted down to the rivers and assembled in long 'trains' of 'bark logs' or light buoyant cradles for floating to the coast. Like mahogany, logwood received its quietus around 1900 when aniline dyes ousted it from the market.

At the end of the year log-cutters from all over the backwoods descended on Belize, blowing their wages to 'keep Christmas' in a wild spending spree. Broke soon after the New Year, they signed up for fresh contracts and disappeared into the forests for another eleven months. It was a tough, free life which they would not willingly change for any other. It was lonely, though, and travellers like Daniel Morris were given a warm, wet welcome.

At Belize slavery never assumed the importance it attained in other British colonies: there were under two thousand slaves at emancipation. In 1816 Superintendent Arthur described 'the kindness, liberality and indulgent care of the woodcutters towards their Negroes, so that slavery can hardly be said to exist in the Settlement'. No colour bar was operated against free coloureds, but the church wardens of St John's laid down that 'the pews on the East End . . . shall be solely appropriated to white and married persons, and no kept mistress shall be entitled to sit in any pew at that end of the church'. White and black sheep were thus separated from white and black goats. Indeed for a small backwoods place there was noticeable prudery. In 1830 some seamen were sentenced to five days' imprisonment and a daily hour in the stocks for 'bathing naked in the River as the Bishop of Jamaica and the Superintendent with their ladies were passing by'.

During the nineteenth century British Honduras became as much a multiracial community as any other West Indian colony. Black Caribs from St Vincent had been deported there in 1798. To the aboriginal Indians of the country were added refugees from across the Mexican border, both Spanish and Indian, after civil war in Yucatan. Firm measures were taken to stop the spread of bull-fighting which these immigrants started to introduce. Chinese, East Indians, Americans (both black and white) and Lebanese were added to the mixture; but the majority of the people today are of mixed race.

Attempts to find alternatives to lumbering have not proved successful. Citrus fruit, bananas and sugar-cane all grow well, but markets and transportation have always been lacking. During the last century a considerable trade grew up with New Orleans that outdid the older connection with Jamaica. Since the Second World War, when incidentally numbers of 'BH' lumberjacks came to work in Scottish forests, air communications have swung more towards Miami. Unless minerals are discovered the country of Belize, as its new leaders plan to call it, is fated to remain a backwater.

The city of Belize, which acquired its own bishop in 1880, grew up with large frame houses surrounded by rambling screened verandas, raised on wooden piles like those of Georgetown, for both towns are built on low-lying river banks. There were ten thousand inhabitants in 1880, 32,824 in 1961. Gardens have proved difficult to maintain owing to waterlogging, rats and salty, sandy soil. The golf course in the 1930s was described by Governor Sir Alan Burns as a course 'with more than one hundred holes, all but nine of them made by land-crabs'.

The Caribbean is an area where natural disasters have to be expected, yet for 150 years there was nothing more serious than a gale at Belize. Then in the middle of the celebrations of 10 September 1931 a terrible hurricane struck. An hour of havoc with winds rising to 160 mph drove the sea out to the cays. An hour later it came back in a tidal wave between fifteen and twenty feet high that swept through the little city, destroying ninety-five per cent of the buildings, killing over a thousand people and leaving a bill for $1,000,000. Thirty years later Hurricane Hattie repeated the disaster. In consequence it has been decided to build a new capital fifty miles inland.

Belize has no harbour, so that steamers have to anchor from one to four miles out according to draft, but the line of off-shore cays provides some protection. Inland the main communications have always been by river, where the Carib Indians excel as boatmen, while the north-south run of the coast has encouraged the use of coastal vessels rather than roads.

If misfortune has struck unexpectedly, so once has good fortune provided an unanticipated windfall. In 1926 Baron Edward Bliss arrived off the coast in his yacht to try the deep-sea fishing. Before he could set foot ashore he was struck by a short fatal illness. In a strange fit of generosity he altered his will to leave his fortune to the colony. Administered since by the Baron Bliss Trust there is an income of approximately £10,000 a year that has provided a number of useful amenities in the form of a museum and art gallery, an industrial school, water supplies, the Burdon canal linking Belize to the Sibun river, and prizes for an annual regatta. In his memory 9 March is celebrated as a holiday as Baron Bliss Day.

Although in 1786 the British government had agreed to give up the Moskito Coast and the majority of the settlers had been moved to Belize, it was not long before English traders were back on 'the Shore', welcomed as they always were by the Moskito Indians, who in 1800 numbered about 1,200. After the battle of St George's Cay the king travelled to Belize to congratulate his friends on their victory, and in 1816 his successor, George Frederick, went there instead of to Jamaica for his coronation. During the Napoleonic wars the semi-official ties between Britain and the Shore were restored. Spain never came back into the picture and it was not until the 1830s that the new republics of Central America showed any interest, because their populations were centred nearer to the Pacific than the Caribbean coast. What was it that attracted British adventurers to this remote shore?

For most of the three hundred miles between the San Juan river and Cape Gracias a Dios the coast is low and swampy with wide shallow mangrove-fringed lagoons, where the mosquitoes (the insects) greatly outnumber the Moskito Indians. Originally 'the Shore' stretched round the corner of Cape Gracias to Cape Honduras near the small Spanish settlement of Trujillo. Twenty miles off Trujillo lie the Bay Islands which the English sailors used as stepping stones on the way to Belize. Between Belize and the Bay Islands and down beyond the San Juan river there was

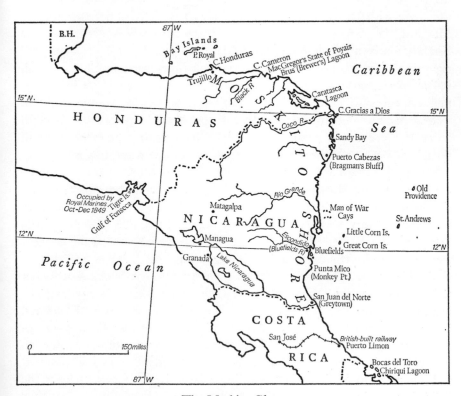

The Moskito Shore

continuous schooner traffic and from there over to Jamaica via the Corn Islands, St Andrew's Island and Old Providence. The Shore was a beachcomber's paradise.

Along it in 1819 came a plausible rogue named Gregor MacGregor. With a concession along the Black (now Paulaya) River from the obliging Moskito king, the Scottish speculator published a prospectus in London for a new gold mine in a subtropical paradise, 'already blessed with the amenities of civilization', to wit, the State of Poyais and 'its well-established capital at San Joseph'. Believing that if one tells a lie it pays to tell a big one, MacGregor went on to describe himself as 'His Serene Highness Gregor, Prince of Poyais, Cazique of the Poyer Nation, Defender of the Indians'. A shipload of gullible colonists arrived and were only saved from total disaster (after seventy had died) by a relief party sent out from Belize. The rescue operation cost the British settlement more than £4,000, not a penny of which was ever recovered.

Of a more reputable character was Thomas Young who lived on the Shore between 1839 and 1841 and left a description of his experiences. The king, Robert Charles Frederick, used to dress in naval uniform. He had decreed that his people should provide English traders with food and assistance with travel. Young distinguished three divisions: the original Moskitos, the Caribs (descendants of deportees from St Vincent) and the Sambos, a mixed people of Indian and Negro origin. British traders were exporting sugar, tobacco, mahogany, logwood, hides, sarsaparilla, cochineal, indigo, silver, coconuts, mules and cattle. In exchange came in liquor, muskets, cutlasses, knives and ammunition; items which, Young admitted, were doing no good to the morality of the Moskito people. Of benefit, however, were cotton goods, shawls with large showy patterns, reels of thread and trouser buttons. The *entrepôt* for all this trade was Belize.

During the 1820s and 1830s Belize developed a valuable *entrepôt* trade, not only with the Moskitos but with the emergent neighbouring republics of Guatemala, Honduras and Nicaragua. In 1834 there arrived in Guatemala a very keen consul-general named Frederick Chatfield, who saw infinite possibilities for British trade – and territory too if the government wanted it. He reached his headquarters via Jamaica and Belize, establishing a friendly liaison with the Superintendent there. A schooner took him to Fort San Felipe, where the sloop HMS *Thunder* was engaged in a survey of the Bay of Amatique and Lake Izabal, as part of the general interest in possible canal routes over which the Guatemalans were co-operative. From the coast Chatfield travelled by mule for seven days to Guatemala City. There he found two Belize merchants, Marshall Bennett and Thomas Gould, busy in obtaining a large land concession near the Belize border, in return for a thousand muskets. On condition that they exploited the resources and introduced settlers during the next twenty years the land would then become the property of their company. This was typical of the concessions extracted from the emergent governments. At the same time Bennett and Gould were anxious to oust other British merchants. Among their rivals was a Guatemalan of Irish origin, Colonel Juan Golindo, who had obtained a neighbouring concession. As a keen nationalist Golindo was infuriated by Chatfield's view that once a British subject, a man could not renounce his nationality. He also opposed the monopolistic ring that Bennett and Gould were attempting to create.

Although warned before leaving London that all assumption of superiority would shock the pride of the new nationalists, Chatfield proceeded to do just that. Typical of the Victorian Englishman, so convinced of his country's imperial destiny and the benefits to all who came under its sway, Chatfield became overbearing in the extreme, so much so that he got away with it. For seventeen years he was the dominant foreigner in Central America, hated perhaps, but imperturbable. A San Salvador newspaper of 1850 groaned: 'The ravages of smallpox, cholera, civil war, tyranny, barbarism . . . all these pass away. . . . But there is an evil, horrible and interminable, there is a living curse which corrodes the vitals of Central America – and this is Chatfield, the eternal Agent of England.' The explanation for Chatfield's long survival was the presence of Lord Palmerston at the Foreign Office for thirteen of Chatfield's seventeen years in Central America. They were birds of a feather, and there were times when the consul seemed to lead the Foreign Secretary on. Gunboats were waiting in the Pacific as well as the Atlantic to protect British nationals from interference in their commercial exploits. In 1849 Chatfield ordered the occupation of Tigre Island in the Bay of Fonseca by Royal Marines to encourage the settlement of a debt owed by the government of Honduras.

In 1837 there arrived to take up the post of Superintendent at Belize Captain Alexander Macdonald, a man of the same ilk as Frederick Chatfield. Consequently it was not surprising that he saw no reason for consulting Chatfield before he took action. When complaints reached Belize that the Nicaraguan Colonel Quijano had occupied the little town of San Juan, Macdonald descended on him in a naval sloop and took him for a ride up to Cape Gracias to impress on his unwilling guest that San Juan was part of the Moskito Shore under British protection. Macdonald and his naval friends treated the affair as a rollicking adventure, 'drinking lots of champagne, toasting Queen Victoria, King Frederick of the Moskito Nation, her ancient ally, the Queen and Family, the Duke of Wellington, the Army, the Navy, Commander Douglas [of HMS *Tweed*], and the memory of Lord Nelson in Silence'.

During this remarkable cruise HMS *Tweed* called at the Corn Islands, and there Superintendent Macdonald ordered the liberation of the ninety-eight slaves, promising £25 a head compensation to their owners. It was never paid. Eighteen years later the owners were still asking for their money. This was in parenthesis to the main Quijano affair. An indignant clamour arose in Central America that almost brought together the members of the recently defunct United Provinces. San Juan was reoccupied by Nicaragua, repossessed by King Frederick, retaken by Nicaragua. Palmerston, Foreign Secretary again, sent two gunboats in 1848. An expedition up the river to rescue two British subjects kidnapped in Quijano fashion fought a minor engagement in which fifteen sailors and marines were killed and wounded. Leaving his small force at the head of the river, Commander Granville Lock crossed Lake Nicaragua and forced the government to accept the Treaty of Managua, acknowledging San Juan as part of Mosquitia, as the coast was then being called. To emphasize its British-protected status, the town was renamed Greytown after Sir Charles Grey, then governor of Jamaica. Three years later the Bay Islands were declared a British colony. This marked the peak of British bellicosity. That same year Consul-General Chatfield was recalled, and his successor, Charles Lennox Wyke, pursued a more conciliatory policy. In 1859 Britain ceded the Bay Islands to the Republic of Honduras; next year Mosquitia went to Nicaragua with the proviso that the king should be allowed a great measure of autonomy and Greytown should become a free port.

Shortly before the last British sell-out, Captain Bedford Pim paid a visit to Mosquitia in the sloop HMS *Gorgon*, a sail-cum-paddleboat based at Jamaica. Greytown was a miserable little place with wooden frame houses and a few grass-grown streets, where it was said to 'rain thirteen months in the year'. The sallow British consul, Dr Green, however, denied this defamation. He had lived there for twenty years and found the climate healthy. The river-mouth harbour had silted up, for which Pim blamed the operations of the American Transit Company, and the *Gorgon* had to anchor outside the bar in rough water. He found the Moskito king at Bluefields, a pathetic figure on a lonely shore. George Augustus Frederick was a bachelor, living in a large American two-storey frame house owned by Consul Green. Of pure Indian blood, he was short, slight but well built, and lived with the Queen Mother and two sisters, Princess Victoria who was married to a Moskito, and the other whose English husband had gone off. The ladies were very simply dressed. The King, dressed in a white suit and a felt hat, gave the English visitors a friendly welcome, sending his one black servant for beer – warm, but wet and welcome. Speaking without any trace of accent, King George told Pim that he felt like an Englishman, and there were the works of Shakespeare, the poems of Byron and the novels of Sir Walter Scott on his shelves to prove it. Unfortunately, from the Englishmen he and his ancestors persisted in admiring, he had adopted a liking for liquor, but he was civil enough to behave himself when Pim took him on a cruise up the coast. Bluefields was a small place. A beach-comber type named Rahn who lived on a cay at the entrance to the bay was agent for the Royal Mail ships that called occasionally, and there was a Moravian mission. Pim liked the place so much that he obtained a concession from King George Augustus Frederick and returned in 1863 to promote a railway up to Granada, but he failed to find the financial backing.

Across at Great Corn Island there were about 280 inhabitants, white Creoles and Negroes, with English or Irish names like Quin, Forbes, Francis, Hooker and Nansank. A man named James Bowden was chief magistrate, with a vague connection with Belize. It was a delightful place with crystal-clear water and white sand beaches that have today turned it into a Nicaraguan holiday resort. The fertile soil produced a variety of tropical fruit and ground-provisions and the sea provided fish and turtle. It was a tropical paradise. Little Corn Island was a cattle pasture. Further away were Old Providence and St Andrew's Island. Providence had about three hundred inhabitants; St Andrew's, which had had no permanent residents in the old Puritan days, now had between four and five hundred people, all of English extraction. Although the Republic of Colombia had laid claim to these islands they were still virtually self-governing. English is still spoken there to this day.

Similar conditions prevailed on the Bay Islands. Once again there were the English, Irish and Scottish names: Eden, Cooper, Bodden, Warren, Woodville, Kirkconnell, McNab, Macdonald. For long the Bay Islanders tried to ignore their transfer to Honduras. Although only Spanish is taught in the schools today, half the population is bilingual. During the nineteenth century schooner-building produced ships that sailed the Caribbean and Gulf of Mexico, profiting from the frequent civil wars, smuggling and gun-running, at times carrying arms for both sides. In the 1930s the little settlement of Port Royal – the Jamaica connection is significant – was described as 'entirely nailed together in a wooden tangle of planks and logs that is a triumph of architectural socialism: each house supports the next and the burden of the public way is shared'. As it was built on stilts over the water, boats and canoes were conveniently kept underneath. In the houses were Union Jacks and pictures of George v. The Honduran authorities had attempted to ban the use of English in vain.

The final Moskito curtain was not drawn until 1905. During the Honduras-Nicaragua War of 1893 Royal Marines were landed on the Shore to protect British lives and property. A private army of Moskito Indians and Jamaica Negroes, who had come in with the banana companies then operating, drove out the Nicaraguan troops, but agreed to incorporation in the republic again next year. But the Moskito king was not satisfied, still hankering for a return to British protection, so that by the Anglo-Nicaraguan Treaty of 1905, although Britain finally renounced any claim to a protectorate, the king was removed to Jamaica where he lived on a small pension until he died three years later.

Although the Moskito Coast and the islands associated with it constituted the biggest areas of British interest outside Belize during the nineteenth century, the activities of British subjects within the republics of the Main and Central America were by no means insignificant, especially in the two decades after Waterloo, the years in which the new nations of America were emerging. The key to understanding the timing of the struggle for independence by the countries of South America lies in the Napoleonic wars. That twelve-year European struggle loosened the control of her colonies by Spain and gave the Creole patriots their chance. It also opened the door into Spanish America for British commerce. With the first surrender of Napoleon in 1814, however, and the restoration of Ferdinand VII to his throne, the Spanish government made strenuous efforts to reassert its authority. As General Morillo arrived in the Caribbean with ten thousand Spanish troops, Simon Bolivar the Liberator sent an urgent appeal to Luis Mendez, his commissioner in London, to raise a force of British volunteers. Here was a golden opportunity for British merchants with surplus war stocks on their hands to sell them in South America and establish valuable new markets. Protesting their love of liberty rather than their hopes of gain, they encouraged the recruitment of mercenaries. In December 1817 four ships carrying 120 officers and six hundred other ranks set sail for the Spanish Main. It sounded a godsend for discharged servicemen. In all, during the next three years over five thousand English and Irish volunteers crossed to South America.

Among this considerable body of volunteers motives were extremely mixed. There were idealists going to fight in the glorious cause of liberty; there were adventurers and fortune-hunters; there were debtors escaping from their creditors. Some of the recruiting officers made their pile by the sale of commissions before ever setting foot aboard, caring little if the new officers, resplendent in bright uniforms though they were, had had any military experience or not. Prominent among these unscrupulous people was the Scottish scallywag, Gregor MacGregor – Colonel, of course, but not yet Cazique of the Poyer Nation. His Hibernian Regiment achieved little save a few Falstaffian adventures at Porto Bello and Rio Hacha. Of the two thousand men and a few families he sent to the

Caribbean only three saw Britain again – and one of them was Gregor MacGregor.

The vanguard of 1817, flaunting the titles of 1st and 2nd Venezuelan Hussars and 1st and 2nd Venezuelan Lancers, were to form a British brigade. Their organizer, formerly Lieutenant but now Colonel Gustavus Hippisley, had been authorized to offer British rates of pay and a bonus of $200 for officers, $80 for NCOs, on landing in South America. Nobody ever saw the bonus because Bolivar's government had nothing in the treasury: his Creole soldiers fought without pay. Hippisley soon left in disgust, which was good riddance, for his place was taken by Lieutenant-Colonel James Rooke, a fine leader. Of the six hundred who had sailed from England only 150 reached Angostura (the modern Ciudad Bolivar) on the Orinoco. Shipwreck, disease and desertion had taken their toll.

A second wave of one thousand men as reinforcements, together with some Hanoverians, captured Barcelona on the Main and marched across the eastern Andes to Maturin, enduring appalling privations that left alive only fourteen officers and 130 other ranks. Bolivar then assembled the survivors and reorganized them. Colonel Rooke was given command of the 'Dragoons of the Guard of Bolivar'; Colonel Arthur Sandes commanded a rifle battalion of four hundred Indians with British officers, which became one of Bolivar's crack units and fought in every engagement of his Andean campaign. A second rifle regiment with British and Hanoverian officers was commanded by Major J. Macintosh. Lastly, a small all-British unit of sixteen officers and 130 other ranks, known as the British Legion, also accompanied Bolivar into the mountains. The two thousand Irish recruited by Colonel John D'Evereux took part in the capture of Rio Hacha and then disintegrated, some reaching Jamaica, others Canada.

Once the dross had been cast off the small cadre that remained performed useful service. The campaigns of Bolivar have filled books of their own and make reading as incredible as the exploits of Cortez, Pizarro and the sixteenth-century Conquistadors, but because such small numbers of them were present the British mercenaries played no decisive part in the wars of liberation. Nevertheless it can be claimed that they showed their Creole fellow-soldiers the use of the bayonet and improved the cavalry tactis of the cowboy *llaneros*. Their part has been acknowledged at the battles of Boyaca, where a bayonet-charge went in with effect to open the way to Bogotá, and of Carabobo in 1821, which led to the investment of Caracas. The remnant of the British Legion, combined with that of Macintosh's rifles as the Albion Regiment, marched south to Popayan and took part in the Battle of Picincha, high up on the volcano, which liberated Quito, while the indestructible Sandes was present at Ayacucho in Bolivia, the final victory of the war in 1824. The British did not win the war but they were there.

Besides the regimental officers there were numbers of British on Bolivar's staff. Sandes served until 1830 when his rifle regiment was disbanded. He lived on in Venezuela and left his name in the country. Thomas Manby settled in Bogotá. When he died in 1881 public honours were paid to his memory as the last survivor of 'the glorious British Legion'. Charles Minchin who fought at Carabobo settled in Coro on the Main. Recalled to service in 1855, he became a Venezuelan general and minister of war. Colonel William Ferguson died in 1828, defending Bolivar from a would-be assassin. Then there was Belford Wilson, the son of General Sir Robert Wilson, sent by his father to serve as an ADC. For out-riding Paul Revere – he is credited with covering 1,800 miles through the Andes in nineteen days – he was promoted from captain to colonel and remained with Bolivar till the Liberator died in 1830. Subsequently Wilson served as British consul-general in Peru and Venezuela.

Two Irishmen also rose to fame. Daniel O'Leary started as a cornet in the 2nd Venezuelan Hussars. After fighting at Carabobo he joined Bolivar's staff, on which he became chief ADC. He retired to Jamaica in 1832 to write his memoirs (the principal source for the biographies of Bolivar) and then performed various missions to Chile, the United States and Spain. He married the sister of General Sucre and founded one of Bogotá's leading families. Finally, Francis O'Connor, the brother of Fergus the Chartist, who came out with the Irish Legion, served as a staff-officer in Peru and finally settled in Bolivia. But the great majority of the five thousand British mercenaries passed forgotten into limbo, save for a tablet on the front of the Capitol in Bogotá in memory of the British Legion.

In Central America there were no mercenaries because Spain made no military attempt to suppress the independence movement. There was, on the other hand, considerable commercial activity by European nationals in which British people played their part without ever attaining the dominant role as they did in Argentina, and to a lesser extent in Chile and Brazil. In Central America and Mexico, situated as the area is on the southern door-step of the United States, the main activity has been American. In the first half of the nineteenth century the chief spheres of British commercial interest lay in Australia, New Zealand and South Africa. What commercial activity there was round the shores of the Caribbean was of an individual nature. Thus Captain Charles Cochrane and Lionel Gisborne did some exploration in Panama for possible canal routes; Royal Navy vessels carried out some useful charting; mining prospectors searched for gold and silver; a few Englishmen went coffee-planting in Nicaragua and Guatemala. Perhaps the most important line of business was banking; examples are the

Bank of London and Mexico, founded in 1864, and the Bank of London and Montreal which opened branches in the Central American republics. A successful Scottish banker was James Walker, who arrived in Mexico in 1888 as a clerk in the Bank of London and Mexico and ended his connection with it as manager, when he transferred to the management of the Mexican Bank of Commerce and Industry. In 1907 he was described as 'one of the most hospitable of the British colony, entertaining lavishly at his beautiful home with its spacious grounds in the suburbs'.

By far the most important British subject to make his mark in Mexico was Weetman Pearson, first Viscount Cowdray, who visited the country on holiday in 1889 and was invited to undertake the construction of the Mexican Grand Canal to empty the lakes of the inland drainage basin which periodically caused flooding in Mexico City. This successful contract led to others: for harbour works at Vera Cruz, harbour works at the Atlantic and Pacific termini and the reconstruction of the Tehuantepec Railway. In all Lord Cowdray's firm, S. Pearson and Son Ltd, completed works exceeding £14,000,000 in value which led on to the acquisition of a substantial stake in the Mexican oilfields. Other family interests included a jute-mill at Orizaba, tramway and electric power companies and cattle ranching.

It was men like Lord Cowdray who built up the high reputation enjoyed by Englishmen throughout Latin America. Scrupulous in carrying out the terms of every contract, particularly the completion date, and conscious of the sensitive character of his clients, Cowdray endeared himself to the Mexicans as few foreigners succeeded in doing. He always made the maximum use of Mexican engineers and labour, looking after the comforts of his employees and expecting them to endure no conditions that he was not prepared to share with them himself. When President Porfirio Diaz came to set the first dredger working on the Grand Canal, his large party was entertained at a banquet laid in the hull of the second dredger, decorated in the Mexican national colours with coloured candles on the tables and a sugar model of the dredger before the presidential place. At a Christmas dinner given later for the employees, the local village president, magistrate and padre were thoughtfully included among the company and were loud in their toasts of 'Salud, Señor Don Weetman Pearson!' As the engineer-in-charge described the scene, 'In fact they drank his health so often that it slightly affected their own, and we generally assisted them into their saddles at the close of the festival.'

Lord Cowdray was accustomed to spending about three months of every year in Mexico, where his son Harold was in permanent residence, managing the oil business. The family dispensed lavish entertainment as the custom was in the Mexican capital, joining in a round of dinner and luncheon parties, dances, picnics, riding parties and polo matches, not only with the British colony but with their numerous Mexican friends. Too often the Englishman abroad spends so much of his leisure with his compatriots that he earns a reputation for aloofness and snobbery; yet to the young man newly out from home the British club provided a haven where he could keep up with the English news and eat more cheaply than he could in the city restaurants. There were impromptu entertainments called 'smokers', the ubiquitous amateur dramatics and rarer musical evenings. The British are not the only clubbish people in foreign capitals. For every British club there was and is an American, German, French or Italian institute.

Like most foreign concerns in Latin America, the Cowdray businesses became affected in due course by revolution. After the fall of President Diaz in 1911, Mexico's prosperity was ruined by six years of civil war, and foreign nationals found themselves faced with delicate and sometimes dangerous situations that called for the exercise of tact, fortitude and courage. Thanks to skilful local management the Anglo-Mexican Oil Company continued to function and prosper throughout the First World War, producing vital supplies for the Royal Navy. In 1919 the company was taken over by the Royal Dutch group. Mexico's political upheavals continued until in 1937 and 1938 railways, public utility companies and oilfields were nationalized. After compensation was eventually paid, nationalization was seen to be only right, but without foreign capital, enterprise and expertise Latin American countries could never have reached their present status.

Down on the Isthmus of Panama the main activities were conducted first of all by the French in the abortive de Lesseps canal project of 1879–88, and then by the Americans who completed their lock-canal in 1914. Both these ventures made use of Negro labourers from the British West Indies, as also did the several American fruit companies that started their extensive banana plantations in most of the republics after 1870. British companies built only two major railways outside Mexico: the line from Puerto Limon to San José in Costa Rica and the Dorado Railway from Santa Marta, which was one of Lord Cowdray's many enterprises. During the greatest period of British activity, between 1880 and 1914, British communities were to be found in all the republics. If a cross-section of their various occupations had been taken these would have been found to include some or all of the following: diplomatic and consular service, export and import business, shipping, oil, railways, public utilities, manufacturing, shopkeeping, banking and insurance, planting and mining. These permanent residents were joined from time to time by scientists, geographers, anthropologists and archaeologists. Through the influence of faceless and nameless Britishers with their passion for sport the Latin Americans were introduced to association football which today surpasses in popularity the baseball and basketball introduced by the Americans. The First World War, the 1930 slump and the Second World War progressively reduced British activity in the area to a trickle of its former volume. In 1965 exports to Britain averaged less than three per cent and imports from Britain less than five per cent of each country's total overseas trade.

12
SAILORS AND SOLDIERS

A statement that the main activity of British servicemen in the Caribbean over three and a half centuries was dying might be spared from dismissal as a gross exaggeration by acceptance as a warrantable hyperbole. Records are far from complete, but a half-calculated guess would be that there are between 150,000 and 200,000 British graves, both earthy and watery, marked, unknown or forgotten, under and around the blue waves of the Caribbean and its neighbouring waters. To quote the figures of only four expeditions: there were over 3,500 deaths at Cartagena in 1740, 6,500 at Havana in 1762, 20,000 in Haiti and 40,000 in Martinique during the French Revolutionary War. On garrison duty alone the death rate among British troops was eighteen per cent at Barbados between 1796 and 1805, and twelve per cent at Jamaica between 1817 and 1836. The main cause of all these deaths was not the enemy but disease. Mortality was high wherever British soldiers and sailors served, but in addition to the occupational diseases of typhus, dysentery and scurvy, men posted to the West Indies had to face the ravages of malaria and yellow fever. Every contest between Britain and France was refereed by 'Yellow Jack' and a knock-out was banned. It was yellow fever and not the French that foiled the British attempt to capture Haiti; it was yellow fever that defeated Napoleon's attempt to win it back from the slaves; it was yellow fever that saved Jamaica from the French in 1741.

The course of the fever was swift and horrible: usually it killed in three days. As it spread at lightning speed through a ship's company men panicked and sickened; when they started the fever they threw up their hands and died, but a few tough, resilient and courageous people survived. One such case was the Rev. Richard Rawle who caught yellow fever in 1852 when he was principal of Codrington College. He received the typical treatment. The doctor bled him till he fainted, then he was dosed with calomel. The pain in his back and limbs was agonizing. More bleeding and

The eastern Caribbean, showing principal changes of sovereignty

more calomel followed and he would have surely died but for the devoted nursing of his wife and a friend, who fed him on toast and water, gave him saline draughts, bathed him in warm water, applied leeches, put ice on his head. After three days he passed the crisis and lived to become Bishop of Trinidad. Soldiers and sailors who started yellow fever had not the nursing that undoubtedly saved Richard Rawle. Fortunately it was not permanently virulent and years could go by without an epidemic. Newcomers were more susceptible than old residents, so that the death-rate was always high among troops and crews just out from home. And all the time the real enemy was hiding in the corner-cupboards and breeding in the water-cisterns – the stegomya mosquito, unsuspected for two hundred years.

Because of the importance of the West Indian colonies during the eighteenth century, they were carefully guarded. Between 1739 and 1763 the usual army and navy dispositions were one regiment each at Jamaica and the Leeward Islands, three ships at Jamaica, one at the Leeward Islands and one at Barbados. During wartime the numbers of troops and ships were greatly increased. Because the colonies were islands the navy played a more important role than the army, so that it is not surprising to find that the bearers of nearly all the famous names in British naval history served in the islands during some period of their careers. The first of a long line, Vice-Admiral John Benbow died at Jamaica in 1703 from wounds received in action against the French. There is a memorial to him in Kingston Parish Church.

Next came Vice-Admiral Edward Vernon, famous for his association with the rum ration. Contrary to popular legend, however, it was not he who introduced it: he had it diluted and gave his nickname, 'Old Grog' – earned by the grogram cloak he affected – to the mixture of rum and water which he introduced and issued, half at midday, half at sunset. Previous to Vernon's orders in 1740 the men had been issued with half a pint of neat rum, which had proved too much even for sailors' hard heads, rendering men incapable of duty by sundown. The generous rum ration – the only attraction in naval service – derived from the daily *gallon* of beer issued to the Elizabethan navy in home waters. Because beer did not keep on long voyages, half a pint of brandy or rum was issued in its place. So Vernon reduced and split it between noon and sunset, prescribing an issue of one gill of rum and three of water on each occasion. In the tropics lemon juice and a little sugar were usually added. Various admirals modified the ration from time to time until by 1850 the evening issue had been abolished in favour of drinks like tea and cocoa.*

Partially successful in his conquest of naval drunkenness, Vernon enjoyed only partial success also in his campaigns. In 1739 he was acclaimed for his capture of Porto Bello, but two attempts to capture Cartagena failed, partly through the old bogey of lack of co-operation from the army commander, partly on account of yellow fever. Serving as a surgeon's mate was Tobias Smollett, who left an account of the soldiers' experiences in his novel *Roderick Random*. Among the North American troops was Lawrence Washington, who admired Vernon so much that he named his estate Mount Vernon after him, leaving it on his death to his famous half-brother, George. With Sir Chaloner Ogle, who relieved Vernon, was a young officer, Edward Hawke, the future victor of Quiberon Bay, while his contemporary victor at Lagos, Edward Boscawen, went to Cartagena with Vernon as a volunteer. Four years before his great victory at Cape St Vincent in 1798, Sir John Jervis was the naval commander at the capture of Martinique.

But the greatest naval names in eighteenth-century Caribbean history are those of Nelson and Rodney, each of their careers typifying various aspects of naval service conditions in their time. In all, George Rodney

* In 1970 the single issue ended.

spent eight years in the West Indies. From 1761 to 1763 he was commander-in-chief, Leeward Islands Station; from 1771 to 1774 he commanded at Jamaica; from 1779 to 1782 he was back at the Leewards. Nelson's West India service totalled six years. From 1777 to 1780 he was stationed mainly at Jamaica, coming out a second lieutenant and going home a post-captain; between 1784 and 1787 he was senior captain at the Leeward Islands. There were two other brief visits – discounting his boyhood voyage on a merchant ship – the first with Hood in 1782, the second while chasing Villeneuve in 1805. Rodney and Nelson never met on West India service. Rodney, forty years Nelson's senior, ended his career in the Caribbean while Nelson was rising through the captains' postings.

In Rodney's first command, unusual co-operation with the army led to the capture of Martinique in 1762. An infantry officer there left a tribute to the sailors' part in the campaign: 'It is droll enough to see them tugging along, with a good twenty-five pounder at their heels: on they go, huzzahing and hallooing, sometimes uphill, sometimes downhill, swearing, blasting, damning, sinking, and as careless of everything but the matter committed to their charge as if death or danger had nothing to do with them.' It will ever be surprising that such service could be given by men, half of them pressed, many of them unwell, living on overcrowded gundecks without the smallest amenity – save the rum – and subject to a code of discipline that prescribed twenty-five lashes with the cat-o'-nine-tails as the minimum penalty for even the slightest offence. On this occasion their efforts were wasted because Martinique was returned to France at the Treaty of Paris in spite of Rodney's recommendation that Britain should keep it for the reason that the island possessed in Fort Royal the best natural harbour in the Lesser Antilles, strategically situated to windward of the islands to the north of it. When war broke out again less than twenty years later, Fort Royal provided the French with a secure base from which to threaten the British islands. Rodney had to fight then from the second-best haven at Gros Islet Bay, St Lucia. Barbados, although to windward, possessed only the open roadstead of Carlisle Bay. But the main British base in the eastern Caribbean developed at English Harbour, Antigua, of which the islanders made a present to the British Government in 1725. Twenty years later it was in use as a careenage and storage depot, but St Lucia continued to be used as the advance base against Martinique.

Every sailor, officer or rating, took cheer when war came, because war provided the chance of earning prize money. Impecunious officers like Rodney and Nelson kept a keen watch for enemy sails. For years Rodney had no luck. After the capture of Martinique, just as he was on the point of embarking on a plundering cruise along the coast of Hispaniola, he received orders to await and give assistance to an expedition under General the Earl of Albemarle and Admiral Pocock, dispatched to capture Havana. He never forgot his chagrin when he heard that the enterprise had led to the capture of £3,000,000 worth of booty. Pocock and Albemarle received £123,000 each; a naval captain's share worked out at £1,600 and on down the scale to army privates who received £4 1s 8d and ordinary seamen, £3 14s 9¾d each. This was strictly in accordance with recognized scales, but there was such an outcry against the discrepancy between the highest and lowest that they were amended. In the seventeenth century the King had received a fifteenth and the Lord High Admiral one-tenth of the value of each prize, but the royal rights were waived after 1708. For the next hundred years all booty was divided into eight parts. One-eighth went to the Admiral of the station, two to the commander or commanders; one-eighth was divided among the captain of Marines, the naval lieutenants, the ship's master and the doctor; one-eighth among the lieutenants of Marines, Army lieutenants, principal warrant officers and Marine sergeants, and one-eighth among the naval ratings and army other ranks. The more, the less merry! The best haul for the lower deck came in 1748 from the capture of the Spanish frigate *Hermione* by the RN frigates *Active* and *Favourite* when the ordinary seaman's share worked out at £485. Lieutenants drew £13,000, and the two captains collected £65,000 each. Seamen did not expect to make fortunes, but captains and flag officers often did. Rodney's predecessor, Sir Hyde Parker, is alleged to have made £200,000 in prize money during his tour of service in the West Indies.

Rodney had to wait until 1781 before a fortune fell into his lap when he captured the Dutch island of St Eustatius and took prizes with booty as valuable as at Havana. Yet quixotically he attempted to give it away – to George III for the conduct of the disastrous war against the American colonies. 'I do not look upon myself entitled to one sixpence, nor do I desire it,' he wrote; 'my happiness is having been the instrument of my country . . .' With equal gallantry George declined Rodney's offer and ordered the booty to be distributed in the customary manner. Rodney used his share to pay off his debts and buy a London house, but he was not to enjoy his riches for long, because most of them went in the settlement of damages awarded against him in a long series of lawsuits brought by the merchants of St Kitts.

Nelson made no fortune either. While waiting for an answer to his suit for Fanny Nesbit, he wrote to his friend Cuthbert Collingwood: 'My dear boy, I need some prize money.' Dreams of prize money kept the career officer serving for in 1793 rates of pay were inadequate. The captain of a first-rate drew £28 a month, the captain of a sixth-rate, £8 8s od. A first lieutenant's pay varied from £4 to £9 2s od according to the rating of his ship. A rear admiral earned £48, a full admiral, double. On the lower deck, a cook was paid 25/–, an able seaman 24/– and an ordinary seaman, 19/–. These rates of pay were increased during the Napoleonic Wars. Poor as it was the naval pay was better than the army because the sailor was fed. In 1795 a private's pay was sixpence a day with fourpence for messing. Two years later it was raised to one shilling and stayed there till 1891. Officers' pay remained low until the twentieth century. Until the Crimean War an ensign's pay was 4/6d a day, which did not cover the cost of his messing; it was assumed that officers had private means. Purchase of commissions continued until 1871, when it was abolished. As late as 1860 it cost £1,300 *by regulations* to purchase a captaincy in a line regiment and £4,500 for a colonelcy. In fact as much as double had to be paid. Except in expeditions like that to Havana the army had fewer chances of booty than the navy, but a system of rewards was encouraged by regulations. Thus by 1793 the captor of a cannon was paid £20, colours won £10 and a horse, £12. This was chicken-feed, so the soldier rewarded himself by pillage and expert foraging. The best reward for meritorious service was promotion. Occasionally a pension was awarded.

In the West Indies awards were frequently made to officers for meritorious service by the colonial legislatures, often on a generous scale. After the Demerara Rebellion of 1823 the Court of Policy distributed presents magnanimously: to the O.C., Troops, 500 guineas for plate and 200 guineas for a sword; sums of 100 and 200 guineas to other officers, but to Lieutenant Brady of the 21st Fusiliers, who had defended Mahaica Post against large numbers of slaves, 1,000 guineas was voted. The most munificent recognition of services was that made by the Jamaica assembly after Rodney had saved their colony by defeating the French at the battle of Les Saintes: they spent over £8,000 on a commission to the sculptor John Bacon for his design of the Rodney memorial that still stands in the square at Spanish Town. Of more value to Rodney was the barony and pension of £2,000 a year voted to him by the British Parliament.

The eighteenth century was the age of privilege and patronage. When Rodney arrived in Jamaica in 1771 as commander-in-chief, he was accompanied by an entourage of young gentlemen anxious to secure some of the lucrative offices there. The Navy storekeeper at Port Royal drew a salary of only £300 a year, but the perquisites of office were alleged to be worth another £3,000. Unfortunately for the place seekers, the island was enjoying a healthy period and nobody obliged by dying in office and creating a vacancy. Rodney himself at this time applied for appointment as Governor of Jamaica, but was turned down because he lacked the right contacts. During the eighteenth and nineteenth centuries most of the governors were appointed from the higher ranks of the army and navy, an exceptional appointment being that of Admiral Charles Knowles who started his career on the lower deck and ended, after serving as admiral, in the King's House, Jamaica. Sir John Moore for a short time was governor of St Lucia, and Trinidad's first British governor was General Picton, afterwards killed at Waterloo in 1815.

It was perhaps stretching the accepted standards of his day to the limit when Rodney appointed his own son a post-captain at the age of sixteen, but apparently the boy held the job down. Another youthful appointment of his later distinguished himself as Admiral Sir Sydney Smith, defender of Acre against Napoleon: Rodney gave him his captaincy at eighteen. By comparison Nelson, a post-captain at twenty, was old.

Rodney's greatest feat was his victory over De Grasse at Les Saintes, between Dominica and Guadeloupe, on 12 April 1782. Coming as it did after the surrender of Yorktown, the news was greeted with the wildest enthusiasm in England and Rodney returned to a hero's welcome. In fact it could have been a greater victory than it was, for only four French ships of the line were taken. If Hood had had his way there would have been many more, but Rodney was justifiably cautious. He did not want to leave the Leeward Islands upwind of him until he was assured there were no further French ships to attack them once he had lost the weather gauge by sailing after the French towards Haiti and Jamaica. As it was he had captured De Grasse and his flagship, the *Ville de Paris*, the greatest battleship in the world. Although they were left with a considerable fleet, the French gave up all idea of further attempts at Jamaica. They saw at the Saints and admitted that the British Navy was one hundred years ahead of them, and this was due as much to Rodney as their defeat in battle, for Rodney had brought out with him as his private physician, Dr Gilbert Blane, whose influence in improving the health of the British sailor is recognized as second to none. Due to Blane, appointed as Commissioner for the Sick and Hurt by his patron, attention was paid to cleanliness and ventilation on the ships, soap was issued for the first time and lemon juice virtually eradicated scurvy. It was Blane who recommended that petty officers should carry tourniquets on them to bring quick action that saved wounded men bleeding to death before they could be taken to the surgeon. He could make the justifiable boast that on the twenty-two British ships at St Lucia there were not twenty-two men who could not come to quarters. Among the French fleet the old, filthy conditions prevailed. When the fleets went into action the British sailors were far healthier than the enemy.

The experiences of Nelson exemplify other aspects of naval life. His greatest share of booty was £800 from the capture of a French ship off the North coast of Jamaica when he was Captain of the *Hinchingbrooke*. Before that ship arrived at Port Royal, Nelson had been in command of Fort Charles there, daily expecting a descent on the island by the French. A

Islands and Towns

A view over Kingston to the harbour in 1870. Note the shingle roofs and the absence of corrugated iron.

Top A Duperly daguerrotype of King Street, Kingston, in 1850, looking north towards the Blue Mountains beyond the spire of the Parish Church.

Bottom The Court House, St John's, Antigua.

Top Fort George, guarding Scarborough, the tiny capital of little Tobago, drawn in 1793 when the island was captured from France for the second of three times.

Bottom Scarborough Bay, Tobago, 1834.

Kingstown, St Vincent. Drawn by Lieut Caddy, R.A.

Top The Pitch Lake, Trinidad, sketched by R. Bridgens in 1851.

Bottom Looking down on Falmouth Harbour, Nelson's Dockyard and English Harbour, Antigua. A greetings card of 1830.

Brimstone Hill, St Kitts, sketched by Lieut Caddy, R.A. In January 1782, the French fleet under De Grasse arrived off Basseterre. The Governor, Major-General Thomas Shirley, retreated to the fort on Brimstone Hill, where he withstood a month's siege, bombarded by the guns intended for the fort, which he had been forced to abandon on the beach because the planters had refused to provide slaves to carry the guns up the hill. The island was saved by Admiral Hood who brilliantly outmanoeuvered De Grasse, in a prelude to Rodney's victory at the Saints in April.

The scenic beauty of the West Indies is nowhere more impressive than in the Blue Mountains of Jamaica. The Peak rises to 7,402 feet. On the northern slopes the average rainfall varies between 120 and 200 inches a year; the southern slopes form a rain shadow area, giving Kingston an average rainfall of only 34 inches per annum. Blue Mountain coffee, once world famous is no longer grown.

simple plaque commemorates his association with the fort. In February 1780 Captain Nelson in the *Hinchingbrooke* took part in a small expedition of five hundred men who were sent to the Moskito Shore to capture Lake Nicaragua and control the passage to the Pacific by that route. Following in the path of Henry Morgan and his buccaneer friends more than one hundred years before, Nelson played a prominent part in the attack on Fort San Juan near the effluence of the river from the lake. Then, as in so many of such forgotten expeditions, fever struck and Nelson was invalided back to Jamaica on another ship, for the *Hinchingbrooke* was immobilised by the death of nine-tenths of her crew. Her captain might well have ended his days on the Moskito Shore.

Carried ashore at Jamaica, Nelson was nursed back to health by Cuba Cornwallis, a free negress who had nursed him before, famous for her cures of many other officers. Reaching convalescence Nelson was invited to Admiral's Pen, the official residence of the commander-in-chief, provided by the colony of Jamaica. Sir Peter Parker had seen to the rising star's promotion and now his wife nursed the invalid when he suffered a relapse. He was far from well when he sailed home. It took him a long time to recover his full health.

Already Nelson was known as an outstanding officer. In 1784 on the Leeward Islands Station, where he found himself second-in-command to Sir Richard Hughes, who had distinguished himself by losing an eye in an accident while he was killing a cockroach, Nelson made himself unpopular with the colonists by insisting on the rigid enforcement of the navigation acts. His one-eyed chief was inclined to see nothing of the encroachments of American ships, but Nelson had four of their captains arrested. As in the case of Rodney a few years earlier, the local merchants sued the future hero for damages to the tune of £40,000. Fortunately for Nelson the Admiralty persuaded the Treasury to pay up.

The outstanding captain was also marked in another way by the arrows of Cupid, for he tended to fall in love with every pretty girl he came across. In Antigua he fell for the wife of the Commissioner of the Dockyard; on the rebound after their parting, he fell for Fanny Nesbit, the widowed niece of John Herbert, president of the council of Nevis. Herbert kept Nelson waiting eighteen months, for his niece was also his housekeeper and he insisted on keeping her services till he retired. Meanwhile Nelson found himself ostracized by island society for his over-conscientious enforcement of the acts of trade. Indeed the wedding might have been a flop, but for the fortuitous arrival of HMS *Pegasus*, commanded by no less a person than His Royal Highness Prince William Henry, a service friend of the ardent suitor. Immediately the atmosphere changed. On Sunday 11 March 1787, all members of the island community attended the wedding, staged by the custom of the day, not in the local church but in the spacious hall of Montpelier, John Herbert's palatial great house. Deep bows and low curtsys marked the entry of His Royal Highness with the bridegroom on his arm. Inside he changed bridegroom for the bride and graciously gave Fanny Nesbit away. Shortly after the completion of a week's honeymoon the newly married couple sailed home on separate ships, Nelson so ill once more that he took on board a puncheon of rum in which to have his body preserved should he succumb during the voyage.

Generally quarrels with the colonists like Rodney and Nelson's were exceptional and relations between colonists and servicemen were friendly. Governors and admirals sometimes quarrelled over pressing, for navy ships too often arrived short-handed and captains attempted to seize merchant seamen. Governors then found themselves having to mediate between the petitions of merchants affirming that the next convoy would be unable to sail through shortage of hands and an ultimatum from the admiral that if his ships remained undermanned the convoy would sail unescorted. In the press-ganged navy the desertion rate was high, encouraged by the merchant captains who took full advantage of the less rigorous and better paid conditions on their ships. Thus Vernon in 1742 complained of 'not less than 500 having deserted from the hospital in Port Royal since my being in command; which I believe to have all been seduced out and gone home with the homeward-bound trade, through the temptations of high wages and 30 gallons of rum, and being conveyed drunk on board their ships from the punch houses where they are seduced'. Port Royal had changed little since the days of Morgan.

Impressment went out slowly in the long peace after 1815, accompanied by an improvement in service conditions that included the gradual reduction of flogging until it was abolished in the army in 1881. In the navy flogging was never technically abolished: it was 'suspended in peace time' in 1871 and in war time eight years later. Earlier in the West Indies there had been the anomalous position, during the emancipation campaign, when a slave could not by law be given more than forty lashes, while a soldier could be sentenced by a court martial to as many as a thousand. As the nineteenth century advanced increasing attention was paid to hygiene. Until 1857 no uniform was issued to naval seamen. Then cloth was provided and men were required to make their own to an official pattern: white trousers, blue jackets and straw hats with a name band. For tropical service white drill and a wider straw hat were issued. Below decks men were allocated fourteen inches width of deck for slinging their hammocks, a seemingly impossible arrangement circumvented only by the absence above of the watch on deck. In the eighteen-sixties attempts to improve ventilation were made by the use of windsails and pumps. The installation of steam engines and iron hulls made the improvement of ventilation still more urgent. Fixed cowls for directing air down to engine rooms made their appearance, then steam-driven fans, and finally electric fans from 1900. In the eighteen-sixties also quinine was first issued as a prophylactic and vaccination against smallpox was made compulsory.

To reduce the risk of desertion, captains cut shore leave to the minimum and withheld pay to the maximum, on the principle of 'Keep the pay, keep the man'. When they did manage to get ashore seamen amused themselves simply with drink and women. Following the custom in English naval bases, many a captain favoured having women brought aboard, allowing his ship to be turned into a Hogarthian stew. Thus Captain HRH Prince William Henry (later King William IV) issued an order: 'The First Lieuten-ant to see all strangers out of HM Ship under my command at gunfire, is by no means meant to restrain the officers and men from having either black or white women on board through the night, so long as discipline is unhurt by the indulgence.' Sometimes a planter would oblige by providing each member of the crew with the loan of a female slave. Occasionally women managed to hide themselves aboard between ports. After action against the French off Martinique in 1780 Rodney discovered there was a woman on *Sandwich*, who had stepped into her man's place in a gun crew when he was wounded. Rodney had her brought before him. After reprimanding her for breaking regulations, he rewarded her with ten guineas for the courage she had shown.

Such cases were exceptional. Ashore nobody took any care of British seamen until the twentieth century. They were to be seen all too frequently lying drunk in the streets of the unhealthy ports. Hauled on board by the petty officers, they were flogged for their drunkenness – and given their rum ration in which to drown their pain and sorrow. After the great naval victories, however, opinion of the British sailor changed. By the time of the First World War the pattern of shore leave had changed. When a Royal Navy ship came into port there was a round of football and tennis matches, golf, cricket and shooting. Not that Jack Tar turned Puritan: he still enjoyed 'his wife in every port' and his drinking bouts in the port dives.

Navy men could never have survived without a sense of humour. Captain Bedford Pim, whose experiences on the Moskito Shore have been quoted in the last chapter, left an account of an experience in Port Royal. He received the following invitation:

Miss Josephine Johnson presents her compliments to the Captain of the *Gorgon* and hopes to have the pleasure of his company at a *Dignity* on Monday evening at 8.30.

Now Miss Josephine Johnson was a washerwoman who looked after officers' clothes. Being no snob, Captain Pim went along, smartly turned out in 'whites'. There was a band from Kingston and food could be purchased from street vendors. He was asked to contribute 'a few bits' towards expenses. Then he looked for some dancing. There was 'a good bevy of women', but the heat was stifling and the *bouquet d'Afrique* was noticeable. He danced with a Haitian mulatto, then with a Jamaica Creole, but his attempt to make conversation was snubbed. 'I come here to dance, Sah,' his partner informed him, 'I no come to tark!'

The British soldier in the West Indies led a more sedentary life than the sailor. Soon after the first barracks had appeared in the seventeen-eighties, it was discovered that the hills were healthier than the coastal plains, so that regiments were constantly moved around. The soldier's daily round was filled with ceremonial drill and guard duties, punctuated by frequent reviews and inspections. For a full-dress parade a soldier of Wellington's time needed two hours to prepare. Useless but popular because they provided a spectacle for bored colonists, parades were colourful sights. In 1797, shortly after the capture of Demerara the Queen's Birthday was celebrated by such a show: the British troops and Demerara Volunteers in scarlet, the still present Dutch troops in blue and detachments of Royal Artillery on the wings. The parade was followed by a banquet and ball. General Sir George Nugent, while Governor of Jamaica, spent much of his time on reviews and inspections. His wife often accompanied him, noting in her diary: 'Rise before 3 . . . off to Kingston for a review of the Kingston Militia in a glorious sunrise . . . N. set off at 4 a.m. to review troops at Stony Hill . . .' and next day, 'Up at 4 a.m. to review troops at Up Park Camp . . .' Early morning parades were sensible, but very often they were held in the heat of the day and spoilt by the number of men fainting. Best of all the local people loved a military band, beating Retreat on the local barrack square or leading the troops through the streets to some parade for which an excuse was never difficult to find.

Most of the drilling was supervised by NCOs with only the duty officer present. Lieutenant Thomas St Clair of the First Regiment of Royals wrote his reminiscences of the two years he spent on garrison duty in Guiana between 1806 and 1808. His light duties allowed ample time for shooting and making expeditions up the rivers of the country. There is little mention of military duties in his journal, except for the monthly muster parade which all officers were obliged to attend, and his turns as duty officer. St Clair was fortunate in his commanding officer, Lt-Col Robert Nicholson, who proved himself kindly and attentive to the comforts of his subordinates. The regulation uniform for West Indian service was then a tall, round hat with cockade and feather, regimental jacket and duck pantaloons, with sash and small dirk hanging from a waist-belt to the side. The colonel's hair was cut strictly to regimental orders and tied in a thick queue on the nape of his neck. St Clair shared a large airy room in the Eve Leary barracks until after only a week in Georgetown he was posted to Berbice.

Without admitting that he followed the custom himself, St Clair described how, 'The first thing generally done by a European on his arrival in this country is to provide himself with a mistress from among the blacks, mulattoes or mestees, for here they are to be found in all different shades of colour. The price varies from £100 to £150. Many of these girls read and write. . . . Tasteful and extravagant in dress they are inviolable in their attachment. They perform all the duties of a wife except presiding at table.' Two officers had their mistresses living in their barrack rooms with them, one a beautiful young mulatto, the other a fine handsome black. Although at first shocked by the custom, St Clair came to appreciate its better side for he saw two officers' lives saved by the devoted nursing of their women. The girls seemed to suffer from no stigma among their families, who regarded the girls' relations with the officers as a lawful temporary marriage. Because of their excesses men in the tropics usually showed a higher death-rate than women, who frequently were 'married' as many as four times. 'It has frequently happened that a widow has buried four husbands,' observed St Clair, 'but it is rare to meet with a man who has survived one wife.'

When the time came for his transfer to Berbice, Thomas St Clair was invited to share the Colonel's gig, while their baggage and the dog he had brought out from England travelled by schooner. They were in no hurry. The sixty-mile journey took six days, three of them spent at a plantation waiting for heavy rain to stop. There were no inns along the road but the planters were hospitable. Arriving soaked to the skin the two officers were given a change of clothes, a good dinner and joined in a rubber of whist. Next morning St Clair found his boots had been burnt by a slave putting them to dry too close to the fire. To save the man a flogging, he made no complaint.

From Fort St Andrew's near New Amsterdam, Nicholson took St Clair to call on the Governor of Berbice, General Murray.* They were rowed to the town in the garrison boat, manned by six Negroes. At Fort St Andrew's St Clair was befriended by a Captain Yates – later a general – then a mad young officer who took the newcomer hunting. On Crab Island they shot parrots for the mess pepper-pot, often up to their armpits in mud and water, surrounded by a cloud of mosquitoes. On their return to the fort,

---

* Later transferred to Demerara and there during the 1823 Rebellion.

they had to hurry to clean up and change in time for mess dinner. The colonel warned them that it was unwise to expose themselves to 'the damps and heats' of the climate, and surely enough it was not long before St Clair was down with fever, caused of course by the mosquitoes and not by the miasma of the swamps as people of the time supposed. There was little yellow fever in Guiana in St Clair's day. The men kept good health except for drinking 'that vile beverage rum'.

During his attacks of fever, St Clair was drenched with quinine by the surgeon – one of the earliest instances of its use. Once he was treated more drastically by being laid naked on the floor and dowsed with buckets of cold water. Everybody suffered from malaria, or ague as it was still called. There are no hills near the coast of Guiana, but the sick were sent to convalesce at plantations near the sea, especially at Mahaica which enjoyed the healthiest reputation. To give him the maximum sea air, St Clair was posted to Fort Myers, a small emplacement of two guns at the mouth of the Berbice river. His quarters were 'like a card-house built by boys on a table' – a room eight feet square with a bedroom above reached by a ladder, but at least he had a view of the sea. His main duty was to report on all ships entering the river. Many of them failed to salute. Then the fort opened fire, the first shot ahead and the next aimed direct. He could signal across the river to Fort St Andrew's and there was a chain of signal stations along the coast linking Berbice with Fort William Frederick on the Demerara river. After recurrent attacks of fever St Clair was sent to Barbados on three months' sick leave. There he was taken in by a relative and made a good recovery, but an assistant surgeon of artillery just out from home, who was very careful of his health, was dead in ten days.

On his return to Berbice, St Clair was taken back to Georgetown as ADC to Colonel Nicholson, now acting governor of Demerara during the absence on leave of Governor Bentinck. It was the sort of luck every young officer must have dreamed of. The colonel, 'gayest of the gay', plunged into a round of dinners and balls at which his young protégé was delighted to assist. Through Georgetown* on his way to a home posting came the sporting Captain Yates, who sold him his English-bred bay mare. She made him a lot of money in racing matches until he met his downfall by losing a bet with a nondescript American to the tune of a hundred 'Joes', and that before a large crowd of heavily betting officers and civilians including the acting governor.

During the French Revolutionary War when there was heavy fighting in the Lesser Antilles and high mortality among the British troops, five

* It was called Stabroek until 1812.

Negro regiments were raised in the hope that they would prove better inured to the tropical climate. On 2 May 1795 the *London Gazette* carried orders for the formation of the 1st West India Regiment, with officers and NCOs seconded from British units. Into this new regiment was incorporated the remnant of the Carolina Corps of American Loyalists and their slaves, formed in 1779, who had been moved to Jamaica after Independence. The Loyalist Corps contributed the Carolina Laurel in the regimental crest of the 1st West India Regiment. Also in 1795 out of irregular troops known as the St Vincent Rangers, the 2nd West India Regiment was formed. The experiment proved successful: by 1799 there were no less than twelve West India Regiments. During the nineteenth century continual changes were made until in 1888 all units were amalgamated in the single West India Regiment with two or more battalions as occasion demanded.

Not surprisingly the formation of black regiments aroused the suspicion of the planter assemblies, but time allayed their fears. After the rebellions in British Guiana and Jamaica in 1823 and 1865 the colonial legislatures voted money for mess plate in appreciation of the loyal service performed by the West India Regiments. They also earned praise from commanders-in-chief like Sir Ralph Abercromby and General Picton, first governor of Trinidad. In 1807 both 1st and 2nd Regiments had as their commanding officer in turn, Lt-Col Benjamin D'Urban, later governor of British Guiana and Cape Colony.

After the Napoleonic Wars there were difficulties over recruitment. West Africans rescued from slavers were invited to enlist, then in 1826 a company of the regiment was sent to Sierra Leone to use that settlement of freed slaves as a recruiting base. This led to the regiments being employed on service in West Africa. Recruitment was also carried out concurrently in the West Indies, the 1st regiment drawing most from Jamaica, the 2nd from Trinidad and the eastern Caribbean. Later the regiments were regularly moved round between most of the islands and West Africa. They performed meritorious service in the Ashanti War of 1872–3. When the 2nd West India Regiment returned to Barbados the Assembly presented the regiment with a congratulatory address, entertained the men to a dinner and gave a grand ball for the officers. Jamaica gave them an address of welcome, and in British Guiana when the band of the 2nd West India Regiment came to leave, the ladies of Georgetown presented it with a silver cornet and baton. The West India Regiment had won its place in West Indian hearts.

Service in the regiment was popular with the European officers. When Lt-Col Nicholls died at Up Park Camp, Jamaica, in 1844, he had served twenty of his forty-nine years in the army with the 2nd Regiment, and left two sons serving in the regiment. His record was beaten, however, by Lt-Col Whitfield who in 1868 was given a commemorative dinner by the officers on completion of forty years' service with the unit.

In 1858 the West India Regiments were issued with their resplendent zouave uniforms. Perhaps it was a sign of their mainly ceremonial duties, for there was really no fighting in West Indies, with the exception of the Morant Bay Rebellion and an attack by Mexican Indians on Orange Walk, British Honduras in 1872. As a result of six hours' spirited defence, three DCMs were awarded. Mid-century saw the West Indies providing nearly two-thirds of the troops employed in garrison duty in the islands. Yellow fever, rife at that time, caused a high demand for their relief of imperial troops. Although the rank and file showed resistance to the terrible scourge, this did not apply to the officers who died as easily as any other Europeans. As late as 1897, when the cause of it was on the brink of discovery, twelve officers in one battalion died of yellow fever.

By 1905 imperial troops had been withdrawn from West Indian garrisons with the exception of Jamaica. During the First World War the 1st and 2nd battalions of the West India Regiment served in the Cameroons, East Africa and Palestine, winning five DSOs, nine MCs, eight DCMs and a number of military medals. After 1915 eleven battalions, mostly pioneers, known as the British West Indies Regiment were also recruited and earned a mixed reputation. They were disbanded soon after the war. In 1927 the old West India Regiment was also disbanded, with the exception of the band, which, as the Jamaica Military Band, has survived to the present day, still dressed in zouave uniform.

When the Second World War broke out, although many West Indians were anxious to serve and many did so, making their way independently to Britain for service in the Navy, Army and RAF, official recruitment was deferred until 1944, with the exception of local defence forces. Then War Office files became sadly mixed. Instead of reforming the West India Regiment with its valuable traditions, confusion with the less meritorious British West Indies Regiment led to a decision to create a completely new regiment composed of contingents from no less than ten different colonies. Known as the Caribbean Regiment, it was an interesting touring exhibition of West India people but it never was given the chance to develop into an efficient fighting unit: the war ended before it saw action. In the West Indies local forces were stiffened by Canadian and American troops, the latter centred in their bases acquired in exchange for fifty obsolete destroyers, but unlike the British colonies in the Far East, the West Indies suffered no enemy attacks other than U-boat sinkings.

When in 1958 the West Indies Federation was created a decision was made to revive the old West India Regiment, but it was as stillborn as the political union it was intended to defend. With the subsequent grant of independence each ex-colony has formed its own regiment. The last British regiment was withdrawn from Jamaica in 1962.

13
INTO THE TWENTIETH CENTURY

As too often happened in imperial days, social conditions in distant colonies were allowed to deteriorate until they led to violent disorders before alleviating measures were taken. This had been the case in Jamaica in 1865, and it was to occur again throughout the Caribbean in 1938. In the meantime Jamaica was given a new constitution and the eyes of successive Secretaries of State for the Colonies were warily directed to the Caribbean for a number of years.

Sir John Peter Grant, the governor sent to relieve Eyre, was a carefully chosen high-calibre administrator from India. With the obstructive Assembly out of the way, Grant ruled as a benevolent dictator with a small legislative council of officials and non-officials, all nominated by himself. Argument and debate were out; the watchword was action. Grant's eight years in office saw eventful changes. The parishes were reduced in number from twenty-two to fourteen; the police force was remodelled; the judiciary and magistracy took on their modern shape; the government medical service and public works department were formed; irrigation works from the Rio Cobre were started; East Indian immigration was resumed, government schools appeared to augment the church schools, and Kingston became the capital. By 1871 Jamaica and Trinidad received their cable links with the United Kingdom, an amenity which all inhabitants could use but none more than the governor – it tightened Whitehall's grip on colonial governments. Although the other colonies had suffered no disturbances like the Morant Bay Rebellion, during the next decade Crown Colony government was extended to all except Barbados, which kept its seventeenth-century Assembly down to independence in 1966. After 1884 in the various legislative councils, where government ex-officio and nominated members usually outnumbered by one the elected members representing a selection of the population, governors kept executive control of their colonies. Generally good sense prevailed, but imagination and initiative became slowly smothered under bureaucracy until in the 1930s the troubles attendant on the world slump led to political activity and demands for self-government.

Meanwhile the main business of the British West Indies continued to be agriculture, and the main crop, sugar. Although the slaves were emancipated in 1838, the West Indies have remained enslaved to King Sugar down to the present day; it is still the leading export in Barbados, St Kitts-Nevis and British Honduras, and second in value in Jamaica, Guyana and Trinidad. More important than the value, however, are the numbers employed and so dependent for their living on the sugar industry. Economically, sugar production in these countries is unjustified. Its continuation is entirely dependent on Commonwealth and international sugar agreements, which apportion production quotas and control prices. Before the present-day arrangements came into force, however, the West Indian sugar industry made extensive efforts to save itself, cutting production costs to the bone. In the process sugar companies like Booker Brothers in British Guiana, Caroni in Trinidad, and Tate and Lyle in Jamaica, took the place of many individual planters; the number of factories was greatly reduced; scientific methods were applied to cane-growing and sugar-making, and management efficiency became remarkable.

'Down in Demerara' at the beginning of the present century the Overseers' Messes were a distinctive feature, run on army lines, with young men from Scotland, the north of England and Barbados. Sometimes suffering from the inexpert catering of managers' wives, the overseers, many of whom saw military service in the First World War, won the right to organize their own catering under a mess president. The change of president at the end of each month provided the excuse for a special 'farewell' dinner. As the salary of an overseer started at less than £40 a year and never exceeded £130 the prospects of marriage were remote. It was not surprising, therefore, that overseers sought female consolation from the coolie lines, for as Kipling said: 'Single men in barracks don't grow into plaster saints.' Shooting, fishing, racing and rugby were more publicized forms of relaxation, the mule race 'for gentlemen riders' at Port Mourant providing some unpredictable results. If an overseer gave offence to an East Indian labourer, the latter might say he was 'going to Krasbi', his name for the local immigration agent. By the 1920s few could have explained the origin of this term, which was a corruption of the surname of James Crosby, a graduate of Trinity College, Cambridge, who held the office of Immigration Agent-General and Protector of Immigrants from 1850 to 1880. So staunchly did he champion the humble Indians' rights that his department became known as Crosby Office; he was Burra Crosby

Sahib and all the other officials, Chota Crosby Sahibs – a strange footprint to leave in the sands of time.

Attention has been drawn to the way the Jamaica planters resigned themselves to ruin after emancipation. It will not be surprising, therefore, to read that the chance of salvation from enslavement to sugar came through no effort of theirs, but from the chance call of an American schooner at Port Antonio in 1869. Because the few bunches of bananas he had shipped from there sold well in New Jersey, Captain Lorenzo Baker of Boston returned to the island and persuaded a few of the small settlers in the parish of Portland to plant bananas and sell them to him. From this small beginning grew the multimillion-dollar banana business of the Caribbean headed by the mighty United Fruit Company that developed from the small Boston Fruit Company founded by Baker. Being a northerner, Baker was pleased to help the ex-slaves of Jamaica, but before long the peasant growers could not supply the bananas to meet the rising demand in America, so Baker proceeded to buy derelict sugar estates in Portland and grow his own fruit. By 1883 Baker's company was using steamers; ten years later it owned thirteen estates. The Jamaica planters were slow to turn to banana-growing, referring to it in early years as 'a backwoods nigger business'. Not until a government medical officer, Dr (later Sir) John Pringle and his friend, John Kerr, showed there was profit in bananas, did their cultivation commend itself to estate-owners. Eventually the industry assumed a dual character, supported by both small and large growers. It spread to all parts of the island that were well watered, either by rain or irrigation. By 1910 the export exceeded fourteen million stems a year and was worth five times the value of sugar. By that time the United Fruit Company had developed into a monopolistic menace, operating extensive concessions in the republics surrounding the Caribbean and engaging in fratricidal wars with other American companies. It swallowed the Elders and Fyffes Shipping Line, formed under subsidy from the United Kingdom and Jamaica governments to carry bananas to Britain, but it never succeeded in capturing the monopoly of banana-planting in Jamaica; the government and the small settlers prevented that. The Jamaican peasant showed no more enthusiasm for working on United Fruit estates than he had on the sugar plantations, and although many of them crossed the Caribbean to work in the 'banana republics', those with land clung to their independence until in 1929 the government helped them and equally independent-minded estate-owners to form the Jamaica Banana Producers Association, with no fewer than 7,694 members. It has never looked back.

The Caribbean would not be the bitter-sweet place it is if it had allowed banana-planting to enjoy uninterrupted progress. Although requiring far less capital than sugar, bananas are more vulnerable to hurricanes and 'northers' than cane is, and they are susceptible to leaf-spot disease, which is curable, and Panama disease which is not. In recent years sugar has overtaken bananas in export value. In the Lesser Antilles banana-growing has been introduced commercially only since the Second World War, in the Windward Islands.

In British Guiana rice-growing gradually increased as an alternative to sugar. Introduced from Georgia in 1853, it did not begin to reach noteworthy production until the end of the century when over six thousand acres were in cultivation. By 1921 the area under rice had reached 55,911 acres and expansion has continued, until recently Guyana rice has been supplying most of the English-speaking West Indies. In Trinidad citrus fruit has taken second place to sugar, and citrus comes next after bananas in Jamaica. There the Sharpe family of Trout Hall have pioneered with crossed varieties like the ugli and the ortanique. There is an active Citrus Growers Association.

There are many other crops which are grown, have been grown or will grow in the fertile, well-watered, extremely variegated terrain of the West Indian islands. In the mountains it is possible to grow most sorts of temperate fruit and vegetables, but there is little point in such experiments when the variety of tropical trees and crops is so great. Tobacco, the first crop of the English colonists, is still grown for local consumption and Jamaica cigars have a world-wide reputation. In that large island, from which it is so difficult to get away, coffee was second only to sugar for most of the eighteenth and nineteenth centuries. Competition from Brazil since 1900 slowly killed the Jamaica coffee industry, except for its Blue Mountain strain that commanded the highest prices in world markets and came from not more than a dozen small, precipitous estates. It was not surprising therefore that when Blue Mountain beans were introduced into East Africa in the early years of this century they soon gave to Kenya coffee the same high reputation. But today, although Blue Mountain coffee can still be purchased in English shops, there is hardly any coffee being grown in the Blue Mountains of Jamaica. Cocoa, once important in Trinidad, is grown there and in the Windward Islands only in small quantities. St Vincent has long been known for its arrowroot, Dominica for its lime-juice and lime-oil, while Jamaica (again) enjoys its name for ginger and pimento, its single indigenous crop, much appreciated by continental sausage-makers and by the handful of connoisseurs of Pimento Dram, a palatable liqueur made by steeping pimento-berries in rum.

But the social importance of all this great variety of produce lies in the way most of it is grown: on the small holdings of less than ten acres owned by thousands of peasant proprietors. The start of this landholding revolution has already been described, but it was not until the 1890s that it was given any official encouragement by government purchase of derelict or unwanted sugar and coffee estates, the division of them into small lots and their sale on easy terms to 'small settlers'. To educate the new proprietors in proper cultivation techniques agricultural societies were formed in Trinidad and Jamaica. At first they were inadequately staffed to deal with the numbers of farmers, but gradually improvements have been introduced until the Jamaica and Trinidad Agricultural Societies have become the driving force behind peasant agriculture, organizing demonstrations and shows, distributing literature and employing a staff of skilled inspectors whose advice is available to all members. In British Guiana the Royal Agricultural and Commercial Society was founded much earlier, in 1844, before peasant cultivation was encouraged. In consequence it has directed its interests more to estate than plot management as well as covering subjects of a historical and cultural nature, running a library and museum, and publishing an informative magazine entitled *Timehri*, a Carib word for the engraved hieroglyphics found on certain rocks.

In addition to the purely farming problems of soil erosion, crop disease and stock improvement, the agricultural societies had to cope with the social evil of predial larceny, the theft of estate crops and produce. It was a curse from which the planters had suffered, but whereas on a large estate it amounts to fractional losses, on a peasant's small plot it can entail the loss of all of his crop. Typically, Governor Eyre had prescribed flogging as both a punishment and a deterrent, but predial larceny went on to such an extent that it was discouraging land settlement. In 1909 the Jamaica Agricultural Society was authorized to appoint Vigilance Officers or Authorized Persons who were licensed to arrest on suspicion anyone they met or found in possession of produce obviously not their own, and the onus of proving his innocence was placed on the arrested man. This system helped to reduce the trouble but over 2,500 Authorized Persons were still considered necessary in 1935, and thirty years later the problem still existed.

Human predacity is perhaps all the more difficult to bear in lands where nature is always liable to stage spectacular disasters in the form of hurricane and earthquake. Hurricanes have continued to cause enormous damage. They cannot be controlled, but radio warnings of their approach enable measures to be taken to preserve lives at least, though not to protect crops. The nearest approach to this lies in insurance, although premiums are naturally high. A hurricane always leaves hundreds of people homeless. As a result of three centuries of experience, relief measures come swiftly to hand from government sources, but individual subscriptions to relief funds still play a valuable part, not only from distant places like London's Mansion House, but from island to island. Within a year of suffering three hundred deaths and losing the roofs off almost every house in 1898, the people of St Vincent were subscribing to a relief fund for fellow colonists in the Leeward Islands. If people have no money to spare, their sympathy is always welcome.

Four years after the serious hurricane just mentioned, St Vincent hit the headlines with the eruption of her Soufrière volcano in the north of the island. It was not the first eruption. There had been an eruption in 1812, but the north of the island was then thinly populated and there was little loss of life. In 1902 over two thousand people died. Because the story of the earlier event had been largely forgotten, people failed to take warning from the earth tremors round the 3,500-foot mountain which had started during the previous year. Suddenly on 7 May a semi-solid, black, gaseous cloud, raining hot mud and stones, rolled down both the eastern and western slopes of the mountain. By comparison with Martinique, the French island next but one to the north, St Vincent suffered lightly, for there, on the day after the Soufrière erupted, Mont Pelée completely obliterated the garden city of Saint-Pierre and its forty thousand inhabitants. There was one survivor – the single prisoner in the gaol. Today both volcanoes are sleeping.

During the last hundred years earthquakes have shaken Port of Spain once, in 1888, and Montserrat on two occasions, in 1896–7 and during the four years between 1933 and 1937, but the worst earthquake happened at Kingston in 1907 when eight hundred people lost their lives and, between the quake and the fire that followed it, two million pounds' worth of damage was done. On this occasion the British government made a grant of £150,000 and a loan of £800,000. Many of the buildings had been covered by insurance. West Indians have learnt to live with these dangers. Hurricanes hit crops but blow round sound buildings; earthquakes destroy buildings but spare crops. They are preferable to the war damage suffered in so many temperate countries.

Until the twentieth century minerals played no part in the economy of the British colonies in and around the Caribbean, with the exception of British Guiana where the discovery of gold and diamonds in the 1880s caused a minor rush. The Dutch had taken no interest in the hinterland of that large country, which is almost the size of the island of Great Britain. The early British explorers were naturalists rather than prospectors. Charles Waterton, who penetrated to the Amazon tributary of the Rio Branco in 1812, was more interested in the Amerindians and the secrets of their arrow poisons than in gold, and Robert Schomburgk, sent out by the Royal Geographical Society in 1834 to complete the work of von Humboldt, was more thrilled with his discovery of the Victoria Regia water-lily than he could have been with diamonds. The great forest belt which begins nowhere more than fifty miles from the coast had been lightly tapped for greenheart and mora, but until machinery came into use it was too difficult to bring out timber for more than two miles to a river. It was the rivers that provided the lines of communication, and upon them grew up a small hardy community of boathands, managing with great skill and intrepidity the numerous small falls and rapids of the Essequibo, Mazaruni and Cuyuni rivers. Long narrow boats, forty by seven and a half feet, blunt at both ends like a punt, were paddled by a crew of sixteen hands. On small platforms at each end the bowman and the steersman (who was captain) guided each boat through the swirling waters. To obtain a captain's certificate a steersman had to have years of experience and pass a stringent oral test – a written exam would have been beyond him. Broad in the shoulder, the typical bowman was remarkable for his exquisite flow of invective and a sense of showmanship that kept chance passengers enthralled throughout the long hours of a river journey. The introduction of the inboard engine altered the design of the boats and the size of the crews and led to the decline of Bartica, where the three great rivers meet, from a rip-roaring frontier station to a quiet river port.

Gold and diamonds never amounted to very much. Over the forty years up to 1922 gold exports were worth under £10,000,000. In that year diamonds worth more than £800,000 were exported. By then, however, a more valuable mineral was beginning to be exported: bauxite from Mackenzie on the Demerara river. This has since become Guyana's most valuable product, accounting for nearly half the total value of the country's exports.

For too long Jamaica was kept struggling with little except agricultural produce, until at the end of the Second World War bauxite was discovered all over the limestone areas of the island. In twenty-five years it has risen to the top of the export table and provides a valuable source of revenue for the government of a newly independent country. Four companies, British, Canadian and American, have raised production to make Jamaica the world's greatest bauxite producer. But it is Trinidad which is the most prosperous island, thanks to its oilfields. Production started in 1911 and oil now accounts for three-quarters of the total exports, which run at nearly double the value of Jamaica's. Another valuable asset is Trinidad's remarkable pitch lake, which today provides the asphalt for surfacing world-famous thoroughfares like London's Piccadilly and the Mall and New York's Broadway. Long ago Sir Walter Raleigh used the pitch for caulking his ships and in 1850 another famous sailor became intrigued with it: Thomas Cochrane, tenth Earl of Dundonald, who, after breaking his Royal Navy career to command the navies of Chile, Brazil and Greece, sailed into the Gulf of Paria at the age of seventy-four as Commander-in-Chief,

America and West Indies Station. He experimented with the pitch mixed with coal as a fuel for his steamships. He even imported a load of the stuff and paved a street in Westminster, but it was considered too smooth and dangerous for horses. So the asphalt and the oil waited for exploitation until the invention of the motor car. It should go without saying that today Trinidad has the best roads in the West Indies.

About the turn of the century industries started to appear in the larger colonies, but sugar factories are still the biggest industrial plants, with the possible exception of the bauxite plants in Jamaica and Guyana and the oil refineries in Trinidad. Light industries provide matches, cigarettes, soap, shoes, condensed milk, beer and mineral waters, confectionery, cosmetics, leather goods, clothes, paint, cooking oil, and of course rum.

Yet the most popular industry in the Caribbean at present is the tourist industry which operates in hotels instead of factories and consists of selling sunshine, white sand and turquoise sea-water to ever increasing numbers of visitors from North America and Europe. Although the first hotel opened in the Bahamas in 1861, it was the Jamaica Exhibition of 1891 that really started the tourist business. By the 1930s Montego Bay was well known and there were a few hotels along the north coast. Barbados, too, had a small select clientele, but it has been since the Second World War that tourism has really boomed, with cheap air travel and the package tour. Hotels have appeared like mushrooms in almost every island. In 1961 some quarter of a million tourists visited Jamaica and spent about £13,000,000; in Barbados the tourist trade is reckoned to be worth over £5,000,000 a year.

The majority of the tourists come from the United States and so form a considerable part of the American influence that has impinged upon the West Indies for many years. Two hundred years ago Americans and West Indians were fellow colonists, grumbling in sympathy over the restrictions on their trade imposed by the Navigation Acts. If there had not been so many absentee proprietors the West Indies might well have joined the Americans in the War of Independence. After the war Britain made futile attempts to stop the then American foreigners from trading with her colonies. It was a natural trade between tropical and temperate zones and exceptions had to be made. It increased enormously following the banana shipments and was augmented by the development of West Indian labour migration into the United States from the end of the nineteenth century. It should not therefore be surprising that West Indians buy their medicines in a drug-store instead of a chemist's and then sit down and eat a meal there, which nobody can do in an English chemist's shop. West Indians fill their car tanks with gasoline, or just 'gas', instead of petrol, and half their cars are American with left-hand drive. They shopped in supermarkets before

British housewives had heard of them and came to appreciate the benefit of air-conditioning. Men wear Palm Beach suits, women study American beauty culture and their children make a bee-line for the soda-fountain.

But the English-speaking West Indian has not merely copied American and English ideas: he has added those that he fancied to his own and has produced local variations to the general pattern of western civilization that pertains throughout his home region. Today population figures are small compared with the developing countries of Asia and Africa. The total number of people has yet to reach five million, but with the exception of the mainland countries of Guyana and Belize, which are the largest and the emptiest, the islands are now crowded. Of these Barbados is by far the most densely populated with more than 1,400 people to the square mile; Grenada is next with over six hundred; St Vincent has more than five hundred; Trinidad, about five hundred and Jamaica over four hundred. It was not surprising, therefore, that immigration had largely stopped by the turn of the century, although immigrants from India continued to arrive until the Indian government put an end to it in 1917. Long before then an anomalous position had arisen, for from the 1850s emigration from the islands had started, to Panama to build first the railway, then the de Lesseps canal and finally the American project. The attraction was the high wages compared with those at home – a man could earn three or four times as much. West Indians formed the majority of the labour force on the banana plantations in Central America; they went to Cuba (and so did a few white managers) to work on the sugar estates. Many sent their savings home. It was reckoned that Barbadians working on the Panama Canal were remitting £60,000 per annum to post office savings accounts on their crowded island. Many of these emigrants settled permanently in their places of work; others came home after a few years, stirring their stay-at-home brothers' ideas on the question of wages. After 1930 the falling demand for labour in the republics exacerbated unemployment in the island colonies, where popular protests against the low wages there – 1s 6d to 2s 6d a day – led to the riots of 1938. Out of the economic and social distress of the time trade unions were born, which in turn gave birth to political parties demanding self-government and the right to correct their own troubles. During the last war many West Indians joined the forces and saw the possibilities of employment in Britain. Between 1953 and 1961 150,000 Jamaicans alone emigrated to the United Kingdom. Emigration has thus become a West Indian tradition, as well as an economic necessity to keep pace with rapidly expanding populations. The savings they send home are also a valuable contribution to the economy.

It is perhaps in the matter of diet that West Indians have developed one of the customs that distinguish them most from English and American people. At home West Indian labourers have grown accustomed to a diet in which starchy foods predominate. Lord Olivier (*Jamaica: The Blessed Island*) gave the following typical diet-sheet for 1930–5:

6.30 a.m.	Coffee and a piece of bread or yam	1d
Noon	2 large plantains, boiled	1d
	Large piece of yam	$\frac{1}{2}$d
	Rice, cooked	$\frac{1}{2}$d
	Okra	$\frac{1}{4}$d
	Salt fish	$\frac{1}{4}$d
7.30 p.m.	Pork, $\frac{1}{2}$ lb	3d
	Beans, ackee, coconut oil, peppers	2d
	Total daily cost	$8\frac{1}{2}$d

Other favourite starch foods, referred to as 'bread-kind', are breadfruit, sweet potato, cassava and maize. With the exception of avocado pears, green vegetables are not popular except in soup, and little fruit is eaten except mangoes and oranges. Small wonder that when they come to Britain, West Indians club together to eat their traditional fare cooked in a hot and spicy way. To cater for these tastes, in British towns where West Indians predominate special shops have grown up to supply their favourite requirements. In the Caribbean, higher up the social scale, many of the local vegetables appear on the dining table to accompany European dishes so that the best of both worlds is enjoyed. Turtle, which used to feed the indentured servants of the seventeenth century and became a fashionable dish in English society in the eighteenth, is rarely seen today, except in out-of-the-way places like the Cayman Islands. Trinidad has small tree-oysters and Barbados, flying-fish pie. The gourmet appreciates paw-paw, pineapple and Bombay mango at breakfast; fried plantain or yampie as a lunch vegetable; guavas and coconut cream as a sweet, and barbecued sucking-pig or curried goat on a picnic. Black crab, mountain mullet and the old pepper-pot are rarely found these days.

Drinking fashions, too, have changed. The planters' claret and madeira disappeared in the nineteenth century, giving place to gin and whisky. Rum was usually drunk as a punch, except by the working man who downed his tot of white, smelly rum straight and followed it with a little water. In the eastern Caribbean after the introduction of ice, first brought down in great blocks from North America about 1845, the 'swizzle' made its appearance and became popular as an aperitif from Antigua down to Georgetown and remote Berbice. There were three requirements besides the rum: ice made from soft water to form a head, a narrow glass and a swizzle stick cut from the roots of a small bush. It was customary, as with the workman and his

tot of white rum, to down it in one. An old rhyme epitomized the swizzle
habits of the 1880s:

> Essequibo for length,
> Demerara for strength,
> The City for plenty of ice,
> But Berbice likes it strong,
> And Berbice likes it long*
> And often, which really is nice!

In Jamaica swizzles were unknown. In the 1930s it was not fashionable to
drink rum, for whisky cost 8s 6d a bottle, but with the war and rising
taxation rum has come into its own.

There is a romantic tone in the accounts of life and travel in the last two
decades of the last century. Steamers were none too comfortable in those
days and passengers got off them at the earliest opportunity. In the small
islands, as they landed on the beach from the rowing boats that brought
them from the ship, they were met by washerwomen who could finish
laundering clothes in a day and fruit sellers with their luscious basketfuls.
At Carlisle Bay, Barbados, there was always a cluster of shipping, perhaps a
visiting cruiser, several steamers, Danish, Norwegian and English barques
and brigs, fishing vessels and inter-island schooners. Around them all like
flies the multicoloured bumboats clustered with their oarsmen offering
trips ashore, or fruit for sale, or just passing the time in idle curiosity. Once
ashore visitors were besieged by beggars, as they never are today. They
were pathetic and yet not without that irrepressible sense of humour and
showmanship that characterizes the West Indian Negro. One of those
forgotten visitors left a graphic description of the welcoming chorus:

Beg you a penny (or sixpence), massa – beg you a penny! I'm de one dat saw,
spoke to, pointed at, touched you (as the case may have been) first. I see you
come from de ship, dear massa – beg you a penny! I'se old, (or young, has a baby,
loss me husban'), is sick, was sick, cut me han', is hungry. . . . Give me a penny
to buy bread – to give to me mudder – for the chil'en – for me own self – for
charity – for de lub o Heaben!' For any reason, for all reasons, for no reason.
'Beg you a penny – jus' one. Look at me, pity me,' and so on, up and down the
gamut, from A to Izzard, in solo, duet, in chorus, crescendo, diminuendo,
staccato, fortissimo, pianissimo, and always and at all times very much the
reverse of non troppo.†

The Negro was on his way up from slavery and it was a long road.
Attention has been drawn to the great influence of the missionaries at

---

* Referring to the double-size planter's glass.
† Paton, *Down the Islands, A Voyage to the Caribbees*, London, 1888.

emancipation and the optimism with which the new freemen set their feet upon that road, but as the nineteenth century advanced and economic depression led to social distress, many of the ex-slaves became disillusioned. Particularly in Jamaica, as they moved into the interior they became separated from church and school and a wild undisciplined generation grew up. Under slavery marriage had been discouraged and although the missionaries made many converts, mid-century clergy like the Rev. Richard Rawle, principal of Codrington College and later first Bishop of Trinidad, were upset at the high rate of illegitimacy. It is a feature that still persists, at a level as high as seventy per cent. But it would be quite wrong to dismiss the West Indians as promiscuous. They are uninhibited about sex and many of their legally unrecognized unions are remarkably permanent – and not infrequently they end up in church with the children in attendance. These people treasure their individual independence. The men are as reluctant to sign a contract of marriage as they are to sign a contract of labour, and the women treasure their freedom as much as the men. In consequence West Indian Negro society has developed as a matriarchy, with the women holding the home together, mothers out working and grandmothers looking after the children, while the men may be overseas or working – for a time anyway – on a sugar estate, or building a new hotel, working as a waiter, as a taxi- or lorry-driver, eventually returning home to a hero's welcome, dispensing treats to his family and relations before disappearing once again on his adventures. Of course this is a generalization, about which criticism is perfectly acceptable, but it does contain a great measure of truth.

There are many other people living as respectably by western standards as normal people do in Europe and America. There is a tendency for people of mixed race to monopolize the civil service, for white people to confine themselves to business and farming, but by and large West Indians do not make anything of such distinctions. Now that independence has come, the emphasis lies in being a Jamaican, a Trinidadian, a Barbadian or a Guyanese, regardless of the colour of one's skin.

No tourist can come away from the West Indies today without hearing calypsos and listening to a steel band, yet forty years ago there were no steel bands and the word 'calypso' was confined to the eastern Caribbean. It was not used in Jamaica then. The origin of the word is uncertain. Coming from Trinidad it may well have derived from the French *carrouseaux* and then passed through a slow metamorphosis: *carrisseux – calisseau – caliso – calypso*. A calypso is hardly a song but rather a spoken or intoned story or comment on the news, or a celebrity in the news, accompanied by drumming and guitar strumming. It contains rhymes of a sort (usually in couplets) but no regular metre so that its fascination for the visitor lies in the way the singer manages to fit in any number of words to each line, reminiscent of the limerick about the man of Japan who

'always tries to fit into the last line as many words as he possibly can.'

At the annual carnival there are calypso competitions in which the singers appear under such fantastic names as Lord Melody, Iron Duke, King Pharoah, Zebra Killer, or even Attila the Hun. In Guyana the Essequibo boathands and the lumberjacks used to paddle and heave to shanties, but the petrol engine and the tractor appear to have killed these songs. In Jamaica there have been folk songs from before emancipation. Monk Lewis heard one about a cruel slave-owner named Bedward, who used to have seriously sick slaves who were unlikely to recover taken and left to die in a nearby gully to save hospital expenses:

'Take him to the Gully! Take him to the Gully!
But bring back the frock and board.'*
'Oh! Massa, Massa, me no deadee yet!'
'Take him to the Gully! Take him to the Gully!
Carry him along.'

In the late nineteenth and early twentieth centuries topical songs appeared that have now become classics: the Banana-Boat Song; the ruined huckster's lament known as 'Linstead Market'; 'Run Mongoose' epitomizing the adventures of the smart alec; songs about trouble with donkeys, stealing mangoes, cooking rice and peas, admiring a pretty girl and teasing a saucy one, and other themes of everyday life. Since the last war the calypso has come to Jamaica and the word is used for the old folk songs as well as recent topical compositions.

The steel band also originated in Trinidad. In the 1930s, following a police ban on carrying bamboo stems in carnival processions – they had been used more for concussion than percussion – the local musicians started using dustbin lids for drumming. This led to experiments with all kinds of metal objects retrieved from rubbish dumps until a selection of them was developed to produce not only a beat but tunes.

Where there are folk songs, there is also folklore. The West Indian Anancy Stories have become as famous as those of Uncle Remus about Brer Fox and Brer Rabbit, even finding their way into a set of infant readers widely used in Britain; but shorn of their dialect they suffer from emasculation. Then there are the proverbs – over 1,300 of them, some with English equivalents, some of purely local significance. For the rhythm of their music and dancing and the vivid realism of their folklore, the West Indians have drawn most on their African heritage. As long as they lived

* The board on which the sick man was carried.

under colonialism the islanders remained inhibited in their cultural pur-
suits, slavishly copying the ideas of the ruling race, and the British expatri-
ate is not usually recruited from the ranks of the intelligentsia. In 1934
there was not a single bookshop in Kingston, the largest city in the West
Indies, although there were books on sale in two department stores. In the
late thirties, however, the stirring began that has led to the present flourish-
ing growth of West Indian art and literature. Poets, artists, sculptors,
novelists are all hard at work, observing and recording the scenes of their
environment, capturing the bright light, the vivid colours and the dark
shadows of their tropical world; describing the warm humanity, the pathos
and the humour of West Indian peoples.

Houses range in variety from hovels to small palaces. Shacks that dis-
figure the fringes of so many towns are the result not so much of poverty
and indolence as of insecurity of tenure: nobody is going to spend money
on a building on land which is not his own. On their own land peasants
build neat little cottages and wash them in white or bright colours. Many
of the eighteenth-century great houses still survive. Some are still private
residences, one at least is a tourist hotel, others are preserved as national
monuments. Perhaps the most interesting architectural link with the past
has been the stone-by-stone removal of a sugar factory from the north
coast of Jamaica and its re-erection as the chapel of the University of the
West Indies outside Kingston. Elsewhere cement and corrugated iron, that
aesthetic curse of the tropics, have produced functional but ugly little
houses. Hurricane and earthquake encourage the building of low, flat
dwellings, and the bungalow reigns supreme in the suburbs. Successful
merchants and businessmen, however, have had some attractive houses
built in recent years. The old ideas have survived in places: the wide
veranda, the jalousies, the deep, wide storm drains to carry off the water
of tropical downpours. Before the days of electric fans and refrigerators
wide verandas on two sides of a house were essential for keeping the
family cool, with migration from the morning to the afternoon shade. In
Guiana planters relaxed in 'Berbice chairs' with extending wooden arms on
which weary legs could be rested and a convenient hole was cut within
hand-reach for securing the often-raised glass. Semi-porous earthenware
filters cooled drinking water. Hammocks were also popular, and rocking
chairs. A peculiar feature in Georgetown houses was the almost universal
substitution of the shower for the bath, due largely to the tea-coloured
water of the city's supply canal. Every house had a wooden vat or tank for
storing rain-water and every shower-room had two roses, one with brown
water for soaping and the other with fresh for rinsing. Since the war the
Lamaha Canal water has been treated and clarified.

Throughout these English-speaking lands there are only four towns with more than ninety thousand inhabitants: Kingston, with its enormous suburban environs, contains over 377,000 people; Port of Spain in Trinidad and Bridgetown (with suburbs) in Barbados both have ninety-four thousand people, but it is Georgetown, Guyana, with its present 168,000 population, which has the most unique character and unusual history. Although it took the French to start it during their brief occupation of 1782-3, the Dutch developed it in their homeland tradition with drainage canals, dams and kokers, as the control sluices are still called to this day. Renamed Georgetown in 1812, the old Dutch name of Stabroek has survived in the market and ward of that name. In 1820 its population numbered 9,191 and consisted of 1,460 whites, 2,505 free coloured people and 5,226 slaves. Because it is six feet below spring high tide level, the alluvial clay on which the town is built is always waterlogged and during the rainy seasons the roads were well-nigh impassable. Early efforts to improve these conditions gave the chief thoroughfare its name: Brickdam. Because of the soft soil and the plentiful supply of forest timber, Georgetown grew up as a wooden city with its houses raised on wooden or brick piles to keep them above flood level and bring them into the steady Trade Winds which keep the temperature down to a bearable level. Floods were a serious drawback until the present sea-wall was built by degrees between 1860 and 1892, but a far greater menace was fire. There have been four serious conflagrations in the last 150 years and at least six minor outbreaks, the worst occurring in 1945 when the business centre was completely gutted. The damage exceeded £4,000,000. This has led to rebuilding in concrete. Because of the fire-risk stress has always been laid on efficient fire-fighting. In 1812 there were two fire-engines and the first to arrive at a fire received ten 'Joes' (about £30) divided among the crew. The first man with a bucket of water received five Joes. Every lot-holder had to keep two leather buckets ready and pay a tax of one per cent of his property value for the maintenance of the fire service. This tradition has come down and the modern fire-brigade is extremely efficient.

Georgetown has always been noted for its social gaiety. From early days dinners were held in celebration of St George's, St Andrew's and St Patrick's days and the King's Birthday. Around 1890 fourteen graduates of Oxford and Cambridge had instituted an annual dinner. Earlier there had been a Theatre Royal but it did not last in the absence of any leisured classes. In 1858 the Georgetown Club was founded. It was a hospitable place, 'where the sound of the swizzle stick was heard all day'. Officers from Her Majesty's ships were especially well treated, enjoying honorary membership for the period of their stay and having most of their drinks paid for. A social centre open to all developed along the sea-wall, where the citizens of Georgetown went in the hour before sunset to take an airing and gossip with friends and acquaintances. Although the beaches, surprisingly, are not muddy, the sea is a murky brown and Georgetown has never had a chance of becoming a seaside resort or a tourist centre.

During the nineteenth century the Anglican Church awoke to its responsibilities and grew to become a beneficent power in the British colonies. Until 1824 all Anglican clergy had come under the jurisdiction of the Bishops of London, none of whom ever visited the distant churches of their diocese. Once local bishoprics were created, however, a great difference became apparent. Starting in Jamaica and Barbados, by the end of the century there were bishops in Antigua, St Vincent, Trinidad, British Honduras, the Bahamas, and British Guiana, constituting the Province of the West Indies under their own archbishop. Until 1870 the Anglican Church was the established church, with its clergy paid from British government funds. Apart from their spiritual duties, the bishops were actively involved in education. The first Bishop of Guiana, William Piercy Austin, was the son of an Essequibo planter. When he was consecrated in 1842, Queen Victoria described him as the youngest and handsomest bishop in her dominions: he was thirty-four and stood six feet two inches in his stockings. In 1892 there were great rejoicings at the celebration of his golden jubilee in Georgetown's new cathedral, the tallest wooden building in the world. By then he was also Archbiship of the West Indies. He died later in the year.

The man who succeeded him as archbishop was Enos Nuttall, Bishop of Jamaica since 1880. Strangely, he had arrived in Jamaica in 1862 as a Wesleyan missionary but entered the Church of England four years later. Unselfish and of great charm, he employed his boundless energy in long tours of his diocese which made him known and respected from one end of Jamaica to the other. A colonial bishop needed to be fit, for travel was not easy in the eighties. Typical of his experiences are extracts from his diary of 1885:

'On 22 July left [Kingston] by first train with horses and buggy for May Pen. On to Chapelton. . . .' He made his way across the central mountains. . . . 'Near Albert Town road very rough. Mr. Shearer had kindly sent me a pair of horses so as to rest mine. . . .' On 28 July he had reached Falmouth. Next day he drove thirty miles to St Ann's Bay. The following night he spent at Moneague, twenty miles away. Then on 31 July, 'Got up at 3 a.m. Got away by 4.30. Reached Bishop's Lodge before 12,' i.e. a journey of forty miles in seven and a half hours. It is not clear, but one hopes for the sake of his horses that he travelled from Spanish Town by train. Next year he went to Highgate in St Mary's Parish. . . . 'Rain, bogs and broken roads. . . . Rain, but good congregations. We left after the service, but it was almost impossible to get to the main road. We had to drive through people's grounds and through the bush to avoid the bogs in the main road.' He went on to Port Maria. . . . 'Blew a hurricane all night. Trees across the road . . . river swept through buggy. All my clothes in tin cases, as well as most of those I had on very wet.' Confirmation candidates made their way to church through rivers with water up to their armpits, and he had to hold a second service for those who had been delayed.

Bishop Nuttall was a great traveller. Apart from pastoral visits he made many voyages to England and America, raising funds, looking for clergy. He travelled for meetings of the Provincial Synod all over the Caribbean from Belize to Georgetown. In fact the Provincial Synod was the earliest organization to work on a complete West Indian basis. Nuttall built churches and founded St Peter's College for the training of local clergy, but his interests were island-wide. As chairman of the Jamaica Schools Commission for thirty-three years he played a leading part in island education; he was chairman of the boards of the Mico and Shortwood Teacher Training Colleges, played an active part in the progress of Jamaica College and Kingston College, and in 1889 was interviewing the Registrar of London University over the possibility of starting a West Indian university. In 1898 he founded the private nursing home which still bears his name. He took a keen interest in the foundation of the Jamaica Agricultural Society and was attending the opening session of the West Indies Agricultural Conference at the Mico College when the 1907 earthquake occurred. He played a leading part in the relief work and served on the delegation sent to England for help. Four years later he was one of the two Jamaica delegates to the coronation of King George v. When he died in 1916 at the age of seventy-four, the attendance at his funeral was the greatest ever known in Jamaica, and all the shops closed in respect for Jamaica's leading citizen.

Archbishop Nuttall was not the first to advocate a university. For three years from 1873 to 1876 an abortive attempt was made when Sir John Peter Grant was governor to start a university in Spanish Town, but it failed for want of suitably qualified candidates. Attention was therefore given to secondary education. In the Lesser Antilles it was difficult to start grammar schools for lack of funds and numbers to support them, and attempts to centralize secondary education in Barbados failed through inter-island jealousy. Small schools like the Grammar School in St Vincent with two masters and a handful of boys could not expect to achieve much. Queen's College in Guyana, so named in 1876 when the government took over the Anglican school founded in 1842, and the Queen's Royal College in Trinidad, founded in 1859, have been the leading schools in their countries, supplemented by other good schools run by the Roman Catholic Church, but it is Barbados that has been the most successful country with its education, reducing its percentage of illiteracy to nine per cent, the lowest in the

Caribbean today. Illiteracy is comparably low in British Honduras, Antigua and St Kitts. Jamaica has eighteen per cent, Guyana and Trinidad about twenty-five per cent. The highest percentages are in Dominica and St Lucia with forty-one and forty-eight per cent respectively.

The University of the West Indies was founded in 1946 with HRH Princess Alice of Athlone as Chancellor. The headquarters and the four faculties of arts, natural science, social science and medicine are on an attractive site at the foot of the Blue Mountains in Jamaica. There are branches, for agriculture and engineering in Trinidad, for arts and sciences in Barbados, together with an Institute of Education. Since 1965 Guyana has started its own university.

It has been in the realm of sport, however, that the West Indies have become best known, particularly in athletics and cricket. In Jamaica cricket started to become organized with the foundation of the Kingston Cricket Club in 1863. In 1895 an English XI paid their first visit to the West Indies and played a series of matches round the islands. At St Vincent England were all out for sixty-three and the local XI scored 139 for nine. Two years later the tables were reversed. In 1900 the West Indies sent their first touring side to England, under the captaincy of the Hon. R.S. Warner, a descendant of the founder of St Kitts, while in the English XI there was playing at this time another descendant, the famous 'Plum' Warner. The best playing fields in the West Indies developed in Guyana, where the clay soil gives as fine a pitch as any around Cambridge. In Georgetown they shave the grass completely off the wicket and play on the bare clay, which, to the despair of the bowlers and the joy of the batsmen, never crumbles. Introduced by expatriates in the early days, cricket has become the monopoly of the local peoples. Enthusiasm reaches down to the small boys who play their games with paraffin tins for wickets and palm frond ribs for bats. Lawn tennis came in shortly after cricket. Soccer is popular, especially among the schools, and down in the south-eastern Caribbean rugby football was played before the war between inter-colonial XVs made up of ex-patriate oil men, police officers and overseers. There was a Demerara rowing club, and in Jamaica polo has been popular among planters and Kingston businessmen for many years.

But the oldest sport in the West Indies is racing. Lady Nugent attended race-meetings in her time. Three-day meetings were held on Kitty Estate in Demerara in 1811 with horses from Barbados and Trinidad competing against the local steeds, and in 1829 Governor Sir Benjamin D'Urban founded the race course that still bears his name, on the edge of George-town. Racing was popular with all classes of the people. In Trinidad Governor Lord Harris opened the first race-meeting on the Queen's Park Savanna in 1853 and they have continued without a break ever since. The most sophisticated racing takes place in Jamaica. There the race course has been moved three times to make way for new houses of the expanding town, the last move being to the Caymanas Estate on the way to Spanish Town. Other sports like golf, shooting and fishing, both in the rivers and in the sea, have become increasingly popular. Islands in the sun are ideal for sport, once one can decide to stop basking in it.

In the last seventy years the Caribbean has ceased to be the graveyard it still was at the end of the nineteenth century. In its last decade the causes of both malaria and yellow fever were traced to the mosquitoes that carry the germs. From the 1850s the use of quinine as a prophylactic against and cure for malaria had been widely practised with beneficial results, but the cause of the disease remained a mystery. In 1895 Major Ronald Ross traced the carriage of the germs to the anopheles mosquito, and his discovery helped the American army surgeon, William Gorgas, working in collaboration with the Cuban Dr Carlos Finlay during the Spanish-American War, to prove that yellow fever was carried by the stegomya mosquito. By 1901 they had cleared yellow fever out of Havana. To the tropical world, and the Caribbean in particular, the discoveries of Ross and Finlay and Gorgas were as momentous as the discovery of gold and silver in Mexico and Peru. They made possible the development of banana plantations along the previously unhealthy and avoided shores of Central America; they saved the lives of hundreds of engineers and labourers constructing harbours and port works all the way from Vera Cruz to Rio de Janeiro, and they enabled the Americans to complete the building of the Panama Canal, where the lives of thousands of West Indians were in danger. Gorgas took charge of the health services there and the scourge of the notorious Isthmus of Darien was eliminated.

The opening of the Panama Canal in 1914 changed the Caribbean from a backwater into a world trade route, greatly improving communications by the increase in the number of ships passing through on their way to the antipodes and the Pacific coasts of North and South America. With the development of air travel the islands have found themselves valued as stepping stones between North and South America. The elimination of yellow fever and malaria came in time to encourage the tourists, and now the airlines ferry them to and from the islands.

Unhurt by the two world wars, but with sufficient problems of their own to balance that escape, the newly independent nations within the Commonwealth are attacking the twin enemies of poverty and ignorance with the same verve and self-confidence displayed by the first English colonists over 350 years ago against Spaniard and Carib and hurricane. They would not be West Indians if they followed a uniform pattern. So it is that Jamaica,

Trinidad, the Bahamas and Barbados have chosen dominion status with governors-general while Guyana has preferred to become a republic within the Commonwealth. Antigua, St Kitts-Nevis-Anguilla (with a question mark in front of the last one), Dominica, St Lucia, St Vincent and Grenada are internally self-governing Associated States, and Montserrat, the Turks and Caicos Islands, the Cayman Islands and the British Virgin Islands remain, willy-nilly because of their size, as colonies. Barbados is the most densely populated and the best educated; Trinidad is the richest; Jamaica is second richest and has the largest population; Guyana is the biggest and emptiest; British Honduras is the second biggest, second emptiest.

And what of the British heritage in these Afro-Asian-American countries? Language, law, Christianity, democracy, education, sport and social customs – all these are British and will survive more surely than British influence is likely to do in any of our former dependencies in Asia and Africa. At least there is hope that this will prove true, or 'when puss gone will ratta take house?'

NOTE ON
THE BIBLIOGRAPHY

When I first went to Jamaica in 1934 it was my intention to write a book on the history of the island compiled from original sources. With the object of making a fresh approach, therefore, I deliberately avoided reading the standard works like Edward Long (1774), Bryan Edwards (1819) and W.J.Gardner (1873). When I left Jamaica in 1940 I had not proceeded very far and the typescript of the period 1655–1702 never saw publication, but I have used it for that period in this book.

A transfer to then British Guiana enlarged my viewpoint, and short service with the Caribbean Regiment in 1944–5 gave me an introduction to the representatives therein of the ten British West Indian colonies. They all had distinguishing characteristics stemming largely from their differences of historical background: whereas Bermuda, Barbados, the Bahamas and the Leeward Islands have had a wholly British colonial experience, the Windward Islands were once French, Jamaica and Trinidad were Spanish, British Guiana was Dutch, while little Tobago had belonged to Spain, the Netherlands, France and Britain in turn. From away in the west came the men of British Honduras, so long only half owned by Britain as a 'settlement' and promoted to colony status only in 1862.

From this experience I learnt that it is a mistake to generalize about the West Indies and West Indians. They exhibit distinctions as marked as those of the Scots, Irish, Welsh and English, differences that are becoming more accentuated as each island diverges into independent nationhood. When it comes to the task of writing a history about the region, however, it is difficult to avoid generalizing because sources vary in value from island to island. The Windward Islands are the worst off, Jamaica quite the opposite, containing as it does the main faculties of the University of the West Indies and the much older West India Reference Library of the Institute of Jamaica, founded by the pioneer Secretary of the Institute, the late Frank Cundall. For readers who wish to keep abreast of research and cultural activity in Jamaica, I would recommend the excellent *Jamaica Journal* which the Institute publishes quarterly.

I do not regard this work as more than an outline. When the English publishers kindly invited me to undertake the writing of the book I was asked to include the activities of British people in the whole of Latin America and was limited to seventy-five thousand words. I had not been engaged in the research for very long before I realized that the canvas was too great for such a small brush. Accordingly it was agreed to reduce the subject to the Caribbean and to extend the length to what has become nearly a hundred thousand words. My plea was based on the fact that the length of British association with the Caribbean has been much more extensive than the British connection with other regions of the world featured in this series. More than four centuries have passed since Hawkins and Drake first sailed into the Caribbean, and nearly three and a half since the first English colonies were founded at St Kitts and Barbados. Only in India is the British time-line as long. In the Far East and Africa, apart from the West Coast, the British story dates only from the nineteenth century.

In four hundred years of history it is not surprising that some interesting events have come to be forgotten, so I have found space for the early attempts at colonization in Guiana and the Amazon and at Old Providence between Jamaica and Panama; the early years of Barbados and Jamaica are equally fascinating and too often forgotten; I have attempted to place the colourful Buccaneers in their right perspective, and have repeated the sad story of the Scots at Darien.

For the sixteenth and early seventeenth centuries I have relied most on A.P.Newton's *European Nations in the West Indies,* J.A.Williamson's several books, including his less well-known *The Caribbee Islands under the Proprietory Patents* and *English Colonies in Guiana;* V.T.Harlow's *Barbados 1625 to 1688* and his biography of Christopher Codrington; and lastly my still-born *English Jamaica,* which provided considerable detail, based as it was on the *Calendar of State Papers, Colonial* and seventeenth-century authors like Hickeringill, Ligon, Esquemeling and Hans Sloane.

The most valuable sources in a social history are the diaries and journals of individual colonists and visitors. Partly due perhaps to the lassitude engendered by a tropical climate, nobody in the West Indies produced an account comparable to those of Pepys, Evelyn and Parson Woodforde. Nevertheless John Baker kept a journal during his residence in the Leeward Islands from 1751 to 1757 as well as on a return visit in 1766 and 1767; Janet Schaw left a glimpse of life in Antigua and St Kitts in 1774–75; but by far the most informative and interesting is Lady Nugent's journal of her experiences while her husband was governor of Jamaica from 1801 to 1805. 'Monk' Lewis's *Journal of a West India Proprietor* describes two short visits to Jamaica in 1816 and 1818. Thomas St Clair's *Soldier's Sojourn in British Guiana* covers the years 1806–8 and is valuable for the light it throws on social conditions in the colony generally as well as on a soldier's life there.

Other valuable sources are the biographies of Drake and Hawkins in the sixteenth century; Morgan, Christopher Codrington and Sir Thomas Warner in the seventeenth; Rodney and Nelson in the eighteenth; and Bishops Rawle and Nuttall in the nineteenth and twentieth centuries. Henry Kirke's *Twenty-Five Years in British Guiana* covers the last twenty-five years of the nineteenth century in that rather literature-impoverished former colony.

In recent years a valuable contribution to knowledge about the Caribbean has come from American university presses which have been publishing books about that region, literally on their doorstep. These are clearly indicated in the bibliography and the most important sources are referred to in the text.

FURTHER READING

For a chronological account of the main events in West Indian history, the reader is referred to J.H.Parry and P.M.Sherlock, *A Short History of the West Indies* (London 1963), which includes the non-British countries in outline; for more detail, Sir Alan Burns's *A History of the British West Indies* (London 1954).

There is a mine of information, which I discovered too late to use, in Jeannette Marks's *The Family of the Barrett* (New York 1938). Now out of print, it is difficult to come by. It traces the histories of the families of Robert Browning and Elizabeth Barrett, both of which had connections with Jamaica from 1655.

Since I completed my manuscript the following valuable books have appeared:

Michael Craton and James Walvin, *A Jamaica Plantation : the History of Worthy Park, 1670–1970* (London 1970).

Eric Williams (Prime Minister of Trinidad), *From Columbus to Castro : A History of the West Indies* (London 1970).

Edward Brathwaite, *The Development of Creole Society in Jamaica 1770–1820* (London 1971).

In the Cass Library of West Indian Studies the following reprints have recently appeared:

W.Bridges, *The Annals of Jamaica* (1820).

Thomas Southey, *The Chronological History of the West Indies* (1827).

N.M.Crouse, *The French Struggle for the West Indies, 1665–1715.*

Père Labat, *The Memoirs of Père Labat.*

Thomas Coke, *A History of the West Indies* (1808).

L.M.Fraser, *A History of Trinidad 1781–1813.*

E.L.Joseph, *A History of Trinidad* (1838).

W.J.Gardner, *A History of Jamaica* (1872).

Sir Robert Schomburgk, *A History of Barbados* (1848).

John Davy, *The West Indies before and since Slave Emancipation* (1854).

Thomas Atwood, *The History of the Island of Dominica* (1791).

Charles Shepard, *An Historical Account of the Island of St Vincent* (1831).

Lastly, for the value of their social background there are the novels of Edgar Mittelhozer of Guyana and V.S.Naipaul from Trinidad.

BIBLIOGRAPHY

Auger, Hall, Gordon and Reckford, *The Making of the West Indies* (London 1961).

H.M.Bailey and A.P.Nasatir, *Latin America, the Development of its Civilization* (London 1960).

J.Harry Bennett Jr., *Bondsmen and Bishops* (California 1958).

Richard Blome, *A Description of the Island of Jamaica* (1678).

British Guiana Handbooks.

Robin Bryans, *Trinidad and Tobago* (London 1967).

Sir Alan Burns, *History of the West Indies* (London 1965).

Stephen Caiger, *British Honduras Past and Present* (London, 1951).

Calendar of State Papers, Colonial.

Cambridge History of the British Empire.

Gertrude Carmichael, *History of the West India Islands of Trinidad and Tobago, 1498–1900* (London 1961).

Colonel J.E.Caulfield, *One Hundred Years History of the Second Battalion the West India Regiment* (London 1899).

E.K.Chatterton, *Sailing Ships and their Story* (London 1909).

Wayne M.Cleghorn, *British Honduras – Colonial Dead End, 1859–1900* (Louisiana 1967).

Julian Corbett, *Drake and the Tudor Navy* (London 1917).

Virginia Cowles, *The Great Swindle* (London 1960).

Brigadier-General Cruickshank, *Sir Henry Morgan* (London 1935).

Frank Cundall, *The Life of Enos Nuttall, Archbishop of the West Indies* (London 1922).

Frank Cundall, *The Governors of Jamaica in the Seventeenth Century* (West India Committee 1936).

Daily Gleaner (Kingston, Jamaica).

R.C.Dallas, *History of the Maroons*, 2 vols. (1803).

Noel Deerr, *The History of Sugar* (London 1950).

Vincent Roy D'Oyley, *Jamaica: Development of Teacher Training Through the Agency of the Lady Mico Charity from 1835 to 1914* (Toronto 1964).

Bryan Edwards, *The History, Civil and Commercial, of the British Colonies in the West Indies*, 6 vols. (London 1819).

Gisela Eisner, *Jamaica 1830–1930* (Manchester 1961).

L.E.Elliott, *Central America* (London 1924).

A.B.Ellis, *History of the First West India Regiment* (London 1885).

Johann Esquimeling, *The Buccaneers of America* (reprint) (London 1893).

Thomas Gage, *The English American* (ed. A.P.Newton) (London 1946).

Shirley Gordon, *A Century of West Indian Education* (London 1963).

Elsa V.Goveia, *Slave Society in the British Leeward Islands* (New Haven 1965).

Richard Hakluyt, *The Principal Navigations* etc.

Vincent T.Harlow, *Barbados 1625–85* (Oxford 1926).

Vincent T.Harlow, *Christopher Codrington 1668–1710* (Oxford 1928).

A.Hasbrouck, *Foreign Legionaries in the Liberation of South America* (New York 1928).

Hickeringill, *Jamaica Viewed* (London 1661).

David Howarth, *The Golden Isthmus* (London 1966).

Jamaica Information Services, *The Morant Bay Rebellion*.

Charles Farquharson, *Journal 1831–32, A Relic of Slavery* (ed. A. Deans Pegg) (Nassau 1957).

Journal of the Society for Army Historical Research, vol. XL (1961).

Peter Keenagh, *Mosquito Coast* (London 1937).

Henry Kirke, *Twenty-Five Years in British Guiana* (London 1898).

Richard Kent (editor), *Letters from the Bahamas Islands 1823–24* (London 1657).

M.G.Lewis, *Journal of a West Indian Proprietor* (London 1834)(Culmer 1948).

Michael Lewis, *A Social History of the Navy* (London 1961).

Richard Ligon, *A True and Exact History of the Island of Barbados* (London 1657).

Christopher Lloyd, *The British Seaman* (London 1968).

Christopher Lloyd and J.L.S. Coulter, *Medicine and the Navy*, vol IV (Edinburgh 1963).

Edward Long, *The History of Jamaica, or General Survey of the Ancient and Modern State of that Island*, 3 vols. (London 1774).

Donald Macintyre, *Admiral Rodney* (London 1962).

Dorothy Marshall, *Eighteenth Century England* (London 1962).

Percy F.Martin, *Mexico of the Twentieth Century* (London 1907).

John Masefield, *On the Spanish Main* (London 1922).

A.E.W.Mason, *Drake* (London 1941).

George Mather and Charles Blagg, *Bishop Rawle, a Memoir* (London 1890).

P.A.Means, *The Spanish Main* (New York 1965).

D.Morris, *The Colony of British Honduras, its Resources and Prospects* (London 1883).

Lady Nugent, *Journal* (ed. F.Cundall) (London 1939).

A.P.Newton, *European Nations in the West Indies 1493–1688* (London 1933).

Vere Longford Oliver, *History of the Island of Antigua*, 4 vols. (London 1894).

Vere Longford Oliver, (ed.) *Caribbeana* (Miscellaneous Papers of the British West Indies) (London 1910).

Lord Olivier, *The Blessed Island (Jamaica)* (London 1931).

Carola Oman, *Nelson* (London 1947).

S.Pack, *Windward of the Caribbean* (London 1964).

R.Pares, *A West India Fortune* (London 1950).

R.Pares, *Merchants and Planters* (Cambridge 1960).

J.H.Parry, *The Spanish Seaborne Empire* (London 1966).

W.A.Paton, *Down the Islands, A Voyage to the Caribbees* (London 1888).

BIBLIOGRAPHY

Captain Bedford Pim, *Dottings in Panama etc.* (London 1864).

F.W.Pitman, *The Development of the British West Indies 1700–63* (London 1967).

Carey Robinson, *The Fighting Maroons of Jamaica* (Jamaica 1969).

Marco Rodriguez, *A Palmerstonian Diplomat in Central America* (Arizona 1964).

James Rodway, *A History of British Guiana*, 3 vols. (Georgetown 1893).

Janet Schaw, *Journal of a Lady of Quality* (ed. E.W.Andrews) (New Haven 1923).

Joseph Shore, *In Old St James* (Kingston 1911).

Sir Hans Sloane, *A Voyage to the Islands*, 2 vols. (London 1725).

South American Handbook.

J.A.Spender, *Weetman Pearson, First Viscount Cowdray* (London 1930).

Lieut. T.S.St Clair, *A Soldier's Sojourn in British Guiana* (ed. Vincent Roth) (Georgetown 1947).

Joseph Sturge and Thomas Harvey, *The West Indies in 1837* (republished) (London 1968).

Anthony Trollope, *The West Indies and Spanish Main* (republished) (London 1968).

Timehri, Journal of the British Guiana Society.

Claudio Velit (ed.), *Handbook of Latin America and the Caribbean.*

The Voyage of Sir Henry Colt, Knight (London 1631).

St Vincent Handbook.

Aucher Warner, *Sir Thomas Warner, Pioneer of the West Indies* (West India Committee).

David M.Waters, *The Art of Navigation in Elizabethan and Early Stuart Times* (London 1958).

Waterton's Wandering in South America (ed. J.G.Wood) (London 1893).

Colonel H.deWatteville, *The British Soldier* (London 1954).

Henry Whistler, *A Journal of Admiral Penn's Expedition to the West Indies* (1655).

J.A.Williamson, *The Caribbee Islands Under the Proprietary Patents* (Oxford 1926).

J.A.Williamson, *Hawkins of Plymouth* (London 1949).

J.A.Williamson, *English Colonies in Guiana* (Oxford 1923).

J.A.Williamson, *Sir Francis Drake* (London 1951).

I.A.Wright, *Spanish Documents Concerning English Voyages to the Caribbean* (London 1929).

Philip C.Yorke (ed.), *John Baker's Diary* (London 1931).

INDEX